Dedicated to my loving wife Paige, my long-suffering fellow Lion Steve Fuller, Brian Curtin - the best coach I ever worked with, all the players I've ever managed and coached, Millwall FC, Kennington JFC, Ashford Town FC, Tunbridge Wells FC, Lordswood FC and Crystal Palace Ladies for the memories and my sons Alex and Aidan, without whom it wouldn't have happened. We came, we saw, we had a lot of fun along the way. COYL.

This edition published 2023

Copyright © Vinny Shell 2023

Published by Victor Publishing - victorpublishing.co.uk

ISBN: 9798850347369

victorpublishing.co.uk

THE GAFFER

Grassroots football at its best - and worst

**A tale of laughter, tears,
alcohol, burgers,
flatulence, wind-ups,
bants, garbs,
angry dog walkers
& dogs**t Dave...
...oh, and football**

BY VINNY SHELL

CONTENTS

FOREWORD

I love Football. It's the greatest game in the world and it can exhilarate, and it can deflate in equal measures. It can take us to the highest high or lowest low and some of the greatest moments in my life have been as a result of watching my team, Millwall. Who can forget Tim Cahill's winner against Sunderland in the 2004 FA Cup Semi Final or Steve Morison's late winner in the Play Off final against Bradford City? Then there's the classic games beating Sheffield Wednesday 4-2 at the Old Den in 1990 after being 2-0 down at half time or the 2-0 FA Cup victory against the mighty Arsenal at Highbury in 1995. What about the incredible 4-1 victory over West Ham at the Den, a game referred to as 'The Mother's Day Massacre' in which the Lions also managed to squander two spot kicks.

Supporting The Lions has meant enjoying/suffering a mixture of promotions and relegations but that's the typical expectations of a supporter of a less than glamorous club. I can also add to my experiences that of watching my son Aidan play for Millwall Under 14s in a tournament alongside future Millwall captain Sid Nelson or watching my other son Alex perform at the Masters 6-a-side tournament on Sky TV, during which I presented Matt Le Tissier with the Player of the Tournament trophy. Alex also scored for a Brazilian Soccer Schools side in a select game at the Millenium stadium Alex was also fortunate to be a mascot for Millwall in a 2-0 defeat at home to Bristol City, sadly Millwall later went into administration against a backdrop of turmoil.

I can add to those experiences with an amazing season managing Tunbridge Wells reserves with what was essentially an under 21 side, the highlight of which was an incredible 8-2 victory at Deal Town Rangers, it was 2-2 at half time and we produced the perfect half with our centre forward Jon Pilbeam scoring 6 times and midfielder Georgie Hayes, playing the number 10 role, producing one of the best individual performances I ever witnessed. I probably should have retired after this game as it was the highlight of my managerial career. During some second half 'banter' the opposing manager lost it and referred to myself and assistant manager Brian Curtin as 'Fat c**t and ginger dwarf' Yes I was the fat c**t, of course once the final whistle went he shook our hands and said 'we was by far the best team they had played all season' The beer tasted good that day.

My coaching career started at Charing Heath in Ashford on a cold and wet Sunday morning when I took Alex to his first coaching session; there was one hardy soul and thirty eager young impressionable footballers. The following week I was roped in to help and so it began. I ended up managing several local youth sides before becoming Head of Youth Development at Ashford Town and we were fortunate to play our home games at the senior sides ground Homelands.

I managed to get my UEFA B coaching badge and my rise up the ranks continued. I became a bit of a ground snob and was fortunate to manage at Maidstone's artificial pitch and the impressive eco-friendly Dartford FC Princes Park stadium on several occasions, in fact a fixture at Dartford was one of the few times when the first team players would volunteer to play for the reserves, yes it was that good. The food also got better and depending on the result you would stay and enjoy the hospitality over a pasta bake and a pint. But what did it for me was the battle of wits.

I will never forget losing 4-2 to Faversham and 5-1 to Ramsgate in the early stages of the season at Tunbridge Wells. The defeat to Ramsgate was a pivotal point of our season and I remember addressing the team in the changing rooms and saying, 'That doesn't happen again' and the subsequent 3-0 victories over both teams in the return fixtures proved otherwise. I went on to scout for Millwall, coach alongside several professional players at Gillingham FC and manage Crystal Palace Ladies as well as the reserve sides at Ashford Town, Tunbridge Wells and Lordswood. I even coached Socatots to 1–5-year-olds while working for Ashford Borough Council.

Nowadays I'm happy just watching my beloved Lions with my fellow season ticket holders Steve, Bill and Will and while I sometimes miss the hustle and bustle of the match days and the dressing room banter, I'm proud of my achievements and I know that I always tried my best when I coached to whatever age or ability. I can also recollect tales of success and glory and horror stories of bad defeats, red cards, which were usually preceded by the red mist, irate parents and disappointed players. Yes, I made mistakes, but I learnt to swallow my pride and tried to get it right the next time.

I also learnt that you cannot win every game and I in turn taught my players how to lose with dignity and be humble in victory. Some of my greatest achievements weren't even results I remember telling a young

13-year-old Danny Keen that I didn't think he was good enough to play for my Ashford Town Under 14s but if he wanted to work hard and try, I would give him an opportunity. Danny went on to play for the Under 14s and then followed me to Tunbridge Wells Reserves and is now a Personal Trainer. I also remember watching my youngest Aidan make his debut for Lordswood Reserves at The Gallagher Stadium home of Maidstone United at the age of 16 and remember the rest of the team saying what a player he was. Sadly, he like many of my players no longer play but Aidan went on to become a Football analyst and like me he is resigned to watching the Lions to fill his Saturdays.

I've had a few calls to return and finally at the grand old age of 60 I answered the call to coach Hawkinge Town Under 16s so I'm back. We can't all be Alex Ferguson and we can't all win the league or cup, but we can make a difference and have some fun along the way. I know I did. So, if you are ever offered the opportunity to coach then take it, it can be frustrating, but it can also be one of the most rewarding roles you will ever be offered and who knows you might be good at it.

Vinny Shell
The Gaffer

INTRODUCTION

What you are about to read is the story of a season in the life of a Football club. It's not one of the big boys United, City, Spurs, Liverpool, so it's a story bereft of the glamour of the Premiership and the multi-million pound players and their multi-million pound transfers or the billionaire chairmen with their here today gone tomorrow hirings and firings. It isn't a tale of a Salford United and their fairy tale rise through the non-league ranks with additional tales of giant killings.

No, it is the tale of Dalworth United **Under 15**s, a grassroots junior Football team and follows their campaign in the Cheltenham & District **Under 15**s league season 2017/18. A team that last year had their most successful season to date, completing the treble of the League, the Dave Bodkin League cup and the Arthur Goodwin District Cup, an incredible feat that had never been completed in the history of league. A team that lost only one game all season in league and cup. This is the story of the following season told through a variety of sources such as media clippings from the local newspaper and the club website and my own personal take on matters, highlighting the failures and successes of what turned out to be a quite extraordinary season.

The previous season I was just a parent helping out wherever needed, putting up nets, making tea or coffee, running the line (reluctantly) or helping out at training sessions. However, due to the success of the team the treble winning manager of last season was promoted to the U18s and I found myself filling the vacated assistant manager role, the previous assistant manager Vinny Smith being promoted to manager. I gladly took the role as I'd been involved in youth football since my own son was old enough to kick a ball. I remember taking him to the same Rec that Dalworth now ply their trade on one morning for an open football session.

There was one brave soul and about 30 kids and I got roped in and I must admit I loved it. My teaching career meant I could only help out occasionally but when the opportunity to be assistant manager of Dalworth United arose I thought why not, after all my son Nick played so I was there for all his games and took him to training so why not? I got on with the new manager, so I took the level one course during the close season, so was ready for what was to prove to be a roller coaster campaign.

I always intended to keep a record for my own reference but I don't know what made me keep such an in-depth journal including the cuttings, musings, diary notes, it must have been the English teacher in me. I'm glad I did though because, in my humble opinion I believe I have captured a tale of resilience, bravery and sheer determination amongst a group of friends that showed a spirit of which I have never ever witnessed before. Like I said this isn't a tale of the premiership, but it does have has all the passion, drama excitement and magic that is associated with the professional game and I believe it is a testament to the importance of the grassroots game.

Simon Sheppard
Assistant Manager
Dalworth United Under 15s

CHAPTER ONE

DALWORTH UNITED

'And it's hi ho super Dalworth...'

How do you spend your Sunday mornings? Lying in bed, mowing the lawn, walking the dog, cooking a full English breakfast, tidying the garage? I do all of these but the majority of my Sunday mornings are spent standing on a touchline as assistant manager of Dalworth United Under 15s, standing in all conditions sun, rain, wind, in searing heat, the soaking wet and the freezing cold. Shouting instructions, celebrating, groaning, moaning going through the full gamut of emotions. So that's how I spend my Sunday mornings and that led to spending an absolutely amazing season with the parents, players and the man who became a close friend, The Gaffer.

Dalworth United are a successful junior football club in the Cheltenham area. They have a good reputation and have had their fair share of success in producing good players and winning trophies. However, while they have their fair share of success that are alike to most grassroots clubs in that they rely on the good will and help of parents to operate.

Dalworth United is one of the bigger clubs in the area with teams at all levels from under 7s - 18s and they have links to the senior side although they run independently to the senior side. The committee resemble at times a small army with Chairman, vice chairman, committee members, treasurers, secretaries, fixtures secretaries, child protection officers, disciplinary officers, league delegates, results coordinators. These are the official club officials. Then there are the others the refreshments organisers (making tea and coffee and making sandwiches) the volunteer linesmen (usually reluctantly volunteered) the volunteer groundsman (marking the pitch and putting the nets up) then there are the managers and the assistant managers, the hardy souls who give up their own time so that boys and girls can play football, last but not least (and I'm sorry to anyone who I've forgotten)

Then there are the most important people of all: the parents, the parental aspect covers many sub-divisions like benefactors, sponsors, chauffeurs (taking their own children and those others who haven't got transport)

Parents will not only give up lots of their precious free time but will also dig deep for the privilege of seeing their child play football. Match fees, training fees, signing on fees, equipment, such as tracksuits, training kit, football kit. Some clubs, Dalworth Under 15s being one, are fortunate to find sponsors, namely Smith's Construction (The Gaffer's company) so the cost is reduced. If you add petrol, the endless cups of tea and coffee and bacon rolls, burgers, packed lunches, tournament fees, the occasional swift half, it really does add up. Sometimes you do have the pleasure of watching in bright sunshine but mainly you can expect wind, thunder, storms and rain of many varieties light, persistent, torrential and always when it's raining, the cold.

In return you watch and support and cheer on your offspring sometimes it might be for a full game, a half game and it has been known no game time whatsoever, but more on that later. Through the good times and bad they are there and the presentations, although they are a celebration of the teams' efforts and sometimes successes they could equally be a celebration that parents have endured or enjoyed another season and successfully got through it virtually unscathed.

The Dalworth United Presentation Night
I can remember going to my first ever Dalworth United presentation evening at the Dalworth Leisure Centre over 300 boys and over 700 parents and siblings at £10 for a family ticket. At first I thought I had got my nights mixed up and was expecting to see Steps or Toyah or one of the other acts the Dalworth Leisure Centre usually host. Still a glance at the front of the stage and I knew I was in the right place, unless of course the antiques road show were doing a trophy special.

The glare that radiated from the 300+ trophies as the light hit them was almost blinding and again, I was thinking Steps have put on a good light show. Once I manage to turn my head and my gaze is deflected from the treasure trove of trophies, I am met with hundreds of kids fueled on excessive amounts of Coke and sweets, charging around the place, is this *really* not a Steps gig?

The kids turned the dance floor into an ice-free ice rink, if there's no skidding it's not a presentation evening. This area is the designated adult free zone (adult free because no sane soul would step foot in that area) so while the offspring tried their best to ruin their brand new presentation outfits the parents were necking pints and other spirits in an attempt to numb the pain of what was going to be a four-hour ceremony. The Oscars, Olympic or World Cup opening ceremonies, Royal Weddings all a piece of piss compared to the Dalworth United Presentation evening. I bet they don't clap solidly for three hours at any of those events. The worst part is at best you are there to see your son collect his medal, trophy and for that you have to sit through 299 other presentations.

Alcohol is certainly a way of getting through the evening. I do, however, take my hat off to the people who organise these evenings, they are run to precision and managers know they only have 5 minutes for their speeches. Ah, those speeches. I'm sure that managers have a safe at home and once the speech is dispatched to, at best, a disinterested audience it is locked away for the following year when the same speech is recited parrot fashion with only the Manager's Player of the Year, Players Player of the Year and Supporters Player of the Year names changed.

But first, the buffet, and my god what a buffet it is. Rows upon rows of food cooked by an army of Mums and the occasional dad or two. Two thousand triangular cheese, ham, cheese and ham, cheese and onion, ham and pickle and egg (why egg I'll never know) then there's an assortment of other savouries, include the desserts and you are looking at 15 tables of foods, foods full of E numbers when mixed with fizzy drinks creates an army of hyperactive children. While the dazzling banquet of food is indeed a sight to behold actually getting to it requires resilience and patience.

Those three words that emanate from the DJ: "Food is ready", create the same scenario as the Floor Manager opening the doors for a Boxing Day sale. One of complete chaos as a charge to form a queue develops. Negotiating the queue, a queue similar in length to that of the Dalworth foot bridge, to get to the bloody food tests anyone's patient but once again the veterans of presentations past will use this as a way of reuniting with friends old and new.

"Hello John, how's the wife and kids?"

"Hello Bill, it's been ages since we've spoken"

Once reaching the food a new set of skills is required and again you can immediately spot the veterans of previous presentations as they will be juggling two or three even four, if really adventurous, plates of food which, if they successfully manage to carry back to the table deserves recognition. Many an argument has started upon return and that's when the fun starts and I've heard it many times: "I don't like Ham and Pickle sandwiches", "Well I'll swop you for my Cheese and Pickle", "I don't like pickle", "Just bloody eat them" says Mum scraping the pickle off and everyone tucks into the food quickly so that they can re-join the queue for seconds.

Tips for successfully negotiating the Dalworth buffet

Egg sandwiches: Only take egg sandwiches on your first visit and never the second as it is guaranteed that the egg starts the 'perishing' process within 30 minutes of the egg sandwiches being unwrapped but more of this later.

Seconds: For the sake of your health never ever attempt a second trip to the buffet based on the fact that the buffet is visited by in excess of 500 people first time round. A number of these visitors will not have washed their hands after visiting the toilets or picking their noses or scratching their bums.

This will mean that on your second visit to the buffet you are in serious danger of eating such delicacies as cheese and urine, ham and bogey, egg and fingernail dirt sandwiches. It should also be noted that a number of items will also have been 'inspected by the younger visitors and by inspected I mean touched, pawed, fingered, had a chunk taken out of and put back.

The clock is ticking: If you must pay a second visit you will be faced with a limited choice, the stuff no one wants, and with the stage lights beating down on the buffet tables the process of 'curling' initiates as soon as the sandwiches are uncovered. It is therefore a race against the clock before said sandwiches become inedible. On a plus note if you leave it long enough you may end up with a toasted sandwich, although I would advise against the toasted egg sandwich.

The Noah Theory: For those parents and by parents I mean dads, collecting for the entire family, I recommend taking two of everything to ensure that everyone will find at least one thing they like. Well it worked for Noah didn't it!

Once the buffet has been devoured or covered up for later. Yes, this does happen and while the sausage rolls prove that they are made to last, I have no idea why the egg sandwiches are covered up? Really, would you? Finally, we come to the highlight of the evening: the speeches and presentations. This is the moment the managers reel out their almost identical 5 minute speeches.

"It's been a good season…blah, blah, blah…… I'm really proud of the players …… blah, blah , blah…….. Next season we will ….blah, blah, blah…. I'd like to thank the parents……….blah, blah, blah, etc, etc, etc

Occasionally there is a comedian in the midst aka: The manager who drank too much too soon. I've never met one who hasn't been anything other than embarrassing but that's another story. After every speech, the relieved manager retreats to his chair relieved it's over for another year and downs a pint. Once his bit is over he can relax and when all the trophies have finally been dispersed to the four corners then the serious drinking start. In fact you can sometimes tell how good a team's season has been by the court that the manager holds.

Successful season: Manager bought pint after pint as parents gather like expectant chicks round the worm bearing mother, hanging on to his every word listening intently while he recounts his 'war' stories "Oh yes remember Tamworth away 2-0 down then I changed personnel and formation and we won 4-2" Parents will also use this as an opportunity, once the manager has supped enough amber nectar, to pounce and start sending subliminal messages to the inebriated boss "Play my Johnny up front next year" "Give my Billy more game time" "Never ever substitute young Ronnie" in a hope that when he awakes hungover the following morning that he will have digested the messages into his plans for next season.

Unsuccessful season: The manager sits isolated with Mrs Manager, his offspring are doing coke (cola not cocaine) induced laps of the safe area. No one goes near him, instead the parents will form mutinous groups which can turn into disaffected lynch mobs and descend on the Manager's table with their lit torches and nooses braying for blood and change. Sometimes the dads will meet at the bar discussing their detailed plans for how to overthrow him. The self-elected spokesman, or shall we call him the bookies favorite to take over, will hold court and oversee proceedings. The disinterested mums sit around tables discussing anything but football and knocking back wine and Prosecco. The concerned manager cuts a lone figure and he is usually the first one to leave, dragging his unhappy offspring out with him, after he has completed the torturous speech that he has to wheel out "We haven't had a great season, but the boys tried. See you next season. I hope/hope not"

Rather than go through the whole ceremony in one go the committee split it so dads can race to the bar, or to the toilet, to stock up on pints or get rid of the ones that are passing through the system. The real presentation hardened pros will race to the bar, place their order, pay and then race to the toilet before returning to the bar to collect their drinks or they will go in pairs and form a toilet relay queue/piss, pass the piss-stained baton (the money) piss/queue.

The next 'break in proceedings' is for the Dalworth Raffle. The raffle provides a welcome relief that is until you see the multitude of prizes on offer everything from two tickets to a Cheltenham Town fixture to a Box of Soaps donated by someone who didn't appreciate their Christmas present from Auntie Joan and who see this as an ideal opportunity to get shot of it. The raffle itself lasts 45 minutes. With the formulaic grab a prize and pick the next ticket "Ticket 355, hooray! Green ticket, boo!" Fate elects that one table will win more than their fair share of prizes, much to the disgust of the other tables that don't win anything. When this table wins the box of soaps they feel obliged to offer a "that's ok I've won already so I'll put it back" token gesture, they have already won the tickets to Cheltenham Town, a meal for two at the local Indian restaurant, 2 bottles of Prosecco, a bottle of red wine and a large box of chocolates. This magnanimous gesture rather than being applauded is met with a collective groan due to the fact that it simply extends the raffle, much to everyone's disgust.

Raffle over and it's another quick sprint to a) The Bar, overcrowded or b) The Toilet, overflowing. Then there are the brave souls who roam the buffet like zombies searching for flesh because they are a) Starving b) Pissed or c) I have no idea whatsoever.

Then we return to the speeches and trophies. It is at this point I would like to point out that I really feel sorry for the U18s who are last up, actually the management of the U18s. The U18s entourage usually consists of Manager and family, Assistant Manager and family and a handful of players namely the winners of the three awards, the award winners will ultimately turn up late and leave as soon as they have grabbed their awards and given them to their manager for safe keeping.

They are then off down the pub or club to join the rest of their teammates who have 'swerved' presentation night. I am sure that if they could do a live link from the Warehouse (the local nightclub) then the players would. "I'd like to thank (aside: get us a pint in Stevo) my family and The Gaffer and my team mates (aside: oh wait, Tuuuuuuuuuune)" It is guaranteed that the Dalworth U18s, who have the biggest squad in the club, will have least representation on presentation night. The manager will also provide the last and shortest speech of the night.

By the end of the evening the 'battlefield' is full of misplaced trophies, the younger siblings have hit the brick wall and are asleep perched on top of discarded coats. Rogue sandwiches and savouries who attempted to make a break for it lay strewn and wounded across the leisure centre, items of food have been known to make it as far as the car park. The Coke levels are beginning to subside as the players blood sugar levels are returning to normal which all means one thing: It's Dad Time.

The requests begin to flood in and the DJ is spinning the old classics and while the intoxicated and unsteady dads find their voices their co-ordination has sadly left the building along with Elvis. Queens "We are the Champions" becomes "Dalworth are the champions" and the old classic "Hi Ho Silver Lining" becomes "And it's Hi Ho Super Dalworth everywhere we go we're winning" Throw in a bit of "Baggy Trousers" "Come on Eileen" "Going Underground" and Dad's Army have overthrown the Children of the Corn and you know the end of the evening is almost nigh and when the evening does eventually end, staggering dads and sleepy children are navigated to various cars, taxi's and minibuses by tired and irritable Mums. The committee and volunteers hit the dance floor and surrounding areas armed with oversized black sacks to collect the discarded food, paper plates, plastic cutlery and sweet wrappers. Collecting all forms of rubbish they will also collect discarded trophies and an assortment of items of clothing discarded by forgetful children and their reward for staying sober and calm amongst the carnage and chaos, a bunch of flowers or a bottle of something which I would imagine is drunk in its entirety when they are finally home and safe in the knowledge that another successful presentation evening has passed off without any major incidents.

A successful football club will not be successful unless it is run effectively. But despite all the hard work you may only see the committee three times a year, the committee meeting, when they are re-elected, the presentation evening and the Dalworth Football Festival

The committee meetings are a major part of the club's calendar. There is the main meeting, the AGM, when club officials are elected or re-elected and each member presents its reports after the last minutes have been read, actioned and agreed. Then we are 'treated' with the reports from the Chairman, Secretary, Treasurer, Child Protection Officer, Health & Safety Officer, Fund raising committee. The first AGM I attended I couldn't believe how long the meeting was but also how professional it was. It really gave me a sense of the history of the club and the traditions that are upheld and although these people are all volunteers you can see that the club operates in a highly professional manner. The minutes and agenda demonstrate a real professional approach to matters and the meeting flows accordingly. The Bi-monthly managers meetings are less formal and are fairly brief in that each manager presents any issues they may have. The committee then feedback any issues they may have for the managers. All this takes place amidst a few pints and a bit of a chat. There is also a fair bit of banter between managers and a firm pecking order is established. I'm sure that psychologists and sociologists would have a field day at these meetings and especially the AGM.

The Dalworth Football Festival

The Dalworth Football Festival is a monumental event run with military precision and it brings in much needed funds for the club, in fact a successful tournament can virtually fund the overheads for a season. The magnitude of the tournament at times is exasperating and often you forget it's a football tournament as the tea bars, burger stalls, beer tents, ice cream vans, doughnut stalls, raffles, tombolas, face painting, name the teddy, hook a fish, bouncy castles, penalty shoot outs, inflatable five a side pitches seem to swamp the primary objective a football tournament. Actually, the primary objective is to take as much cash from parents as is humanly possible. Entry fees, car parking and programmes, free with the £1 per person entry and that's before you've even stepped foot onto Dalworth Rec. In fact, such is its success people who have no interest in football attend the event as it has almost become a traditional summer fete with a football tournament attached. Someone last year had the bright idea of inviting local craft artists to run stalls and it was a big success. They simply sold a pitch and raked in the cash. Then there was the sponsorship in the form of programme adverts and banners. The beauty of it all was that the committee organised and executed the whole event out of nothing more than the kindness of their hearts and a love of Dalworth.

Such is the standard of the tournament that you will find various scouts walking round in their club tracksuits hoping to spot the next Harry Kane. They scour the multitude of pitches hosting hundreds of players from local clubs from U7s - U18s making notes on their free programmes. These scouts are on the guest list as it is in the club's best interests to raise the tournament's profile by having scouts present, The scouts wander around the pitches chatting to managers and parents but remaining aloof and isolated. Every now and then a little gem will be spotted and you can guarantee word will get round and soon pitch side will be filled with track suited men standing well apart ready to pounce at the first sign of talent. It isn't always a case of first come first seen as a pecking order usually develops with the highest placed club taking first dibs. Unless the talent that is on show is first class a process usually develops and a scout will go and watch a player several times before making a decision but tournaments can set the wheels in motion.

The scouts are a small but important part of the tournament. The real cash cow is the parents and once they step foot on the Rec the task in hand is getting them to part with their hard-earned cash. Any parent that has younger siblings will be ripe for the taking and that is why the committee works so hard on creating the complete experience. A number of parents will bring their own food and drink but last year we upped the ante and once parents unwrapped the sweaty cheese sandwiches they simply paled into insignificance against the deluxe Cheeseburgers or the foot long hot dogs. We even had Dalworths version of Starbucks on site so that the coffee poured from various flasks was like comparing Champagne with water. Committee 1 Parents 0. Once the siblings start tugging at parents clothing for 50p for the penalty shoot-out or £1 for the bouncy castle you knew it was a matter of time before they gave in. The apathy even spread to the parents.

"Do you want a sweaty cheese sandwich?"
"No, I think I'll take a stroll over to the cheeseburger place"
"Ok but stay out of the beer tent"
"Ok love" he says making his way to the cheeseburger place via the beer tent.

Once you've hooked them you know this is going to be a well-trodden route throughout the day however to soften the blow for the sneaky Dad creeping to the beer tent we added a Prosecco tent next door so after Dad had had a quick pint and a cheeseburger he simply had to come back with a glass (plastic of course) of Prosecco and everyone's a winner. Committee 2 Parents 0. While the club wins it's not without the hard work of the committee.

One of the last and most hated tasks on tournament days is managing the Portaloos, once again such is the magnitude of the tournament that the Dalworth Rec public conveniences are too small for the number of people attending. So early Saturday morning some poor soul has to take delivery of twenty Portaloos. On delivery they are immaculate, a plastic palace fit for a King, with well stocked toilet rolls, hand wash and hand sanitiser gels and enough chemical blue to paint an army of Smurfs. By the end of Saturday night at least five should carry a health warning as they will contain blue faeces, blue because however much chemical you put on it, it will not disappear. Another five will have no toilet roll and the rest will have enough fag butts, beer cans, sweet wrappers etc to start your own waste landfill, not to mention the puddles of piss that you have to swim around in. Some poor sod from the committee is tasked with some shit-kicking or shit-flicking or even, in extreme cases, shit-picking to ensure that the loos are all at least half decent and ready for another battering the following day. It really becomes an urban version of 'Deal or No Deal' with users faced with a shit or no shit option as they chose a Portaloo:

"No thanks Noel, I think I don't think I'll chance it. I'll just keep my arse cheeks clenched until I get home or can find an alternative."

I've often thought the club should have a celebrity at the tournament. It's a shame Jim Bowen isn't around for a Dalworth version of Bullseye:

"IIIIN ONE... Shit";
"IIIIN TWO... A puddle of piss";
"IIIIN THREE... A half empty can of lukewarm Fosters (or is it?)";
"IIIIN FOUR... The mystery prize: blue shit and a discarded pair of underwear with skid marks".

The weather also plays a part and if it is a really hot day the portaloos become sweatboxes which when mixed with the variety of smells, or should we say stenches, make them virtually unusable. I have heard that when the Portaloos are collected on a Sunday that the Royal Marines use them for endurance training. Anyone who can spend one hour in there automatically gets a pass into the Marines. For committee members the lesson to learn is if you have volunteered for the tournament, make sure you don't get the last job on the list.

The committee start at seven in the morning until seven at night making sure all the food and drink tents are fully stocked, cooking food and replacing the tomato ketchup, brown sauce and burger sauce bottles as well as refilling the salt and pepper pots and milk cartons and sugar pots, pouring pints, registering teams and making sure everyone knows what pitch they are on, managing pitches and refs, clearing up rubbish, taking money and that's all on the day. Before that comes writing and printing the programme, getting sponsors and raffle prizes, buying trophies, booking referees, booking ice cream vans and booking portable toilets.

So it's a full on 12-hour day and then they have to do it all the following day. At the end of it though the financial benefit pays big dividends and that is why Dalworth United are one of the top youth teams in the county. As a parent though you don't always see or appreciate the work the committee do, instead most of your dealings will be with the manager. The manager can be an isolated figure at times although he will usually have the support of an assistant manager and a team rep although to be fair the team rep is usually taking money or taking complaints about the manager.

So it's the manager that you see on a weekly basis and now that I'm assistant manager I see and hear from Gaffer on a regular basis. The manager's role is a very difficult role and like any professional football manager he is open to criticism but doesn't have the comfort of a 6 figure sum to compensate for said criticism. There are many comparisons and he will be expected to take his coaching badges and won't have the luxuries of St George's Park. Sadly, he has no physio at his disposal so he will have to take a first aid course and will also have to attend a child protection course. This is all time he has to give up of his own accord and that's before preparing training sessions (*"fail to prepare, prepare to fail"*) or picking teams and attending matches. Most managers will have a son in the team which is why they got involved in the first place but it's still a big commitment and sometimes a thankless task

Who'd be a manager?

I've heard some pretty disturbing stories concerning managers at grassroots level. The manager punched on the touchline by an angry parent for substituting his son. The manager who ended up having his car damaged, deep scratches caused by keys, after an argument with an irate parent after the game. The manager who had his Sunday dinner ruined from an impromptu visit from an aggressive parent, who let rip on the manager's doorstep in full view of his wife and kids. I have even heard the tale of a successful local manager who was voted out by mutinous parents simply because his team finished second in the league to their bitter rivals.

These are just some of the stories I have heard of but I'm sure that there are many more and probably a lot more shocking. The stories are all the more disturbing because they were aimed at individuals who don't get paid for what they do and give up their free time to do so. A friend of mine is a UEFA B coach who started coaching at youth level and went on to senior football managing and coaching at Non-League reserve team level and managed Swindon's Ladies team while scouting for Swindon. He told me he made the move up so that he didn't have to deal with parents anymore.

What some parents don't see, or appreciate, is all the time the managers put in preparing training sessions (*"fail to prepare, prepare to fail"*), attending meetings, all the phone calls and emails and the match days too. Yet parents are really quick to criticise and the complaints can be really trivial, so why criticise, or even attack, someone who gives up their time for free?

Everyone's got an opinion

Football is a game of opinions and everyone has one. As soon as anyone starts watching football they are an authority on the game and are keen to share their opinions. Maybe the growth of the football pundit has changed the analytical appreciation of the game. Televised games tend to spend more time on the punditry than they do on the game itself.

Football fans usually have a favourite player but they also support the team and to be fair they pay their money and are entitled to have their say. You could say the same of the parents who also pay their money but they are different in that first and foremost they support one player, their child, or two if you're the owner of the Hayes twins. Win, lose or draw parents' first and foremost concern is their own child.
"We won!"
"Big deal my Johnny only played 10 minutes."
"Danny scored a hat trick!"
"So what my Billy got subbed."

With this in mind you aren't going to please all the parents all the time. In fact it only takes one upset parent to cause trouble for the manager. So, while Danny's parents are celebrating his hat trick with a trip to Pizza Hut the manager is taking a call from Billy's upset parent/s.

Parents also have a greater access to the manager than say an Arsenal or Cheltenham fan so the abuse really is up close and personal and sometimes the level of abuse or violence is frightening and it totally crosses the imaginary line. The respect line was brought in to keep parents from the touchline, however, every Sunday you can still witness parents/linesmen frantically waving offside flags while dodging encroaching parents.

The respect line has many uses, a hurdle, and a makeshift limbo pole, for getting the grass off of boots, although the once proud taut line usually ends up dragging along the floor like an escaping snake. In fact it has many uses except for stopping parents inching towards the pitch. Besides, the best most effective respect line isn't going to stop the verbal abuse that players, managers and referees endure.

The FA have tried to tackle the issues with various campaigns and videos and yet still referees are leaving the grassroots game in droves and we are hearing of more and more cases of outbreaks of violence at junior football matches:

A junior football match descended into violence after a referee sent off parents at the weekend. The incident which occurred at Blackburn Central High School involving two under 16 teams on Saturday sparked calls for police to attend.

Police said they were called to the incident at around 10.50am after a fight broke out between approximately 20 people including both adults and children.

The incident at the school off Haslingden Road has also been reported to the Lancashire FA. Police said no arrests were made but several people were spoken to after the incident.

A police spokesman said: "A fight broke out at a youth football game between two local teams, It was a public order offence and around 20 people both adults and children were involved. Three people were identified by police and had to be spoken to about the incident, No arrests have been made at this stage."

"I ran on to a pitch to stop an assault on one of my players, I stood in the way of an opposition player who gave me and my wife a mouthful of abuse. Others joined in. One lad came over to me and said: 'I've just phoned my brother and he and his mates are going to come down here and shoot you.' I called my team off the pitch. I couldn't take that lightly after what had happened to my team."

"A parent came onto the pitch after the game and told me how awful I was, swearing in my face. He poked me in the chest and told me I shouldn't be a referee, with other awful language as well - that scared me and made me not want to be involved anymore."

Extracts from www.teamgrassroots.co.uk, www.theguardian.com/ football, www.bbc.co.uk

It really is scary that people involved in the game have been intimidated, threatened, beaten up. They say that cases of football hooliganism have reduced but perhaps it's just adopted the grassroots game.

The FA are trying their hardest and the advent of Charter Standard Clubs have made the clubs more accountable and every club has a code of conduct but issuing them and applying them are two different things and it only takes a minority to spoil it for the rest.

So to those about to manage we salute you.

It's football, it's the beautiful game and there's nothing better than the thrills and exhilaration that the game can give you. My mate Tom says "it's not always about winning, it's about seeing the players develop, it's about them doing what they thought they couldn't do, it's about defying the odds and that's why I do it"

I think you can compare it to teaching and the thrill of football is similar to when I see a student get an 'A' for an essay or when they open that final envelope with those all-important results in.

What makes it all the more fantastic is that the grassroots manager and all those other volunteers do it for nothing and for that I take my hat off to all of them.

So there you have a brief insight into Dalworth United. The all-conquering, locally-renowned Dalworth United Under 15s.

Let's move onto season 2017-18. The season starts here.

CHAPTER TWO

PRE-SEASON

'Gutted I'm Sick as a parrot'

Last year saw Dalworth United complete the treble and they did so in impressive style.

Team	P	W	D	L	F	A	GD	Pts
Dalworth United	18	17	0	1	69	13	56	51
Tamworth Rovers	18	12	2	4	56	29	27	38
Kingsbridge	18	10	3	5	55	31	24	33
Phoenix United	18	8	5	5	38	31	7	29
Langton Reds	18	7	5	6	47	42	5	26
Parkfield	18	6	4	8	47	48	-1	22
Leighbridge Lions	18	5	5	8	53	52	1	20
Redbridge Sports	18	4	6	8	35	44	-9	18
Oak Town United	18	4	4	10	36	48	-12	16
Dunstable Colts	18	0	0	18	9	107	-98	0

The undisputed Under 14s champions lost only one game. They also won the Dave Bodkin League Cup and the Arthur Goodwin District Cup. Manager Michael Harris' achievements were rewarded with promotion to the club's senior side, the Under 18s, for the forthcoming season in the prestigious Under 18s county league. Harris' assistant Vinny Smith was asked to move up to the manager's role a role he was quick to accept. So a new season a new managerial team and the success of last season was even attracting media interest from the local paper the Dalworth News.

New Season, Same Goals by Roger Wilkinson sports editor Dalworth News

The treble-winning Dalworth United Under 15s might start the new season with a new manager but they still have the same aspirations and goals. After securing the treble last season Manager and UEFA B qualified coach Michael Harris was asked to lead the U18s in the county league, a position he was quick to accept. Dalworth United are hoping to forge closer links with their local senior side to provide a gateway for its players to progress to senior football and Harris has been tasked with providing the foundation for the club to progress. Such was the success of the U14s team last season that they created quite a buzz and the local scouts were soon flocking to the team's games and this led to striker Danny Webster and goalkeeper Luke Dryland both signing for League Two side Cheltenham Town's academy side. Golden Boot winner and Managers and Parents Player of the Year Webster hit an amazing 51 goals in all competitions and Players Player of the Year Dryland impressed between the sticks keeping an impressive 15 clean sheets in the league and cup.

With Harris moving up, his assistant from last season Vinny Smith was asked to take on managerial duties for the **Under 15**s and to carry on the good work from last season. Smith will have to do it without the services of Webster and Dryland but when you go through a season losing only one game and completing a treble you know you will be inheriting a good squad.

So where do you go next and how do you replace the irreplaceable Webster and Dryland?

Manager Smith is under no illusion he has a tough act to follow in Harris but is quick to lay down his own targets and in some respect in doing so he has created his own pressures:

"The first task is to retain all three trophies and the second task is to go through the season unbeaten. While I can see no reason to expect the success to continue I know I must get 110% effort, determination and dedication to achieve my own goals. We go into this as the team to beat so I have to make sure we don't get beaten"

When asked about the loss of Webster and Dryland Smith said:

"It's a team game and I expect other players to step up and maintain and continue the Dalworth legacy".

Smith has definitely laid down his intentions for all to see and only time will tell if he can come good on his claim.

Smith Says (Taken from the club website)
Welcome to a new season and with the exception of a few changes, notably myself as Manager and Simon Sheppard as Assistant Manager, it's business as usual.

You may have seen my interview in the Dalworth News saying I want to go the whole season unbeaten, well that is my aim. This team has built a fearsome reputation for being winners and winners are what we will continue to be. I'm really looking forward to this season and the fresh challenges that lay ahead and I promise we will continue to be the force we were last season. Michael may have left but the will and desire to win hasn't and that is why we must continue his legacy.

We have our trials this coming Sunday (24th July) and then we start training next Sunday (31st July) at 10:30 on the Rec. The first tournament is on Sunday 13th August. We may have some new faces from the trials but I am more than happy with the squad I have inherited.

The new tracksuits, training kit and home and away kit are on order and should be here in the next two weeks. I will hand out the full details of the tournaments at our first training session. Please can you check the dates so I can record players availability?
The Gaffer

Sunday 24th July

Trials day at Dalworth Rec and the sun is shining, not a cloud in the sky, the birds are singing, the grass has been cut and the lines are all marked out to perfection and all that is missing to paint the perfect picture is Lou Reed crooning Perfect Day. When I turn up at the rec Gaffer (all the players and me are to address him as Gaffer) is already there and is pacing up and down like a concerned kid at his birthday party who is hoping that everyone turns up. Trails can be very tense affairs and the number of players that turn up is usually a good indication of the standing of the team. The Gaffer is really excited and optimistic at the prospect of finding a hidden gem amongst today's trialists.

The first thing I notice is that The Gaffer is using last year's balls and bibs (obviously saving the new equipment for next week). The second thing I notice is he is juggling a number of clipboards each of which has a pen and paper attached, he hands one to me.

"Make sure you get as much info as possible Si"

On examination, I notice the clipboard has attached to it three sheets of identical paper that contain a table detailing players name, contact details, position, club and attributes. The final column bears the title Yes or No. A "Hello Si" breaks my concentration as I look up to find four fellow Dalworth Managers/ Coaches. Gaffer hands each of them a clipboard, the information on these clipboards is different to ours and different to each other as it contains the drills and small sided games that Gaffer wants the coaches to deliver.

The drills are already set up in four different stations and The Gaffer gives a quick demonstration of each drill he has set up. There are a few questions but once addressed everyone is ready to go.

It's my turn now.

"Right Si, when someone turns up, note their details and then when the session starts we will watch each group and make notes on technical ability and attributes."

Gaffer points to the two pitches already set up:

"When the small sided games start we'll compare notes".

I can see why The Gaffer is anxious because you simply do not know how many players will turn up. Gaffer breaks away from me to meet and greet last year's goalkeeper Luke Dryland. Luke has kindly agreed to put any new goalkeepers or existing ones through their paces and that explains the separate station away from all the others. Everything and everyone is in place all we need now are players.

The players start turning up and The Gaffer and I are both scribbling names and details.

"Name?"
"Gary Neville"

Gaffer looks up to see the angelic face of Alex Hayes our midfield 'exterminator'

"Funny Alex"

Alex smiles and moves on.

"Next" says Gaffer, eyes firmly fixed on the piece of paper in front of him.
"Phil Neville".
"Piss off Aidan".
Gaffer doesn't have to look up to realise its Aidan Hayes the other half of our midfield assassination duo and twin of Alex.
"Next"

Gaffer spots a face he doesn't know.

"Name"
"Henry Keen"
"Position" Gaffer will get contact details at the end.

"Forward"

"Club"

"Plumpley Colts"

"Thanks. Next"

This year's squad is here early and Adam Morley, our skillful midfield playmaker, and ever the fashionista, uses this captive audience to show off his new pair of Ray-Bans which Gaffer has to forcibly remove before Adam starts training. He is also wearing a Calvin Klein sleeveless white vest and a ridiculously tight pair of Sergio Tacchini shorts. Plonked on his head is a white silk bandana and he has a pair of Neon Green laceless Puma ONE 2018 football boots with white ankle socks.

At least he is wearing a top which is more than can be said for our baby faced assassins Alex and Aidan who are shirtless until Gaffer barks at them to cover up.

Billy Belafonte is covered up, albeit in food with the remains of an early morning pre-training fry up splattered all over his shirt. He has a touch of egg on his chin, a dollop of tomato ketchup on the side of his mouth, baked bean juice on his white England football shirt and a slick of oil on his shorts that found its way there via greasy hands. Gaffer is less than impressed with Billy who with his unkempt hair looks like he has made his way to the trails via a nightclub and cafe.

To be fair last year's squad look like they have all arrived from last season's final game. There are too many muddy football boots and last year's disheveled training tops and shirts for Gaffers liking. This is in comparison to the trailists who have brand new football shirts and spotless boots fresh out of the box.

Once we have all the information, we do a quick head count and we have a total of 24 trialists, of which there are two goalkeepers, two right backs, three centre backs, one left back, four central midfielders, eleven forwards and one "Well I've never played before but I'd like to be a Jamie Vardy".

There are also twelve of last year's squad, three are missing but all with valid excuses. There are 36 players in total in attendance so Gaffer goes for four groups of eight. Danny Hall is press-ganged into joining the goalkeepers for today so they join Luke. He divides the current squad, splitting them into the four groups. The members of the current squad have already passed judgement on the new faces, some of whom they know from school or have played against them.

"He's unfit"
"He's a hoof ball merchant"
"He's shit"
"Third choice for the school team"

The boys judgements seem harsher than a Sir Alan Sugar verdict on The Apprentice but in reality they were right as one by one the trialists received the dreaded 'No' tick. Straight away you can tell the standard as poor touches and misplaced passes reveal the level of ability on show and our Jamie Vardy wannabe is more Oliver Hardy than the England striker. The current squad, ability-wise, is head and shoulders above the trialists, who are struggling to keep up and this is why you always include your current squad in trials because it gives you a benchmark and if a trialist can replicate the skills and touch of your current charges then you know you might be onto a winner.

Slowly but surely the dreaded "Nos" mount and Gaffer's hopes of finding the next Danny Webster are disappearing faster than chocolate cake at a Weight Watchers meeting. This isn't the only thing quickly disappearing as the hopes and dreams of the trialists begin to evaporate and some seek a quick getaway feigning injuries and illnesses as a way of avoiding the inevitable rejection.

"I think I've hurt my leg"
"I feel sick"

Some just up and go as they disappear into the horizon, Jamie Vardy/ Oliver Hardy at last shows us a quick turn of pace when he spots his way out in the car park and shows us his heels when his Dad turns up.

The Gaffer is in frequent conversation with the four coaches and between the six of us we all draw the same conclusion that out of the 24 who came to impress we agree that there are 2 who may meet the desired criteria. Jez Cherry a tall uncompromising centre back and Greg Chellel a small but aggressive central midfielder, however Gaffer isn't totally convinced by the two players.

"Bloody hell, where are all the good players Si?"
"We've already got them Gaffer"
"Good point Si".

We go into some small sided games with the remaining 30 players, having lost six, and all eyes are on the two possible additions to our ranks. Jez is pitted against current first team centre forward Luke Pilbeam. A rampant

Luke runs Jez ragged and the tall centre back cannot cope with Luke's pace and movement and another hopeful falls by the wayside. This leaves Greg who is pitted against Alex and Aidan Hayes. Alex and Aidan systematically 'set about' him and after a few tackles and 'reminders' that they are there he simply throws in the towel and limps off. The arm he waved to signal his departure might as well have been holding a white flag.

So there you have it 24 trialists and none taken up. We may have got it wrong but looking at the 24 there were none that were better than we already have. Gaffer brings proceedings to an end and gathers the remaining players together. The current squad slope off to one side and Gaffer breaks the bad news to the trialists. Some seem disappointed and others seem relieved. The watching dads waiting for their sons seem more disappointed when they hear the outcome and you can hear the mutterings and mumblings, which it has to be said, were meant to be heard.

"It was a fix son"
"You was by far the best player out there"
"Tamworth trials are next week"

Some Dads are less forgiving and lay into their already shattered sons.
"What was wrong with you?"
"You didn't get stuck in"
"I told you not to pass and have loads of shots"
I heard one boy sum it up to perfection.
"Well why didn't you trial then?"

Sorry, whose dreams have been shattered?

We collect all the equipment in and Gaffer collects the clipboards and thanks the coaches. He did go to put the sheets in the bins but I remind him of Data Protection and I take the sheets for shredding. You can see the disappointment in his face as he realises that it's been a waste of time and that it has been totally unproductive. I try to put a positive spin on proceedings "Well at least we know the players we have got are the best available to us" Gaffer just nods without replying, the disappointment etched on his face. That's all folks the Dalworth **Under 15**s trials have been completed for another year.

Thursday 28th July

Gaffer is picking me up at 6:30pm as we are attending the annual league meeting to collect fixtures and find out who we are getting in the cups. The Gaffer was absolutely buzzing when he picked me up and proceeded to talk tactics, players and expectations for the season for the entire 40-minute journey. The disappointment of the trials is a distant memory and at the forefront of his thoughts is the launch of the new season. There has never been any doubting of his enthusiasm and the preparation that had taken place before a ball had even been kicked is evident. He has been planning for this moment the minute he was offered the chance to step up and he is certainly not going to waste the chance. I even detect an air of arrogance as we entered the venue; no we didn't enter to 'Simply the Best' but Gaffer strolled into the bar like a King addressing his subjects.

There were loads of nods and "Hellos" and acknowledgements but you got the feeling that it could have been a press conference for WWE's Royal Rumble 2017 with lots of egos looking to get an edge over their opponents. The mind games were starting already. I had a chat with the manager of Dunstable City, a really nice guy who despite not getting a point last season was still carrying on. They had however amalgamated with a very good village side and were expecting to ruffle a few feathers this year. The Gaffer remained very aloof almost looking at opposing managers with disdain. It was a really long night and like most league meetings there was lots of red tape and long drawn out procedures not to mention the small point of electing and re-electing the league committee. The only reason the managers were there were for the league fixtures and the cup draws and the committee took their time to ensure that the managers took in every last agenda point before the anticipated fixtures and cup draw were handed out. Yes, no drawing balls out of a bag as Colin the fixtures secretary handed out his typed fixtures list. This was the point where managers scoured the room to 'eyeball' opponents and put the intimidation factor into play. While The Gaffer was busy planning his route to the two cup finals I was simply thinking about the long night's marking that awaited me tomorrow. Despite the late night I still managed a glass or two of red wine and on a school night tut tut!

Saturday 30th July
Gaffer's been on the phone but I was too busy marking to answer, he did leave a 'coded' message though "Just ringing about tomorrow Si but don't worry, everything's sorted" another glass of red wine please dear.

Sunday 31st July
It's a scorching hot day at Dalworth Rec and the boys are all on time but some look agitated by the searing heat already. Without the matching training kits that are still on order, the boys are left to their own devices and they do again resemble a rag tag army. There is an assortment of various teams football shirts on display although the Hayes twins opt for

the optimum tanning 'wife beater' which is accompanied by 80s style Sergio Tacchini 'short shorts' and Puma flip flops, which thankfully they will not be training in. I'm half tempted to offer up a couple of knotted handkerchiefs to complete their look, a look which is again surpassed by Adam Morley who is wearing a bandana, a 'Cradle of Filth' t-shirt bearing a very obscene logo and bright yellow shorts, although the obscene logo is nowhere near as obscene as the ensemble he has thrown together. It really is an assault on the senses however Gaffer, when he eventually turns up, is quick to launch a neon yellow coloured bib at Adam in a bid to save our sense of decency and the reputation of the club. Whilst the bib has the desired effect it also attracts every thunder bug in Cheltenham and Adam spends the rest of the session resembling a demented air traffic controller waving his arms windmill style while moaning as the bugs attach themselves to him to create a weird neon yellow and black speckled kit reminiscent of the old paint splattered effect kits of the 80s. The boys turn up carrying a variety of team bags and boot bags; Johnny Day has his boots tied round his neck, unlike Billy Belafonte who is carrying a McDonald's bag which once contained a Bacon Egg & Cheese Bagel, a Sausage & Egg McMuffin and three Hash Browns. Billy dumps his bag in the bin and then he and Charlie Fisher are playing a Billy devised game in which the aim is for Charlie to guess which McDonalds food Billy ate by smelling his burps. It's a pretty disgusting game and while I can't see it replacing The Chase or even Catchphrase it might have a slot somewhere on Channel 5's schedule but for now it's keeping the boys entertained until training starts.

Back to The Gaffer, who as I mentioned turned up ten minutes after the scheduled arrival time with his son Jimmy. The Gaffer appears on the horizon towing several brightly coloured red ball bags and resembling a cart horse dragging its heavy load. He hands me a training schedule, neatly bound in a binder while trying to catch his breath.

"Here Si, It's all in here, the whole pre-season schedule"

The Gaffer then takes a further ten minutes unpacking the brightly coloured and spanking brand-new cones, bibs, traffic cones, agility ladders and hurdles, all of which are still in their bags. The Gaffer begins ripping at the bags like an excited kid at Christmas, albeit without a Mum to tidy up afterwards. Still it provides a bit of temporary amusement for the boys who chase the bags about, although the Hayes twins have to be brought to task when Alex Hayes tries suffocating his twin Aidan with one of the bags. The Gaffer oblivious to all this carnage takes another 20 minutes to set everything up and slowly but surely the neon cones light up Dalworth Rec and my concerns switch from training ever starting to a light aircraft mistaking the Rec for a runway and trying to land. I'm keeping one eye on the skies in fear of being squashed.

In the time Gaffer sets up the remaining drills, Aidan Hayes punches Alex Hayes in retaliation for the attempted asphyxiation and I have to split the warring twins up. Stevie Carr and Johnny Day play Frisbee with the cones; cones which The Gaffer has already set up for his drills and the whole team decide to take 'a wazz' against the wire fence by the pitch, a fence which separates the Rec from the Dalworth Bowls Club.

I'm sure the bowling club would have welcomed the additional watering it received although such was the saturation that it made that morning's ends slightly unbalanced as one end was fast while the other was very slow, which made bowling very difficult and unbalanced. If there was a commentary it would have been very interesting:

"And Its Arthur Evans, bowling into the heavily piss saturated end..."

I would imagine that the bowling towels would have had to have had a very hot wash later that day. However disgusted the Ladies captain may have been at the free sprinkling of their greens this anger was surpassed by the sight that greeted her as she surveyed the green. Her gaze diverting from the lush bowling green, to the sight of 15 todgers being waved at her as they were being emptied. The boys were also doing their best out of control sprinkler impressions in fact I'm amazed that any urine made it to the Bowling Green until I realised that the boys went for the full effect and had placed said 'todgers' through the wire fence.

The Gaffer, of course, is still oblivious to all of this as I try to prevent a major incident developing between Dalworth Under 15s and Dalworth Bowls Club. While I'm frantically apologising to the Bowls captain I'm ushering the boys in the direction of the training pitch. The Gaffer is still lost in the moment as he frantically paces up and down the Rec counting and recounting his paces. Laying and relaying cones and adjusting and readjusting agility ladders into place.

Then the moment finally arrives:

"Right boys in you come", and The Gaffer prepares to deliver his inaugural speech:

"Last season is gone boys. Last season we finished as champions, now we are just another team trying to win the league. But we are the defending champions and the team that everyone wants to beat. If anyone thinks we can't better last season then you're wrong. I want us to go through the whole season unbeaten. I want us to retain all three trophies and I want us to be the new 'Invincibles' Are you up for the challenge and are you ready to create history? Well, are you up for it?"

The Gaffer pauses, waiting for his call to arms to be accepted. But this is no Richard the Third moment. Instead the silence is broken by Ben Padgham who asks: "Any chance of doing some training Gaffer"

He has a point we are now 45 minutes into the session and not a bead of sweat has been spilt and a despondent Gaffer ushers the boys towards the warm up area he has coned off. He runs through a quick warm up then quickly moves onto a SAQ (speed, agility quickness) drill. He is really putting the boys through their paces and to be fair the boys are responding well and putting the effort in. It is a quick high intensity SAQ drill and Gaffer is both impressed and happy again.

"Right boys, grab a drink, I've got new bottles".

The boys look around amongst the many training items but no bottles can be found. Aidan Hayes pipes up:

"Where's the bloody bottles?"
"Address me as Gaffer Aidan."
"Where's the bloody bottles Gaffer?"

Gaffer surveys the area and you can tell by the look that breaks on his face what comes next: "Oh shit, I've got no bottles".

Aidan quickly bursts into an impromptu chorus of: "Gaffer's got no bottle, Gaffer's got no bottle".

Gaffer glares at Aidan who smiles back with an angelic-come-devil-possessed smile. Once the muffled laughs have died down, Gaffer instructs the boys to grab a drink from the fountain. A disorderly queue is formed and I take up a position between the fountain and the fence, the fountain is situated near to the fence and there is at present a bowls match taking place. Five minutes later and the boys are back in place, thirst quenched and thankfully without the need to empty bladders, which in turn leaves me relieved. I advise The Gaffer of the time, it is now 12:00.

"OK boys let's finish with some keep ball, sort out two teams half in yellow bibs and half in blue". Alex Hayes is the first to notice.

"Where's the f**king balls?"

"Gaffer Alex, it's Gaffer."

"Where's the f**king balls Gaffer?"

All eyes are on The Gaffer who cracks under the pressure as his schoolboy error dawns on him: "Oh f**k, I've got no balls"

Alex picks up the song just as The Gaffer finishes his sentence.

"Gaffer's got no balls, Gaffer's got no balls".

The Gaffer tries his hardest to correct his mistake and rather than putting Alex to task tries to save face by completely ignoring the situation.

"Right boys, let's do a walkthrough of our formation for the season".

Before Gaffer can say 4-4-2, Billy Belafonte brings the session to an abrupt halt:

"Sorry Gaffer, my Dad's here to pick me up".

Before Gaffer can say anything, Luke Pilbeam and Charlie Fisher are also on their way. Gaffer begrudgingly accepts defeat.

"OK, see you Tuesday boys" and starts the tedious task of putting everything back in the bags.

The boys that remain assist The Gaffer, sensing his pain. The Hayes twins however see it as too good an opportunity to miss:

"Gaffers got no players" they sing in unison, sniggering.

Gaffer turns to me. "What did they say?"

"Nothing Gaffer, nothing."

Hayes Twins 1 Gaffer 0.

Walking back to the car Ben Padgham sidles up to me "That was a shocking session Simon, not a great start, Gaffer needs to redeem himself on Tuesday" Pre-Season has well and truly begun.

Monday 31st July

An excited Gaffer is on the phone:

"I've got a great idea for training Si, the boys will be on board and it'll be a bit of fun, bit of team bonding, see you at six tomorrow."

I realise when I get off the phone that: a) I never said a word and b) The

Gaffer didn't actually tell me what the idea was. I am intrigued though.

Tuesday 1st August
I'm 15 minutes early for training and five minutes later Gaffer marches on to the Rec dragging his ball bags, which do include footballs and water bottles. He dumps the bags down and takes out of his pocket a fluorescent pink bib, he proudly holds it up for me to see.

On the bib is a crudely drawn but already fading *W* in black felt tip. The boys slowly start to arrive and once again we have a full turn out by 6:00pm.

Adam Morley is wearing a head-turning pink Real Madrid football top which he has matched with bright yellow shorts and white football socks with lime green Adidas football boots. Alex and Aidan are both wearing Parkas over their football kits, despite the fact that its summer and I keep waiting for them to break out into their own rendition of "*Wonderwall*" although they are more likely to have a Gallagher style punch up than starting their own Oasis tribute band.

Billy Belafonte hasn't got any food about his person but close inspection of his red England top shows evidence that he has recently devoured a Spaghetti Bolognese

"Right boys..."

The Gaffer proudly displays his work of art.

"This is the wally of the week bib, every Tuesday before training we vote for the wally of the week and that person wears the bib at training. Then the following week we vote for a new wally. Right, so any nominations boys?"

Quick as a flash Alex and Aidan Hayes look at each other and then in brotherly unison say "You Gaffer" and the exchange follows:

Gaffer: "Me?"
Alex & Aidan: Yes, you Gaffer"
Gaffer: "Why me?"
Alex: "You've got no balls Gaffer"
Aidan: "You've got no bottle Gaffer"
Gaffer: "Any other nominations?"
Gaffer is almost pleading for another nomination.
Alex & Aidan (beaming) "No, just you Gaffer!"

To say the bib was a tight fit was an understatement. The crudely drawn W immediately doubled in size once sat on Gaffer's portly midriff. It was only the XXL white shirt under the bib that prevented a muffin top effect but the bib did look like a crop top on The Gaffer and breathing became a very delicate operation, in fact any form of quick or sudden movement was completely out of the question. Gaffer spent the rest of the session moving gingerly around the field resembling a geriatric walking footballer. Once or twice Gaffer did break out into a jog and the Hayes twins immediately held out their arms and twiddled their fingers, the same movement that players do prior to their captain lifting a trophy, in excited anticipation that said bib was going to explode from Gaffer's chest like the alien bursting from John Hurt's chest. Despite The Gaffer's discomfort he still delivered a good session and I'm pleased to report that the seams of the bib remained intact, just. The Hayes twins still claimed a moral victory though.

Hayes Twins 2 Gaffer 0.

Thursday 4th August
We are attending a managers' meeting at the Dukes Arms. The committee quickly whizzes through the agenda and then it's a general chit chat over a few pints or in my case four pints of Coke, which leaves me bloated and frequently visiting the loo.

Sunday 6th August
I'm early to training again today and I'm surprised to see The Gaffer already there and once again the Rec is lit up with a kaleidoscope of colours. "Couldn't sleep Gaffer?" I ask.

"Fail to prepare Si, prepare to fail."

The boys begin turning up and in keeping with early season tradition are all the present and correct by the designated time. Gaffer is cheating regarding the bib and just has it round his neck and it's flapping around like a scarf in a storm. Warm up, SAQ and keep ball, the session is flowing and everyone is giving their all and The Gaffer is beaming.

"Right let's finish with a small sided game 8v8"
"Erm Gaffer there's 15 of us"
"I'll make the numbers up, Si you ref"

The game is flowing and there are lots of positives technically but you can tell The Gaffer isn't happy and he is coming across somewhat agitated. He makes his agitations known with a snappy "Come on boys, it's not non-contact" and "I want a proper game situation" but the instructions don't appear to be getting across, until he drops the bombshell in the form of a somewhat crude instruction:

"Get stuck in!"

Now it's OK to make the game a little more match-realistic but the minute he says those words I see the Hayes twins eyes light up and from the little nod of heads they exchange I get the impression that Gaffer may have armed the nuclear warheads.

It's one thing giving The Hayes twins Carte Blanche but it's another to invite them to 'get stuck in' The whole complexion and mood of the game quickly changes and whereas beforehand it was being played in a good spirit it becomes very frantic and starts getting a little bit 'tasty' Slowly but surely players are diving into tackles and getting wound up and whereas before Gaffer's instructions everyone had loads of time on the ball, it's a bit hot potato now. I try to keep a lid on the aggression, which is spilling over, by awarding a few free kicks but the game is getting niggly and it's easier said than done. The Gaffer is not helping matters as he seems to be enjoying the situation and questions every decision I make "Come on Si, that was a great tackle" "It's a man's game Si" the whole game is in serious danger of degenerating into a free-for-all so I try to reason with The Gaffer

"Someone's going to get hurt Gaffer"
"Don't be silly Si, it's like a proper game now and no one's going to get hurt"

And then...

I don't know if you have seen the film 'Platoon' and the scene where the unarmed Sergeant Elias played by Willem Dafoe gets left behind by his Platoon, presumed dead, but he isn't and he is being chased by the Viet Cong and almost toyed with as they pick him off as bullet after bullet finds its target. There's an iconic moment just before he is killed when he raises his arms, all in slow-motion, before the fatal bullets strike and he slumps to the ground dead. Well if you can recollect the film and the scene then keep that image in mind.

The ball is pinging around and every now and then there is a little bit of 'afters'. The Gaffer, rather than trying to curb everyone's over exuberance is making things worse with such comments as "Great tackle" and "Loving the commitment boys".

This simply adds fuel to the fire and the game is now being played at breakneck pace and when Johnny Day fizzes a pass to The Gaffer, who is occupying the central midfield spot (he isn't venturing out of the center circle) Gaffer's first touch is a shocker and he has to stretch to try to retain the ball. However steaming in on The Gaffers blind side is Alex Hayes who gets to the ball first. The Gaffer arrives, approximately a millisecond later, off-balance and waving his leg in the air, like a swimmer testing how cold the pool is. The Gaffer gets a touch on the ball but despite the weight advantage Alex throws everything into the tackle and with The Gaffer having the faintest of contact Alex sends him flying through the air (cue the Elias image) with his arms outstretched.

However, awaiting The Gaffer on his descent is not a Viet Cong bullet but Aidan Hayes who enters the fray a split second after his brother and clips The Gaffer on the side sending him spinning mid-air. Imagine a helicopter spiraling towards the ground, rotors desperately trying to prevent the impending crash; well this is The Gaffer's predicament. The Gaffer cannot escape his fate and crash lands, leaving him in a crumpled mess on the floor.

The Hayes twins offer their (in)sincere apologies.
"Sorry Gaffer"
"Yeah sorry Gaffer"

Then they are off again kicking anything that moves. The Gaffer, pride, right ankle and ribs battered and bruised, attempts to get up quickly but stumbles and collapses as his right ankle gives way. He gets up again, balances on his left foot and manages, between staggered breathes, to address the players:

"That's what I want to see, a bit of passion and commitment, right drinks break lads."

A disheveled and aching Gaffer staggers his way over to the drinks bottles, sits down and summons me over.

"Take my place Si"

Hayes Twins 3 Gaffer 0.

Tuesday 8th August
No training tonight as Gaffer confides in me that he has cancelled it due to his severely bruised right ankle, he offers up photographic evidence via his phone like a kid offering his PE teacher a note to excuse him from

the lesson. The photo reveals a shocking mass of black and blue bruises surrounding the ankle. Of course The Gaffer tells the boys that he has to work rather than giving Alex and Aidan the satisfaction of adding another victim to their ever growing CV. But we know the truth.

Hayes Twins 4 Gaffer 0

Saturday 12th August
Gaffer rings about the squads for tomorrows two tournaments. Gaffer is going to the Langton Reds 5-a-side and I'm taking a squad to the Dunstable Colts 6-a-side. Everyone is meeting at the Rec at 9am.

Smith Says
Tomorrow we get the chance to put all the hard work from training into competitive Football when we take part in the Langton Reds and Dunstable Colts tournaments. I've selected two competitive squads for both tournaments and there is certainly no A or B squad just two teams more than capable of winning their tournaments.

I've opted to enter two teams for two tournaments rather than entering two teams into one tournament so that all the boys get a chance to play this weekend and it gives us the chance to win two tournaments early doors. I will be taking the Reds tournament while Simon is taking a squad to Dunstable. The meeting point for both teams is 9am at the Rec.

I would like to take this opportunity to thank you the parents in advance for the time you give up and I'm sure me and the boys will repay you with silverware.
The Gaffer

Pre-Season tournaments fall into several categories: good or bad, wet or dry, well-run or poorly-run. Either way, they are an established part of youth football and an invaluable source of making pre-season income. They are not only another way to raise funds for the club. They offer a chance to win trophies and bond squads (and parents) together. While managers go with a clear plan (win the tournament) the parents face a different set of dilemmas, Tea or Coffee, Burger or Hot Dog, Factor 10 or Factor 30, gazebo or deck chair. I really feel sorry for them as it can be a long and expensive day.

I can remember attending one which lasted five hours and consisted of 40 minutes of football and despite the fact that we won it the whole tournament it was a long and tedious experience. It can also be very expensive as the tournament organisers try to entice every penny available as parents work their way through gallons of tea and coffee and eat mountains of bacon, sausage or egg rolls in the morning and burgers and hot dogs in the afternoon.

If you attend our tournament I thoroughly recommend the excellent egg, bacon, sausage and mushroom baguette. Frequent trips to the refreshments stalls throughout the day alleviate the boredom that accompanies standing around waiting for the occasional football match. Alongside the food stalls there is usually a sweet stall which encourages players to eat their own body weight in confectionery as they, and I quote: "Need energy for all the football they are going to play". I wonder if the number of emergency visits to hospitals and dentists goes up during the tournament season?

Parents also need to ensure they save sufficient funds for the obligatory post tournament Ice Cream at the end of the day. This is the final act of the day and is bought under the pretence that it is in the form of a token of commiseration or celebration and woe betide the dad that used his last pennies in the beer tent. Shame on you Dad!

For those parents that have attended these tournaments for several years, and survived, they can claim the title of hardened tournament veteran. Whatever the weather they are prepared Sunshine: they are armed with factor 50 suntan lotions, gazebos and ice; Storms: they are equipped with kagoules umbrellas and towels. You can spot these veterans a mile away, the tell-tale signs are the flasks, umbrellas, portable deck chairs, the cool boxes and in some cases the tents. They are the ones who shuffle around the pitches looking for the optimum spot. These are the people who are the first ones to pitch their towels poolside on holiday.

"We've got three games on pitch four, two on pitch six and two on pitch seven so I reckon between pitch six and seven is the best bet"

"East is that way so here should give us maximum exposure to the sun"

"The wind is blowing from the north so I reckon set the gazebo up facing that way"

Once unloaded, pitched and unpacked the next task is to establish the key spots the refreshments and the toilets.

The toilets as we have mentioned can be life savers or life takers depending on the time of the day and whether you wish to risk it or hold on to try to find a pub or fast food place. Once the preliminaries are completed then it is a case of digging in and trying to get through the tournament without any casualties. I'm surprised that clubs don't sell newspapers or cross word puzzle books or offer free wi-fi because the actual waiting between games can be really painful although this is when the parenting skills really come to the fore.

Trying to keep the kids calm and conserving energy between games is a major task especially if you are in charge of Alex and Aidan Hayes. I would imagine trying to keep King Kong shackled is an easier task. Thankfully Grandad Hayes is the calmest, most placid person you could hope to meet and possesses the qualities to keep his grandsons under control for the duration of the longest tournament. The FA have never produced a study on how to survive tournament football and I'm surprised that Fat Boy Slim hasn't produced a tournament re-mix of his classic retitling it Eat - Play –Pee – Repeat.

Sunday 13th August

Tournament day and everyone is bright eyed (sort of) and bushy tailed. Parents gather round The Gaffers new Mercedes Vito Tourer while the boys chase each other in and out of the cars. Adam Morley has got a massive pair of headphones, baseball cap, peak at the back and what look like a pair of plus fours with a check t-shirt and a red body warmer. The Hayes twins are both downing a large can of Red Bull each, which they quickly follow up with a large Monster energy drink, heaven help us all. Billy has made his morning trip to McDonalds and Luke has received an invitation to compete with Charlie for the title of "Whose Burp is it Anyway" champion. Although judging by Luke's face, Billy may have been mixing McDonalds with rancid eggs, such is the look of disgust and gagging that follows Billy's latest belch.

Gaffer is busy handing out letters to parents/designated drivers with the directions to whatever venue their child is playing. Then it's a quick head count and the boys destined for Langton are very excited to learn that they are travelling in The Gaffer's new motor/team bus and parents will follow behind. Sadly the Dunstable lads are not afforded the same luxury and trudge off to the familiarity of their parent's cars. Then its wagons rolling as the cars depart the Rec and its left for Dunstable and right for Langton.

The two squads are as follows:

Langton Reds: Stevens, Day, Belafonte, Morley, Webster, Fisher, Smith (c)

Dunstable Colts: Hall, Sheppard, Carr, Padgham (c), Hayes, Hayes, Haugh, Pilbeam,

Dunstable Colts 6-a-side

The Dunstable tournament is one of the better ones that we participate in and we know it's going to be competitive. My pre-tournament speech is easy though: "Go out and enjoy yourselves and have fun."

Ben then chipped in with his bit and away they went, focused, determined and ready. It's fair to say that the boys certainly enjoyed themselves because they won the tournament and they won it in some style. They didn't concede a goal all day and won the four group games 2-0, 1-0, 3-0 and 1-0 with Luke Pilbeam 2, Brian Haugh 2, Ben Padgham, Alex Hayes and Stevie Carr getting the goals.

The winners of the two groups went onto the final which was against our hosts Dunstable City. It was a tense affair but two late goals from Aidan Hayes and Luke Pilbeam saw us lift the trophy with a 2-0 score line. No one was in any doubt who was player of the tournament though and that honour went to Danny Hall who was unbeaten between the sticks pulling off save after save including an amazing double save in the final when the score line was 0-0.

The football the boys played was at times mesmerising and they won a lot of admirers and praise. In time honoured tradition I treated the boys to an ice cream, although I made the mistake of saying whatever you want boys. The Hayes twins were straight in and were last spotted munching on two ice creams apiece when we left.

What made this feat of gluttony even more spectacular was each ice cream had an ice lolly sticking out of it. On this occasion they thoroughly earnt it though. It did leave me thankful that Billy wasn't in our squad otherwise he would have cleared the van.

I rang The Gaffer before heading off home and was surprised to hear he was already at home the boys having exited the tournament on penalties in the semi-finals. He congratulated me on the win but you could tell he was agitated when he spoke about his team.

"We was poor, but I put that down to the fact that we had to do loads of waiting around and we couldn't get going and then went out on the lottery of penalties."

I later found out that part of his agitation was down to Billy Belafonte and his love of food. The Gaffers brand spanking new team bus had suffered as a result of Billy eating the following:
Two Cheese burgers

Two Hot Dogs
Two Bacon Rolls
Three Kit Kats
Two Ice Creams
Five cans of Coke

Billy apparently was sick in sensational style and not only managed to throw up in The Gaffer's new Mercedes but also took out two of his team mates. I didn't push for more as I could tell The Gaffer wasn't ready to share the lurid details.

Nick filled in the gaps after relaying the conversation he had had with Johnny which went as follows:

"We were driving back along the motorway to Dalworth and Billy who was sitting in the front seat by the window said to Gaffer he felt sick and Gaffer, who was already in a foul mood, told him to stick his head out of the window cos he wasn't stopping. Billy begged The Gaffer to stop but The Gaffer just said "No".

It was at this point that Billy turned a really funny colour, stuck his head out of the window and puked and just carried on spewing his ring up. The only problem was we were travelling down the by-pass and the puke flew back in the back window and covered Adz and Fish who were sitting at the back. This started Fish gagging and he was sick as well which in turn set off Adz. Gaffer had pulled up at this stage so we were in the lay-by with Fish and Adz covered in puke and throwing up. The Gaffer was going absolutely mental and called Billy a 'fat pig' you should have seen it, total f**king carnage"

Apparently that night Gaffer was cleaning Billy's puke off the roof and seats of his brand new Merc.

Smith Says
Congratulations to Si and the boys for their win at the Dunstable Colts tournament. It would have been great to make it a double celebration but we lost the Langton Reds tournament to the hosts on penalties in the semi-finals. It was disappointing that one team pulled out of our group and although we won both our games we then had a 75 minute wait to our semi and we just couldn't get going again. I would say we were the best team in the semi but we just missed out on a final due to the lottery that is penalties. I felt sorry for Jimmy for missing the third penalty but he had the guts to take it so I'm not apportioning blame because we should have won the game in normal time. However we cannot wallow in the disappointment

because it's the league that matters but we have other tournaments to put things right.

Next week we host our own tournament and I'm sure that we will add more silverware to the collection.
The Gaffer

Tournament Results:
Langton Reds Squad: Stevens, Day, Belafonte, Morley, Webster, Fisher, Smith (c)
Beaten semi-finalists on pens v Langton Reds (lost 3-2)
Goalscorers: Charlie Fisher 2, Bobby Webster
Player of the Tournament: Jimmy Smith
Dunstable Colts Squad: Hall, Sheppard, Carr, Padgham (c), Alex Hayes, Aidan Hayes, Haugh, Pilbeam,
Winners v Dunstable Colts 2-0
Goalscorers: Luke Pilbeam 3, Brian Haugh 2, Ben Padgham, Alex Hayes, Stevie Carr, Aidan Hayes
Player of the Tournament: Danny Hall

Tuesday 15th August
There is a very strange atmosphere at training tonight. Not one mention of the tournaments at the weekend Gaffer just completely swerved them and got straight down to business but the boys couldn't resist a bit of banter and although it was taken in the spirit it was meant to be taken, just a wind up. It did wind up The Gaffer who was biting every time.

Gaffer "Right boys, two groups for SAQ drills"
Aidan Hayes "Right boys Dunstable squad over here"

Cue Gaffer stare.

Gaffer "Right sort two teams for keep ball"
Alex Hayes "Dunstable winners in Yellow bibs, Langton losers in Red bibs"

Cue Gaffer glare.

Gaffer "Right mix it up for a small sided game"

(Gaffer realises he has left himself open again and quickly tries to save the situation)

Gaffer "Billy, Stevie, Johnny, Ben, Adam, Alex, Aidan, Jimmy in Red"
Aidan Hayes "That's fair teams Gaffer a mixture of winners and losers"

Cue Gaffer death stare and swearing under his breath.

During the game Alex mishits a shot and it sails wide of the post

Gaffer responds smugly: "Left your shooting boots at home Alex?"

Alex: "Yeah Gaffer, I'm sick as a pig"

Game Set and Match to the Hayes Twins

The rest of the session passes off without too much aggro with The Gaffer graciously accepting defeat, again.

"See you Sunday boys"

Friday 18th August

Gaffer was on the phone for over a hour last night thrashing out the squads for our tournament. After much deliberation and swopping players to and from the two squads he finally came up with the following.

Dalworth United 'A': Stevens, Sheppard, Day, Morley, Webster, Haugh, Pilbeam, Smith (c)

Dalworth United 'B': Hall, Carr, Belafonte, Hayes, Hayes, Fisher, Padgham (c)

Gaffer is consistently reiterating that 'we must win our own tournament' he finally ends the call and the phone feels very hot, which is more than can be said for my dinner, which is as cold as the stare my wife gives to me. Microwave dinner it is then.

Saturday 19th August - The Dalworth Festival

The one ingredient missing from the selection process yesterday was hindsight because we lost Stevie Carr from the B squad with food poisoning, which is very worrying as Stevie's mum Janet is part of the catering team for the tournament.

Gaffer is on the case though:

"That's ok, you can have Johnny Day from the A squad when he gets here"

Which was ok until the boys informed Gaffer that Johnny was on holiday in Cornwall.

"What?" Then the penny dropped.

"Oh yeah he did tell me".

The Gaffer rushes off to the registration tent and is hastily amending the registration sheets. In the end we are left with a squad of seven and one of six, which bearing in mind this is a 6 a side tournament means we are light.

Dalworth Festival Squads

Dalworth United 'A': Stevens, Sheppard, Morley, Webster, Haugh, Pilbeam, Smith (c)

Dalworth United 'B': Hall, Belafonte, Hayes, Hayes, Fisher, Padgham ©

The Gaffer has completed the admin work and is now in full-on managerial mode, pacing back and forth scribbling on a notepad. He thrusts at me a slightly crumpled piece of paper, which looks like he discarded and then retrieved. Scribbled on it are a variety of formations 2-2-1, 3-1-1, 2-1-2, 1-2-2.

"Here Si, you could use one of these".
"OK Gaffer"

Gaffer is mumbling away to himself eyes fixed on his notepad.

"You alright Gaffer?"

He holds up his notepad and without looking at me says:

"Fail to prepare, Prepare to fail."
"Good luck Gaffer"
"Yep, yep you too"

The Gaffer's focus is solely on the tournament and you can see the determination in his face. Second place is not an option today, well not for both teams it isn't.

"Tell the boys it's our tournament, so we *have* to win it"

"Will do Gaffer, I think I'll just tell them not to get injured or sent off and just to enjoy themselves"

The Gaffer rushes off to his pitch for their first game mumbling "Yeah, enjoy themselves."

The two teams are drawn in two separate six team leagues with the top teams progressing to the final. The Gaffer is desperate to win a tournament and what better tournament to win than your own. I can see in the distance, on the pitch opposite us, he is still scribbling away and oblivious to the tournament hustle and bustle that surrounds him.

"We need more burgers in the tent", "We need a ref for Pitch six", "Portable toilet five needs toilet paper", "Anyone got any change?"

I quickly gather my squad in.

"Right boys, no injuries, no sending offs" (this is particularly aimed at Alex and Aidan)

"...and go and enjoy yourselves."

"Stuff that Simon." Captain for the day, Ben interjects.

"Mind if I say something?"

"No, go ahead Ben" and he is off:

"Right boys we're going to win this bloody thing. 1-3-1. Dan in goal, Aidan you OK to go centre back?" Aidan nods his approval.

"Billy on the left, Alex Centre Mid, Me on the right and Charlie up front"

Billy, Alex and Charlie all nod their approval. Ben pauses to look over at The Gaffer who is also in full flow delivering his rousing pre-tournament speech. I'm sure The Gaffer looks over at Ben mid-speech and they appear to be in a Mexican stand-off, eyes locked, before Ben smiles at The Gaffer and breaks off to deliver his own take on things:

"Right boys, everyone know their jobs?"

The boys all nod in acknowledgement.

"Keep it simple, support the player on the ball, keep the ball in their half and if we lose the ball press high." And finally:

"Let's win this bloody tournament!"

Ben is looking directly at The Gaffer when he says his last words. If The Gaffer looks determined to win this tournament then Ben is positively gagging at the bit to take the trophy. The boys break off and take up their positions. Five minutes later we have three points and a +2 goal difference after a convincing 2-0 win courtesy of goals from Charlie and Ben. The A team scrape a 1-0 win, by The Gaffer's own admission, and he is straight in my ear after the game.

"Did you win?" (The draw has meant that each team plays their games at the same time)
"Yes Gaffer"
"Good, good, what was the score?"
"2-0"
"Excellent, who scored?"
"Fisher and Padgham"

"What formation did you play?"
"1-3-1"
"Interesting"

The Gaffer is furiously scribbling away on his notepad and his tournament programme. I note he is keeping a record of each group stage score and keeping his own league table. The information sharing process happens after every round of games.

Dalworth A win their next three games 1-0, 3-1, 1-0 and draw the last 0-0 and in doing so top the group. Dalworth B wins their next four games 3-2, 4-1, 2-0 and 2-1 and therefore also top their group. After the last round of games The Gaffer walks towards me beaming and rubbing his hands together, notepad and programme tucked under his arm and pen behind his ear. "Dalworth A versus Dalworth B in the final"

The Dalworth Festival U14s Final
The Gaffer is frantically pacing up and down before the final barking out individual instructions to the squad.

"Clean sheet and the trophy's ours Billy"
"OK Gaffer"
"Keep it tight at the back Nick"
"Yes Gaffer"
"Adz you take control of the midfield"
"Got it Gaffer"
"Webbo don't forget to track back"
"Will do Gaffer"
"Brian don't be afraid to take em on with your pace"
"Got ya Gaffer"
"Come on Smudge you owe me a goal, you want to lift that trophy don't ya?"
"Yes Dad, er, Gaffer"
"Be ready Luke, impact player"
"Sub again Gaffer?'
"Come on boys it's our tournament"
"It's their tournament too" Billy reminds The Gaffer pointing to the team sitting a stone's throw away.
"Yeah but you want to win don't you?"
"Of course Gaffer, but it's a win-win situation"
"Yeah but we don't want to lose to the B team do we?"

Billy drops the conversation at this point.

My team talk is shorter:

"Enjoy it boys, you've earned it. Ben do you want to say anything?"

"Cheers Gaffer" (I'm a bit taken aback by this reference, pleasantly so)

"Right boys, hold our formation and don't let them get behind us, press high and work in pairs, be patient the chances will come and like Simon says, let's have some fun."

Ben emphasises the word "fun" and turns to The Gaffer (the other one) and has a positively wicked smile on his face. This final could be very, very interesting.

The Final

I'm not going to go into fine details but it was a fantastic final played in a great spirit and the B team won 2-1. At the end of the game the boys shook hands and the A team were magnanimous in defeat, the B team humble in victory. You could sense the real team spirit in the camp and the real winners on the day were Dalworth United. The trophy ceremony was a real credit to the club as both teams stood side by side and there was no division whatsoever between the boys.

Ben accepted the trophy and then handed it to The Gaffer.

"Here you are Gaffer, another trophy for the cabinet, job done".

The Gaffer didn't say anything except a strained "Well done" but his body language spoke volumes.

"See you at training Tuesday boys."
"See you Si."
"See you Gaffer."

Gaffer then rushed to the car trophy in hand and with son Jimmy trailing and disappointed to be missing out on the obligatory post tournament commiseration Ice Cream.

Smith Says

The boys did what I expected yesterday and won our own tournament with both teams reaching the final.

Once again the real winner was Dalworth United FC and I would like to thank all our parents who helped make the tournament a success.
The Gaffer

Dalworth United 'A': Stevens, Sheppard, Morley, Webster, Haugh, Pilbeam, Smith (c) - ***Beaten Finalists***.
Goalscorers: Pilbeam 2, Haugh 2, Webster 2, Morley
Player of the Tournament: Brian Haugh

Dalworth United 'B': Hall, Belafonte, Hayes Alex, Hayes Aidan, Fisher, Padgham © - ***Winners.***
Goalscorers: Fisher 5, Padgham 4, Alex Hayes 3, Aidan Hayes, Belafonte, Hall.
Player of the Tournament: Ben Padgham

Tuesday 22nd August
The boys were in good spirits at training but this was soon dampened by The Gaffer who once again squashed any mention of the tournament at the weekend. He got the boys together and mentioned about the forthcoming Plumpley Colts 11-a-side tournament at the weekend. Plumpley Colts play in the local village league and we enter every year to support their tournament. To make it a more competitive experience, we always play the age group above, however The Gaffer drops a bit of a bombshell when he announces that we are in the Under 15 age group much to everyone's astonishment:

"Why Gaffer? We'll walk the Under 15s competition"

Asks Ben Padgham.

"Well we are, end of" comes the blunt reply.

"Right two laps round the Rec, off you go"

Gaffer looks at me and offers an explanation:

"It'll be good to get a moral boosting win under our belts"

I'm not seeking an explanation so just nod. The Gaffer was incredibly focused tonight and it was a very high intensity session and while the boys gave the effort required there were more than a few grumbles from the players.

Friday 25th August Dalworth News
The Dalworth Under 15s triumphed in their own tournament last weekend. An all Dalworth final saw the B side beat the A side 2-1 in a pulsating final.

Saturday 26th August
No phone call from The Gaffer?

Sunday 27th August
Plumpley Colts Tournament

The final tournament and the boss controversially opts for a 14 man squad leaving a disappointed Johnny Day out as he hasn't trained this week. The mood in the team isn't good and the boys are quick to let their feelings known:

"What's the point? This'll be a walkover" says Danny Hall who then proceeds to spend the entire tournament on the touchline in the role of 'reserve keeper'.

"Waste of time" says Adam Morley who is appropriately dressed all in black today which fits both the occasion and mood of the players. Billy B has a bag of McDonald's breakfast items which he systematically munches through, not even trying to hide it from The Gaffer. Ben throws in: "This is going to be embarrassing" which is met by The Gaffer's immediate disapproval.

"Just be professional and win the tournament" he says arms crossed and already on the defensive. Ben is right though as we win our first group game 7-0. Gaffer is beaming from ear to ear. He gathers the boys together.

"What happened in the second half?"

The boys exchange puzzled looks.

"It was 6-0 at half time, I don't want you to take your foot off the peddle"

More puzzled looks, mixed with disbelief.

"We don't ease up, we keep the pressure on"

The boys dejectedly disappear into the surroundings and The Gaffer is left alone.

The next game is the opposite of the first and this time it's only 2-0 at half time with the boys well and truly stuck in second gear.

"What you playing at?" bellows The Gaffer at the boys.
"Eh? Football" Charlie Fisher sarcastically replies.
"Call that Football?" The Gaffer spits back, as he summons Brian Haugh to replace Charlie.

The boys sense that The Gaffer is spoiling for a fight and all of them, including the Hayes twins, let it drop.

"Get out there and finish them off!"

The boys are still cruising and can't seem to get going but they do manage to score two quick goals.

The Gaffer isn't letting up and is bellowing out his instructions. On the next Dalworth attack the ball is cleared and sent flying into a little pony paddock. The Gaffer races over to retrieve the ball and jumps the small fence before booting the ball back. Without taking his eyes off the game he then steps over the fence and lets out a short but loud agonising scream followed by a "f**king hell".

A quick examination of the fence reveals that there is a little electric battery of some sort that is attached to the makeshift fence ensuring its occupants stay inside. The Gaffer has just proven the effectiveness of the contraption and suffered an electric shock. The action on the pitch has stopped as the players are totally engrossed in the action off the pitch as The Gaffer walks slowly and unsteadily back to our spot.

"Shocking Gaffer, shocking."
"Gaffer is in shock."
"No nookie for Mrs Gaffer tonight"
"Gaffer, toilet is that way" a reference to the fact that Gaffer looks like he has shit himself.

The incident does seem to be the catalyst for the type of performance that The Gaffer demanded. The boys kick into gear and they run out comfortable 8-0 winners.

After the game The Gaffer gets the boys together, surely an unwise move, but before he can deliver his team talk, Alex Hayes sets the wheels in motion:

"Was that better Gaffer?"
"Erm yes Alex much better"
"Yeah I thought we was electric second half."

The initial stifled sniggers soon break out into hysterical laughter as the boys collectively lose it and they don't even try to hide as they all break out into full on belly laughs. Gaffer turns and makes his way to the tea tent for a cup of very sweet tea and leaves us with a parting shot of "Oh f**k off"

The boys win their next game 6-0 and The Gaffer, who has regained his full composure and the use of his right leg is not letting up.

"Get stuck in", "Keep up the tempo", "Press, press, press", "I've got subs here you know."

Even the Hayes twins hardly put a tackle in simply because you can't tackle opponents who don't have the ball. The worst aspect of all this is the mumblings on the touchlines from the opposing parents:

"You'd think this was the World Cup" as each Dalworth goal is met with huge celebrations from The Gaffer. Thankfully both the Dalworth players and parents offer ever diminishing muted celebrations for each goal. The comments from the opposing parents continue:

"He (Gaffer) really want's this badly doesn't he" but The Gaffer is oblivious to the locals choosing instead to wind them up further with comments like "It's men v boys", "It's a poor standard this village league", "We're far superior."

Such is the gulf that even the boys are feeling uncomfortable and are quick to acknowledge their opponents after each game with apologetic handshakes and a sincere if somewhat ironic "Well played."

The final is extended from 20 minutes to 30 minutes and is against the hosts. It's another non-event with the boys 2-0 up after three minutes. They score a further eight goals in the remaining 27 minutes to run out 10-0 winners. The Gaffer is unstoppable now and is in full on celebration mode charging down the touchline, fist pumping, high fiving and back slapping the subs after each goal. The boys fail to reciprocate the enthusiasm though and just want to win the game, get their medals and go home.

The presentation is short, sharp and sweet and the boys, with the exception of Danny Hall who refuses a medal on the grounds that "I didn't do anything to earn it" collect their medals to polite applause. Jimmy Smith collects the trophy and Gaffer snatches it and takes center spot for the photos. The lack of smiles is compensated by The Gaffer who is beaming from ear to ear like the proverbial Cheshire Cat. Smiles are not the only thing missing because Danny Hall has taken off before the photos. Gaffer shouts at me to get in the photo and I shuffle onto the end wishing to avoid a John Terry moment as, like Danny, I feel like my involvement was minimal.

Photos are quickly taken, more out of tradition than desire, and The Gaffer is in his element, chest puffed out, waving the trophy around and replicating a multitude of trophy-winning poses. I was waiting for him to take the players on a lap of honour. Thankfully he didn't. He tries to engage players and parents alike:

"What a win", "Celebrations tonight", "I'll have a few beers out of this" he says waving the trophy about. "Anyone fancy a beer?"

The responses are polite but there's a plethora of excuses:

"Sorry got work tomorrow", "Sorry got to get back for dinner", "Sorry got to pick my daughter up from her friends", "Sorry Billy's got homework to complete." as one by one players and parents trudge off to their cars.

Even the Ice Cream van is bypassed such is everyone's need to leave Plumpley quickly. With regards to the offer of a celebratory drink Gaffer would have had company until Alex and Aidan's Grandad politely lets them know that it was the parents Gaffer was inviting for a beer and not the players.

The Gaffer turns to me.

"Great win hey Si?"
"Yes Gaffer."
"An 11-a-side tournament win is always better."
"Every win is good Gaffer."
"Yeah, but It's good for the players to play 11-a-side and get some minutes."
"Gaffer, you do know Danny Hall didn't play any games?"
"Yeah, but he was reserve goalkeeper today."
"But he can play out on pitch."
"No passengers Si, boys have got to fight for their places."
"But you started the same side all four games."
"You can't change a winning side."

I realise that my arguments are futile and fall upon deaf ears. I make a hasty retreat leaving The Gaffer to bask in his own glory and as I shuffle inconspicuously off to my car I'm sure I heard Gaffer singing "Vinny Smith's Red and White Army" to himself.

I've seen a different side to The Gaffer today and I realised how desperate he was for a tournament win under his management. I just hope it doesn't have a detrimental effect on the season. Johnny Day wasn't picked for today. Danny Hall didn't get any minutes. Charlie was subbed for his comments. In fact none of the boys seemed happy and all this after we won the tournament. On a positive note, yes there is one, Jimmy Smith broke his duck with a two yard tap in.

Smith Says
Perfection is something we all strive for and rarely is it achieved but

today we achieved it winning The Plumpley Colts tournament. We scored 31 goals in four games and kept four clean sheets. We were head and shoulders above our opponents and we won the tournament in style. I'm pleased to say that we looked every bit as good as we did last season and I really do believe we will be a force to be reckoned with this campaign. If we can replicate what we did yesterday then we will go some way to achieving a perfect season. I can't wait to get started.

Plumpley Colts Squad: Stevens, Hall, Carr, Sheppard, Belafonte, Hayes, Morley, Hayes , Haugh, Smith ©, Webster, Padgham, Fisher, Pilbeam

Winners: Beat Plumpley Colts 10-0

Scorers: Pilbeam 8, Fisher 6, Padgham 5, Webster 3, Haugh 2, Belafonte 2, Smith, Morley, Alex Hayes, Aidan Hayes, Sheppard

Player of the Tournament: Billy Belafonte

The Gaffer

Monday 28th August

Gaffer rings me up. "Tomorrow night I want to work on our wide play so I've got a 25 minute session planned for the full backs and wingers. See you tomorrow Si" Short and Sweet.

Tuesday 29th August

We are the last team to set up on the Rec and therefore are left with a small corner of the playing field. Gaffer tried to pull rank over the younger age groups but they aren't having it. "First come first served".

The wide play session is replaced with keepball and ball work. The Gaffer initially has the right hump but is soon handing out praise, albeit self-praise.

"Tactically I was spot on Sunday"

"Boys were well fired up on Sunday; I got the preparations just right"

"Fail to prepare, prepare to fail"

"Team selection was spot on"

"We had every game won before half-time"

The boys just get on with the session but it's a subdued one. Even the Hayes twins don't feel the desire to 'crunch' anyone. In fact the only ray of sunshine is provided by Adam Morley who is wearing a Recreativo red and white polka dot shirt and if that isn't bad enough he has matched it with a pair of green shorts and blue and white hooped socks. It is an ensemble beyond comment and warrants only head shaking from the boys. Gaffer gathers everyone together at the end.

"Right boys, friendly this Sunday down here against our under 14s."

The groans and eye-rolling are not concealed. Here we go again.

Sunday 3rd September

The logic behind this hastily-planned friendly is to give the players another 11-a-side run out (4x20 min quarters) and a chance for The Gaffer to try out formations (4-3-3, 3-5-2, 4-3-2-1, 3-4-3) The Gaffer is also expecting a moral-boosting win before the curtain raiser next Sunday. The reality of it however is total confusion regarding the formations and a game that was ended early due to all hell breaking loose over a decidedly dodgy equaliser and a X-rated challenge.

The Gaffer made a staggering 16 substitutions in 70 minutes and players at times had no idea where they were supposed to be playing let alone what the formation was. The Gaffer at the same time was getting more and more wound up as he couldn't get his instructions through to players who were virtually oblivious to things on the pitch as they were trying to make sense of The Gaffer and his garbled instructions. When the under 14s went 1-0 up in the third quarter The Gaffer blew a fuse and there were some inflammatory comments spat out: "Get bloody stuck in", "You can't lose to this lot".

Then it's the turn of the under 14s' manager, players and parents to lose it when they have a perfectly good goal ruled offside by the ref, Frankie Smith (The Gaffer's nephew). The Under 15s then equalise when Luke Pilbeam bundles the ball and the under 14s' goalie over the line in the fourth quarter. The goal is controversially allowed to stand much to the disgust of the under 14s who vent their anger at the Ref. The game is already boiling over when Aidan Hayes completely takes ball and player out on the touchline right in front of the under 14s' manager. One of the under 14s' substitutes then pushes Aidan over only to be then punched by Alex Hayes.

At this point the players from both teams go charging towards the flashpoint. Parents begin squaring up to each other behind the respect line and both managers are nose to nose in an animated exchange. As the warring factions come to their senses and order is restored the two managers agree to call it a day and despite the absence of UN Peace Forces civility is restored and there are no further incidents.

All mention of the game is struck from the records and neither manager mentions it on the website.

This is the game that never happened.

Monday 4th September

Gaffer rings:

"Si do you think some of the boys are struggling with the formations, do you think it's too complex for them?"
"No Gaffer I just think there were too many changes."

I can tell The Gaffer sounds hurt and jumps on the defensive.
"They've got to be adaptable and change things at the drop of a hat."
"I know Gaffer but it was a lot of changes and lots of substitutions, best thing to do is talk to them at training."
"Yeah, good idea I'll do that Si, see you tomorrow. Oh, by the way, have a look at the website I've updated everyone's profile."
"Ok will do, see you tomorrow."

The Gaffer had been busy updating the club's website with a Meet the Management and Meet the Players section. The Gaffer for some reason had also given all the players nicknames, much to, as we will find out later, the disgust of some of them.

Smith Says
This Sunday we start our league campaign against Tamworth so I thought it was time to give an introduction to the management and players.

Meet the Managers
Vinny Smith - Manager: Vinny was assistant manager last year but stepped up to Manager when Michael Harris left for the U18s. Vinny is a level 1 coach and is a big Manchester United fan.

Simon Sheppard - Assistant Manager: Simon helped with the set up last year so was an obvious choice to take the Assistant Manager role. Simon's favourite team is Liverpool.

Meet the Players
Billy (Beanpole) Stevens - Goalkeeper. The tallest member of the squad at 6'2" Billy spent most of last season as understudy to Luke Dryland but never let the side down when called upon and deserves his chance as No1.

Danny (Dodgy) Hall - Right Back & Goalkeeper. Dan is a solid defender and also Dalworth's back up 'keeper. Danny got the nickname from his early days at Dalworth when he was known for his 'dodgy' tackles and 'dodgy' clearances.

Nick (The Rock) Sheppard - Centre Back. No nonsense, no frills defender. Nick does the basics brilliantly and reads the game well and is the 'rock' of the defence. One of the quietest members of the squad.

Johnny (The Rash) Day - Centre Back. 'The Rash' earned his nickname because he is all over opposing forwards. Second tallest member of the squad and carries an aerial threat at set pieces.

Billy (Harry) Belafonte - Left Back. 'Harry' has got the sweetest left foot and one of the hardest shots too. He was the winner of Goal of the Season last year, a 30 yard screamer against Dunstable City. The teams free kick specialist and a lover of takeaways.

Stevie (Jimmy) Carr - Right Back. 'Jimmy' is the team's practical joker and needs watching at all times. A two-footed player who can also stand in at left back if needed. He is the smallest player in the team.

Ben (The Prof) Padgham - Right Wing. Ben has an analytical understanding of the game and is destined to be a football pundit one day. 'Prof' is a tricky winger with an amazing repertoire of skills and tricks.

Alex (Ron) Hayes - Central Midfield. 'Ron' is a no-nonsense tough tackling midfielder with bags of energy. Terrorises opponents with his tenacity and forms a formidable partnership with his twin. Massive boxing fan too.

Aidan (Reg) Hayes - Central Midfield. 'Reg' is the other part of the midfield partnership. He is superb in the air and pacey too. He loves a battle and a tackle too. A massive WWE fan, who loves to practice signature moves on his team mates.

Adam (Adz) Morley - Centre Midfield. The playmaker and best passer of a ball at the club with a full range of long and short passes. The trendsetter when it comes to fashion and as soon as training or matches are finished. 'Adz' will stick his Dr Dre headphones on. Big Rap fan.

Bobby (Webbo) Webster - Left Winger. Webbo is a speed merchant with a blistering turn of pace that leaves defenders for dead. He is a great crosser of the ball who chips in with his fair share of goals.

Brian (Usain) Haugh - Winger. Two footed winger and quickest player at the club. He can play on either wing and can also play at right or left back. Competes in the 100m and 200m for the district and holds his school's 100m record.

Jimmy (Smudge) Smith - Forward. Jimmy played at centre back last season but had few opportunities so has now been converted to centre forward this year. Strong in the air. Very committed player and this year's captain.

Charlie (Fish) Fisher - Forward. Small in stature but like his hero Messi has two very quick feet and is tricky on the ball. A lethal finisher in the penalty box and has a very good strike rate.

Luke (Deadly) Pilbeam - Forward. He is a tall and strong striker. Deadly is lethal when running at defenders and difficult to shake off the ball due to his size. Last seasons second top scorer.

Tuesday 5th September
This is the last training session before the start of the season. The first ten minutes is spent discussing everyone's nicknames. Johnny Day isn't happy that he is 'The Rash' and even less happy when Stevie recommends some cream he can get over the counter.

"Piss off, Stevie."
"I can also recommend something for that potty mouth too Rash."
"Yeah and I've got something you can have" Johnny lets off the loudest and longest fart which he aims at Stevie much to the amusement off his team mates.

The Hayes twins haven't got a clue who Ron and Reg are until Stevie Carr explains in detail referencing the film 'Legend' to explain.

"The Kray twins were gangsters in the 60s who terrorised London."

The Hayes twins listen intently and are very happy with their nicknames until Stevie goes into more detail.

"Yeah Reg was straight and got married and Ron was gay"

At which point the mood changes and Aidan taunts his brother with.

"Gaylord."
"F**k off."
"Ooh! Stick em up."
"Again. F**k off."
"You're a bum bandit."
"You're f**king dead."

Next thing the two twins are wrestling on the ground and throwing punches at each other until everyone jumps in and they are split up.

Gaffer jumps in, albeit late.

"What the f**k is going on?"
"Why is my nickname the name of a gay gangster?" shouts a hurt (hurt by the punches thrown by his brother) and offended Alex.

"Oh for f**ks sake you can be Charlie and Eddie then."
"Who the f**k are Charlie and Eddie?"

Adz jumps in "They're singers," he then breaks out into song: "*Would I lie to you baby...*"

Alex and Aidan look totally confused.

Stevie again references the film Legend: 'They were Ron and Reg's arch rivals from south London. They tortured people and they weren't gay."

While the twins seem happier, but none the wiser, with Stevie's explanation, the matter comes to a close when The Gaffer calls everyone in.

The Gaffer begins with a 'brief chat' which lasts 30 minutes and everyone has an input. It is a very constructive chat but eats into training time. It's a good session though, what is left of it, and the nicknames are soon forgotten.

Smith Says
The season starts this Sunday and we are ready. It's been a good pre-season and preparations have been good. We have a really tough test for our first game of the season against last year's runners up Tamworth United but we are ready to begin the defence of our title.
I look forward to seeing you Sunday and thank you in advance for your continued support.
Roll on Sunday.
The Gaffer

CHAPTER THREE

SEPTEMBER

'How confident am I? Well as far as I'm concerned it's not who will win the league, it's who will finish runners-up to us...'

Thursday 7th September
I've had to let Gaffer go solo tonight at the managers' meeting due to me being roped in last minute to assist with the year 7s' parents evening. The head of English decided that today was a good day to slip in the car park and sprain his ankle. So instead of sinking pints of Coke, I'm drinking endless cups of tea to alleviate the boredom of the evening.

Saturday 9th September
The Gaffer is on the phone for over a hour. He went through the starting line-up and left a pause after each name, for my approval I'm guessing. During that time I must have said about 30 words and 20 of those were "Yes". The format of the conversation consisted of The Gaffer asking me a question, answering it himself and then asking me to confirm that what he had just said I agreed with.

I could sense his anxieties and he kept repeating "We must win this one", "It's a must win game", "It's vital to get that first win under our belts", "We need three points", "I need to get a first win in charge", "I need to make an impact". I began to feel The Gaffer's anxieties and I felt quite stressed myself after the call. Red wine. I need red wine.

Sunday, 10th September 2014 – Dalworth United v Tamworth United
The curtain-raiser and the excitement of a new season is already starting to kick in. It's quite appropriate that the season starts in bright sunshine mirroring the optimism of a new campaign and a fresh beginning. It's that time of the season where optimism overrules pessimism and everyone believes that this is the season it all changes, although this can be very short-lived if you suffer a humiliating defeat in your first fixture.

It's a time where parity is king and everyone is equal. The sun's rays are beating down, creating a cauldron of heat which is appropriate considering todays fixture promises to be a red hot opener between last year's champions and runners up. Think United v City, Celtic v Rangers, Barcelona v Real Madrid, Fenerbahce v Galatasary albeit on a smaller scale.

This particular season not only brings hope, belief and promise it also heralds new kit and new training gear and I have to say The Gaffer has come up trumps with his choices. The all red home and all white away kit are, and I quote the boys: "bangin'". The all black training kits are basic but effective and the tracksuits are very fetching especially when matched with the red polos bearing the players' initials. There is something inspiring about new kit and it raises everyone.

I can already feel the heat radiating against my face and my new manager's jacket with 'optional initials' is going to have to wait until colder climates for an outing. The choice of 'battle fatigues' today is polo shirt, with initials, and shorts. The boys have all discarded their tracksuit bottoms in favour of an assortment of shorts, much to Gaffer's disgust "Why aren't they wearing the training shorts?"

Adam Morley takes the prize for 'most outrageous shorts', a pink and green flowered Hawaiian effect pair which when matched with the black tracksuit top, which is tied around his waist, and red polo, initials compulsory, creates a very unpleasant colour cascade. Thankfully he hasn't got sandals with socks, just sandals and beats by Dr Dre headphones. Adam is a walking picture of youth influenced by the Premier League. The boys quickly take on Adam's innovative approach and are soon wrapping their tracksuit tops, initials compulsory, around their waists. This is met with a disapproving nod from The Gaffer who stands resplendent in his tracksuit and polo shirt, both with initials.

The Gaffer's company name sits proudly on the back of the tracksuit tops but at the moment it sits on the backsides of the players gently blowing in the cool breeze or in Billy Belafonte's case thrashing about in the wind emanating from Billy's backside. Stevie Day is trying, successfully, to wind up Alex & Aidan by suggesting Alex is wearing Aidan's top. The other boys start to join in adding their threepennorth-worth:
"Yeah that looks like Aidan's top, it's got Aidan's initials on it."
Alex takes his top off to reveal a label with Alex written on it.
"See, it's my f**king top".

The boys burst out laughing obviously Mrs Hayes foresaw this happening and acted quickly to prevent another Alex v Aidan incident. It has to be said if this was horse racing we would win the best turned out award hands down. Business must be very good as The Gaffer has dug deep kitting everyone out although I do feel sorry for Mrs Gaffer because that white kit will be a bugger to clean in the winter months.

The Gaffer has been busy and is already standing in his technical area surrounded by balls, bibs, cones, bottles and first aid kit. The next thing I notice is that the respect line, the line the parents stand behind, on the opposite side of the pitch is further away from the touchline than usual.

Then I notice that there appears to be disparity between the technical area The Gaffer occupies, and that of our opponents whose area seems half the size of ours. I point this out to The Gaffer, who incidentally is beaming from ear to ear. Gaffer winks at me when I notice the difference.

"Mind games Si, mind games."

I'm confused as surely our opponents will just change the boundaries but The Gaffer is happy so all bodes well.

The Dalworth v Tamworth technical areas

So The Gaffer seeks to gain an early advantage over Tamworth and I'm surprised that he hasn't flooded the away team dressing room or got Billy to leave a McDonald's inspired surprise package in the away toilet. Instead he simply marks out two technical areas with cones but gives himself a technical area twice the size of his opponents. He does however nearly hand the advantage over to his opponents as he discovers that while his opponents have a smaller area, theirs is free of canine deposits whereas The Gaffer has given himself a larger area containing not one, not two, but three little packages, one of which appears to be a package left behind by a Great Dane with a love of Indian Food.

The Gaffer is quick to act though as he issues cones to his subs to play a quick game of hunt and cover, as opposed to hide and seek. While the Tamworth management and subs struggle to fit everything in their small area, The Gaffer strides and bounces about his enlarged technical area, avoiding the recently planted cones, emphasising that size does count on this occasion. I really expect The Gaffer to start 'lunging' to again emphasis the size of his area (now there's an image).

The Gaffer runs the boys, who are looking good in their all black training kit, through a quick warm up and then the boys split up for keepball and drills specific to their position: shooting, catching, heading etc. The warm-up is good and the boys look impressive. The passes are crisp, the turns are sharp and the intensity is high.

The Gaffer then gathers the boys in and gives them their final instructions before he issues a brief but puzzling speech:

"Greatness is earnt, it's not a God-given right. Perfection can only be achieved by those that strive for perfection. Do you want to be the team that was great but are no longer great? Do you want to be the forgotten team?"

At this point in my head I see Mel Gibson in Braveheart:

"Aye, fight and you may die. Run, and you'll live... at least a while. And dying in your beds, many years from now, would you be willing to trade ALL the days, from this day to that, for one chance, just one chance, to come back here and tell our enemies that they may take our lives, but they'll never take..."

...and then I'm back at Dalworth Rec, or am I?

"Or do you want to be the Invincibles? They can come to our ground, but they will not take.... OUR TITLE!"

There is then an uncomfortable pause until Aidan Hayes breaks the silence: "Gaffer, do you want me on the right or the left of the midfield three?"

Gaffer shuffles off to the technical area disappointed at the reaction to his speech and the boys take to the pitch for the season's opener.

Such is our need to win Gaffer has opted for an attacking 4-3-3 formation with a standard flat back four and three central midfielders. Up front he is starting with his son Jimmy in the central role and wingers Brian Haugh and Bobby Webster either side of him. He leaves the other two strikers Charlie Fisher and Luke Pilbeam on the bench.

Dalworth United v Tamworth United:
Starting line up

Billy Stevens
Stevie Carr   Johnny Day Nick Sheppard   Billy Belafonte
Alex Hayes Adam Morley Aidan Hayes
Brian Haugh Jimmy Smith © Bobby Webster
Subs: Danny Hall, Ben Padgham, Charlie Fisher, Luke Pilbeam

Kick-off:
If the aim of The Gaffer's speech was to fire up the boys it would seem it hasn't had the desired effect as all the early pressure comes from Tamworth. However the boys set up a quick counter attack and excellent

work from Brian Haugh and Adam Morley carves out a golden opportunity for Jimmy Smith but he cannot get the necessary touch from six yards out and the chance goes begging. This move proves costly as Tamworth break away to create an identical chance to the one we missed but this time they manage to find not only the desired touch but also the net to take the lead in the eleventh minute.

The Gaffer is on the pitch to contest the legality of Tamworth's goal however he is the only one protesting and his protests are not only in vain but soon become a dirty protest as he steps directly in package number four aka 'the undiscovered surprise fourth package'. The Gaffer is now literally hopping mad as he bounces about on one foot cursing "Those f**king dogs", "That f**king ref", and "The f**king defence", before finally dispensing of the package from his boot with the aid of a never-to-be-used-again cone.

It's an even game, despite Dalworth trailing, with chances and possession are equal. Then Jimmy Smith latches onto Adam Morley's through ball and races clear of the Tamworth defence. With the Tamworth keeper bearing down, he only has to square the ball to the onrushing Brian Haugh but panics and miscues the pass, sending the ball rolling to a grateful Tamworth keeper. He then launches a quick counter attack via a big and hopeful punt down the pitch and after one bounce the ball is volleyed home to increase Tamworth's lead. The Gaffer vents his anger and frustrations towards the Dalworth defence:

"Where the bloody hell is our defence?"

The back four hold their hands up but are annoyed that some of the blame is not apportioned to other elements of the team, namely Jimmy Smith. It goes from bad to worse as Tamworth quickly go 3-0 up when Billy Stevens and Johnny Day collide with each other going for a cross and the Tamworth striker is left with an easy tap in.

The Gaffer launches into the defence again:

"Three chances, three bloody goals!"

Stevie Carr responds with: "Well if the bloody strikers put their chances away..."

The minute Stevie said it he felt bad because it was aimed at Jimmy Smith and Jimmy doesn't need anyone telling him he is having a stinker as he knows it. Half time can't come quick enough and during the break The

Gaffer launches into the defence, it's a full on 10-minute rant aimed at the back five and is neither constructive or helpful as he simply reiterates each individual mistake and error and offers no insight other than blame. The defence takes it on the chin, a chin that is firmly planted on the ground alongside their morale.

The rest of their team mates sit silent relieved that they escaped The Gaffer's unconstructive bollocking. Rant over, The Gaffer just leaves himself enough time to make his subs.

"Right we are going 4-4-2. He changes three of the back four and surprisingly puts winger Bobby Webster at left back and Centre Midfielder Aidan Hayes at Centre Back.

Second half line up:
Billy Stevens
Danny Hall Aidan Hayes Nick Sheppard   Bobby Webster
Ben Padgham Alex Hayes Adam Morley   Luke Pilbeam
Charlie Fisher Jimmy Smith ©

Jimmy Smith looks gutted that he is staying on the pitch and is soon clutching his ankle

"Dad, er, Gaffer, I think I've hurt my ankle.""You'll be fine get back on"
"No seriously, it's hurting."
"Don't be silly, get back on, we need you."
"I can't put any weight on it."
"For f**ks sake Jimmy, we need you!"
"We've got other strikers."
"Oh come off then, Luke you go up top, Brian go left wing, Nick take the armband."

Jimmy goes and sits down, a forlorn figure. Despite the misses, his teammates sit with him and Johnny Day offers the striker some consolation: "Head up Jim, no one's having a good game"

Revised Second half line up:
Billy Stevens
Danny Hall Aidan Hayes Nick Sheppard © Bobby Webster
Ben Padgham Alex Hayes Adam Morley   Brian Haugh
Charlie Fisher Luke Pilbeam

As the boys take the pitch for the second half they form a huddle around the centre circle. Nick tells me that Ben Padgham took the lead:

"Come on boys we're better than this, We win together, we lose together, but we are always together."

The Gaffer is looking concerned and almost on tip toes regarding this impromptu gathering and trying to hear what's going on, how he thinks going on his tip toes is going to give him access to the conversation I have no idea.

The Gaffer, fearing a mutiny, seeks me out.

"What's going on Si? What they saying?"

I just shrug my shoulders but The Gaffer looks really uneasy.

Second half

The boys start the second half on fire and within five minutes have reduced the arrears as Luke Pilbeam plays a one-two with Brian Haugh and hits an unstoppable shot past the Tamworth keeper. It's all Dalworth now as Ben Padgham hits the bar and then Adam Morley has one cleared off the line. It's a short reprieve though as Alex Hayes heads home a Bobby Webster cross to make it 3-2. Tamworth are reeling like a boxer on the ropes but the Tamworth manager doesn't bat an eyelid.

 "Keep calm and don't panic."

The Dalworth technical area in contrast is all "oohs" and "aahs" with a few "f**ks" thrown in. That is until Ben Padgham curls a free kick home then it's pure delirium and pandemonium amongst the Dalworth contingent. The Gaffer is charging around the technical area going mental and he is screaming: "Push on, get up, press on for a winner". The Tamworth manager is the complete opposite and a picture of calmness.

"Keep going boys, heads up".

The boys move in for the kill, every Dalworth player except Billy Stevens is in the Tamworth half, and he is closer to the centre circle than his penalty area. In Football they say you are at your most vulnerable when you have just scored and as Dalworth continue their siege on the Tamworth goal a long hopeful clearance from the Tamworth defence sails over everyone and into the Dalworth half. There is now a frantic retreat and before you know it a solitary and lightning fast Tamworth attacker is chasing the long ball being pursued by the rest of the Dalworth team with the exception of the lone figure of Billy Stevens, who goes towards the ball then drops back and then realises he needs to get to the ball before the Tamworth striker.

The race is on. Unfortunately it's a race he doesn't win and the Tamworth striker gets a hefty touch past the onrushing Billy and the ball rolls agonisingly towards the net with the whole of the Dalworth team in pursuit, with the exception of Billy who can just watch in frustration.

The ball gently rolls into the unguarded net to give Tamworth a 4-3 lead. This is all too much for The Gaffer who lets out the loudest and longest "NOOOOOOOOOOOOOOO!" followed by an even longer and louder "FOOOOOOOOOOOOOR FUUUUUUUUUUUUUUUCKS SAAAAAAAAAAAAAAAAKE"

All eyes turn to The Gaffer who has managed to grab everyone's attention, including that of the ref who slowly walks towards him, but not before an irate Gaffer kicks a cone in the direction of the Tamworth technical area, to be more precise, the direction of the Tamworth Assistant Manager and father of the scorer of Tamworth's goal.

Unfortunately for The Gaffer, and the Tamworth Assistant manager, it is a cone carrying a special gift and to say 'the shit hit the fan' is an understatement for what happens next. The Gaffer immediately realises his error on kicking the cone and his loud "NOOOOOOOOOOOOOOOOOOO" and the flying dog turd escapes the attention of the Tamworth assistant manager/parent, who was still in the midst of celebration.

That is until said dog turd found its target. Imagine, one minute you are celebrating a goal by your son to give your team the lead over your closest rivals and the next you have been hit by flying dog shit and sent into a spasm of involuntary gagging. In a matter of milliseconds joy turned to utter disgust. Some might say it was an accident but The Gaffer was still issued a red card for violent conduct (can't wait to see the referee's report) and using offensive language.

The Gaffer took the long walk of shame to the fence by the bowls club, an acceptable distance from the pitch in the ref's opinion, and stood a forlorn figure leant against the fence. He would have tried apologising but Tamworth's Assistant Manager had already rushed off in the direction of the changing rooms. The optimism of a new dawn and a new beginning had quickly evaporated into defeat and dog shit.

By the time The Gaffer had got himself comfortable and rung me on the mobile so that he could direct operations from his phone, Tamworth had wrapped up the points with an extremely well taken fifth goal. For the record the fifth was a four man passing move that resulted in a tap in from six yards. The Gaffer by this stage was a crestfallen figure and after the game he trudged wearily off to congratulate the Tamworth manager and apologise for the incident, even offering to pay for the dry cleaning, it really wasn't pleasant. The Gaffer did make an effort to look for 'Dogshit Dave' (a nickname that came courtesy of the Hayes twins) but 'Dave' had given up trying to clean himself up and beaten a hasty retreat. The Gaffer didn't launch into a repeat of the half time rant and simply said to the boys: "We'll discuss it at training on Tuesday."

I helped The Gaffer pack away the nets and equipment and the pre-match enthusiasm of an ultra-confident Gaffer had been replaced with a post-match despondency and dejection.

"See you Tuesday Si."

I gave Ben Padgham a lift home after the game and Ben was very quick to add his views:

"That was a great start, can't wait to read the match report, I can see the headlines: Dalworth crumble as Smith sees red and shit hits the fan. Still, no doubt about 'Wally of the Week' this week."

Results for Sunday 10th September
Oak Town Rangers 1 - 1 Redbridge Sports
Kingsbridge 5 - 2 Parkfield
Dalworth United 3 - 5 Tamworth United
Phoenix Rovers 1 - 3 Dunstable Co

Team	P	W	D	L	F	A	GD	Pts
1 Kingsbridge	1	1	0	0	5	2	3	3
2 Tamworth Utd	1	1	0	0	5	3	2	3
3 Dunstable City	1	1	0	0	3	1	2	3
4 Oak Town R	1	0	1	0	1	1	0	1
5 Redbridge Sports	1	0	1	0	1	1	0	1
6 Langton Reds	0	0	0	0	0	0	0	0
7 Leighbridge Lions	0	0	0	0	0	0	0	0
8 Dalworth United	1	0	0	1	3	5	-2	0
9 Phoenix Rovers	1	0	0	1	1	3	-2	0
10 Parkfield	1	0	0	1	2	5	-3	0

Smith Says
Not the start we wanted against a team I would consider as likely to be our closest rivals this year. To find ourselves 3-0 down was so disappointing and while the boys showed great character to get it back to 3-3 they again showed their naivety and let their opponents take all three points. I have set high standards for this season and Sunday's performance didn't reach

anywhere near those standards. It was a really sloppy performance and I will leave the boys in no doubt as to what I expect our levels of performance to be. It's still the first game of the season and we have a long way to go and this is where the hard work and improvements begin.

Dalworth United 3 Tamworth United 5
Squad: Billy Stevens, Stevie Carr, Johnny Day, Nick Sheppard, Billy Belafonte, Alex Hayes, Adam Morley, Aidan Hayes , Brian Haugh Jimmy Smith ©, Bobby Webster.

Subs: Danny Hall, Ben Padgham, Charlie Fisher, Luke Pilbeam

Scorers: Pilbeam, Alex Hayes, Padgham

Man of the Match: Alex Hayes

Tuesday 12th September
Gaffer is in a foul mood at training. He is on his own tonight as Jimmy's ankle still isn't right. He hardly says a word and you can see he is simmering inside. He doesn't say anything about last Sunday's game and to be honest the boys would rather leave it in the past. The boys also decide to keep the 'Wally of the Week' nominations to themselves and Gaffer doesn't mention it. In fact hardly anyone says a word until the boys are doing a crossing drill and after about eight lacklustre attempts not one has found the desired target.

This is all too much for The Gaffer and his pent up frustration erupts:

"Put the f**king ball in the f**king box".

The next five crosses go sailing over the target as the boys overcompensate and each one is overhit in an attempt to find the target.

"Oh for f**k sake!" The Gaffer then takes a swing at a stray drinks bottle discarded on the ground and promptly misses which is inkeeping with the standard of the session.

Unfortunately this miss is met with a number of repressed sniggers which simply antagonise The Gaffer even more and in a fit of rage he picks up the bottle and launches it into the distance. Unfortunately an elderly gentleman enjoying a leisurely early evening walk with his Labrador doesn't spot the flying bottle. His dog does, and the man is therefore at a disadvantage and is caught off guard when the rather large dog takes off in an impromptu game of fetch.

The dog isn't the only thing that takes off as his owner is propelled towards the flight of the bottle. The Gaffer, realising the consequence of his outburst races to apologise to the disheveled elderly dog walker, who is now sitting on the ground, and offers an apology.The dog walker has now discovered the source of his dog's excitement, which is currently nestling between his teeth and The Gaffer's apology is met with a curt

"What the f**k are you playing at?" 15-love.

The Gaffer takes offence at the rejection of his apology and responds with:

"It was a f**king accident!" 15-all

"Well stick your f**king apology." 30-15.

Gaffer comes back with an argument ending

"Oh f**k off, you sanctimonious prick!" Game, set and match.

The elderly gentleman straightens himself up and walks off in a huff. Meanwhile Larry the Labrador isn't at all bothered by the commotion as he rips into the discarded bottle while wagging his tail furiously. The crossing drill is quickly discarded for an 8v7-a-side game. Thankfully The Gaffer doesn't take part. He searches for and manages to retrieve the offending bottle and holds it aloft examining the chewed mess before throwing it to one side mumbling.

"I'll have to f**king replace that." The rest of the session passes without any more trouble and Gaffer drags everyone in at the end.

"We haven't got a game or training this weekend" and that's it. Short, sharp and sweet.

Marking and red wine for me this Sunday.

Friday 15th September
Dalworth News - Tamworth take bragging rights
Dalworth United **Under 15**s 3 Tamworth United **Under 15**s 5

An enthralling opener to the league campaign saw last season's runners up Tamworth United defeat last season's Champions Dalworth United 5-3. A topsy turvey game saw Tamworth race into a 3-0 lead through a Turner brace and Huggens. Dalworth came back strongly and goals from Pilbeam, Hayes and Padgham saw parity restored before Huggens completed a brace and Davies grabbed Tamworth's fifth and all three points.

Results for Sunday 17th September
Leighbridge Lions 3 - 1 Parkfield

Oak Town United 1 - 4 Tamworth United
Redbridge Sports 2 - 4 Dunstable Colts
Kingsbridge 2 - 0 Langton Reds

Team	P	W	D	L	F	A	GD	Pts
1 Tamworth United	2	2	0	0	9	4	5	6
2 Dunstable Colts	2	2	0	0	7	3	4	6
3 Leighbridge Lions	1	1	0	0	3	1	2	3
4 Parkfield	2	1	0	1	6	5	1	3
5 Kingsbridge	2	1	0	1	4	5	-1	3
6 Redbridge Sports	2	0	1	1	3	5	-2	1
7 Oak Town Rangers	2	0	1	1	2	5	-3	1
8 Dalworth United	1	0	0	1	3	5	-2	0
9 Phoenix Rovers	1	0	0	1	1	3	-2	0
10 Langton Reds	1	0	0	1	0	2	-2	0

Tuesday 19th September

Gaffer isn't happy again and the atmosphere from last Tuesday continues. Today's session consists of running, SAQ, running, press ups, sit ups and running. The footballs remain motionless on the ground protected by the cones that surround them. Adam Morley dares to get one out during a drinks break and is soon showing off his full repertoire of round the worlds and other tricks and flicks for the others.

He is soon reprimanded by The Gaffer:
"Leave the balls on the ground,"
"OK" says Adam who promptly sits down.

"What are you doing?" says a puzzled Gaffer to Adam.

"Well you told me to leave the balls on the ground."

It does break the tension but it also breaks The Gaffer's patience and he in turn breaks the boys spirit and lungs. Even the Hayes twins are too tired to complain.

Everyone is glad when The Gaffer gives the signal for training to finish, not only because they are, and I quote, "f**ked", but also because the atmosphere is awful. The boys trudge wearily over to The Gaffer.

"Here Sunday at 9:30 and don't be late."

No one says a word and the equipment is packed away in complete silence. Within two minutes everyone is gone.

Saturday 23rd September 2017

Gaffer is on the phone but I'm just going out so I whisper to the wife: "Tell him I'm out." This doesn't work however as eight text messages follow in quick succession.

1. "Alright Si, just tried ringing"
2. "Tried ringing again, I'll text"
3. "Here's the team for tomorrow: Billy Stevens, Stevie Carr, Nick Sheppard, Billy Belafonte, Brian Haugh, Alex Hayes, Adam Morley"
4. "Aidan Hayes, Bobby Webster, Jimmy Smith (c) Luke Pilbeam. Subs: Danny Hall, Johnny Day, Ben Padgham, Charlie Fisher"
5   "I'm going for a 3-5-2 formation"
6. "What do you think of the starting line-up?"
7. "What do you think of the formation?"
8. "Do you think it's OK to start Jimmy, his ankles OK?"
9. "See you at the Rec at 9:30am"

I manage a reply albeit brief.

"Yeah all looks good, see you tomorrow."

Sunday 24th September 2014 - Dalworth United vs Kingsbridge

The boys are up for this one as the vibe in the changing room indicates and it's an opportunity to relegate the Tamworth defeat to memory. The Gaffer goes with a 3-5-2 formation as he feels we lost the midfield against Tamworth and centre back Nick Sheppard has clear instructions from The Gaffer: "Last man at all times Rock".

Starting Line Up: 3-5-2:

Billy Stevens

Stevie Carr   Nick Sheppard   Billy Belafonte

Brian Haugh Alex Hayes Adam Morley Aidan Hayes Bobby Webster

Jimmy Smith © Luke Pilbeam

Subs: Danny Hall, Johnny Day, Ben Padgham, Charlie Fisher

Gaffer's portable tactic board is taken out of the case and while the formation is clear the mass of arrows and instructions that are scribbled on it would flummox a Mensa member.

Billy S pipes up:

"Gaffer, do the arrows mean what area you want me to cover?"

"No that's where I want you to distribute the ball."

Nick wants to double check: "So you want me to play the ball back to Billy?"

"No I want you to drop off."

Ben as usual is the voice of reason, well at least he tries to be:
"Gaffer, do the arrows indicate the movements of the outfield players?"
"Yes and the distribution outlets."
"Well, which is which?"
"Figure it out boys it's obvious".

Gaffer looks uneasy and you can tell he hopes that's the final word, but Alex can't resist.

"If it was obvious Gaffer we would understand it."

With that Gaffer takes the tactic board and sticks it back in the bag.

"3-5-2 formation Nick hold at all times, Stevie & Billy cover the channels, Alex & Aidan support the back three, Adz support the front two".

Gaffer gives the boys a confident nod indicating a) he is in charge and b) he knows what he is doing.

Gaffer takes the boys through the warm up and we are ready to go.

Kick-off
All the good work prior to kick off is quickly undone and any confidence that was built up is knocked out of the boys as within five minutes they are trailing. In an early attack a Kingsbridge winger breaks down the wing and Billy Belafonte is late getting across to him. The winger hits a hopeful cross in the direction of our area and it sails straight into the back of the net. The Gaffer is annoyed but doesn't show it and is surprisingly restrained and rightly so as five minutes later Bobby Webster skilfully manoeuvres his way past two tackles and breaks into the penalty area before being upended. The Gaffer is apoplectic and screams at the Ref:

"Penalty Ref, that's gotta be a penalty. Referee! Ref, Did you not see that? Ref, Ref?"

I nudge The Gaffer and point towards the incident. "Erm, he's given it Gaffer."

Luke Pilbeam grabs the ball and places it on the spot only for Gaffer to intervene:

"Smudge, you're on pens."
"But Gaffer I take the pens." says Luke in total disbelief.
Gaffer isn't up for a discussion. "Smudge, take the pen".

Jimmy reluctantly steps up and places the ball on the spot. It's interesting when you watch penalty shootouts you can sometimes tell who is going to miss by the body language. The reluctant walk to the spot, the facial expressions and any sign of hesitation. All are key factors to determining a taker's state of mind. I really felt for Jimmy, you could tell he was dreading it and sure enough it was a weak kick just off centre that the keeper only had to fall onto to save.

I immediately looked at The Gaffer for a response and he didn't make any eye contact and simply said: "Plenty of time left boys".

To be fair the boys were quick to lift Jimmy and weren't on his case. "Head up Jim". Once again The Gaffer was right as ten minutes later. Luke volleyed Brian Haugh's cross into the top corner to make it 1-1. Luke immediately made his way to our technical area and although his comment of "That's how you put them away" was directed towards the subs it was definitely for The Gaffer's ears. Half time and with the score 1-1, Gaffer gives a short team talk. "Chances will come", "Keep going Jimmy you'll find the net", "Big half lads". He makes a change to formation and it appears to be a 1-2-2-3-2 although it could easily be the 3-5-2 we started with but with a few tweaks. He brings all four subs on with Luke Pilbeam making way for Charlie Fisher much to everyone's surprise and Luke just goes and sits in the corner of the technical area and doesn't say a word to anyone.

The 2nd half line-up looks like this.:

Billy Stevens

Nick Sheppard

Danny Hall   Johnny Day

Alex Hayes Aidan Hayes

Ben Padgham   Adam Morley   Bobby Webster

Jimmy Smith © Charlie Fisher

It takes the boys a while to adjust and early on the ball in the channels has us in all sorts of trouble as the centre backs don't know if they should go for it or leave it to Alex and Aidan who in turn are not sure if Ben and Bobby should be tracking back. Gaffer changes this and goes 3-4-1-2

Billy Stevens

Danny Hall   Nick Sheppard   Johnny Day

Ben Padgham   Alex Hayes   Aidan Hayes   Bobby Webster

Adam Morley

Jimmy Smith © Charlie Fisher

This helps the boys defensively but the attacking impetus has gone until Adam comes off and a surprised Luke comes back on and Gaffer again changes the formation as we go 3-4-3.

Billy Stevens

Danny Hall   Nick Sheppard   Johnny Day

Ben Padgham   Alex Hayes   Aidan Hayes   Bobby Webster

Charlie Fisher   Jimmy Smith ©   Luke Pilbeam

Once again it takes the boys time to adjust to another change in formation but slowly the boys start to get on top and they are pressing Kingsbridge back. The next two chances both fall to Jimmy who puts both agonisingly wide when it looked easier to score. Wave after wave of Dalworth attacks are repelled by a solid Kingsbridge defence who are hanging on for dear life. Kingsbridge use every opportunity to find touch with every clearance and every timewasting tactic known to man is used: Injuries, arguing with the ref, stalling goal kicks. With minutes ticking by Kingsbridge concede a free kick just outside the box and their centre back boots the ball out of play. Before the ball can be retrieved Gaffer grabs a spare match ball and kicks it back onto the pitch in the direction of where the free kick has been awarded.

The ref is facing the Kingsbridge defenders and is about to pace out the ten yards when the spare ball hits him smack bang on the back of the head. A mortified Gaffer quickly apologises but the ref is unaware of the apology and is locked on the 22 players laughing hysterically at his misfortune. The Hayes twins aren't helping matters by pointing at the unfortunate ref. The ref is trying to hide his embarrassment but when he notices that everyone present is laughing with the exception of The Gaffer he has no alternative but to regain some measure of authority by issuing a yellow card to The Gaffer.

When the commotion dies down the resulting free kick is curled over the wall by Billy B and the keeper makes a good save down to his right but can only push the ball straight into the path of Jimmy, who with the whole goal gaping somehow manages to stumble and shin the ball wide of the goal. That's the last chance of the game.

Gaffer unsurprisingly is not happy and berates the number of chances that went begging although he doesn't single anyone out on this occasion. Luke Pilbeam again raises the penalty issue:

"Why aren't I on pens Gaffer? I didn't miss one last year.

"Jimmy's on pens and that's final." You can feel Jimmy's unease and when Gaffer says: "Unlucky today Jimmy." Jimmy responds with "Unlucky? I'm a shit forward, I'm a centre Back, that's my position, I'm not a goalscorer and I couldn't hit water if I feel out of a boat"

Gaffer is a little taken aback but simply responds with: "It'll come Jim" Jimmy just shrugs his shoulders and trudges off to the changing rooms. I feel for Jimmy, he is a good defender but as a forward he is nowehere near as good as Charlie or Luke and everyone can see it. Gaffer wants to build his confidence but in reality he is destroying Jimmy as a player. Yes I'm sure it will come, the problem is no one knows what *it* is.

The changing room is a sombre place bereft of conversation. The boys get changed quickly and in silence and you can tell that two games in this is an unhappy group of players who are harbouring a number of grievances and for a group that is usually so vocal it is a team of players electing to be silent in Gaffer's presence. To the boys credit they don't leave Jimmy hanging and they try to lift him.

"On another day Jim you'd have had a hat trick."
"Head up Jim, we all missed chances."

Jimmy raises a smile but his confidence is shot and you can tell that just by looking at him.

Results for Sunday, 24th September 2014
Leighbridge Lions 7 - 2 Redbridge Sports
Dalworth United 1 - 1 Kingsbridge
Dunstable Colts 0 - 2 Phoenix Rovers
Langton Reds 2 - 3 Parkfield

Team	P	W	D	L	F	A	GD	Pts
1 Leighbridge Lions	2	2	0	0	10	3	7	6
2 Tamworth United	2	2	0	0	9	4	5	6
3 Parkfield	3	2	0	1	9	7	2	6
4 Dunstable Colts	3	2	0	1	7	5	2	6
5 Kingsbridge	3	1	1	1	5	6	-1	4
6 Phoenix Rovers	2	1	0	1	3	3	0	3
7 Dalworth United	2	0	1	1	4	6	-2	1
8 Oak Town Rangers	2	0	1	1	2	5	-3	1
9 Redbridge Sports	3	0	1	2	5	12	-7	1
10 Langton Reds	2	0	0	2	2	5	-3	0

Smith Says
While we earned our first point of the season I'm disappointed that it wasn't all three. We missed a penalty and conceded a ridiculous goal but

still had enough chances to win the game several times over. The chances that we were putting away for fun during pre-season are being missed and we have to get back to the levels of pre-season. We will be working hard to put things right on the training ground and we will get it right. Next week we have an equally tough task with Leighbridge Lions but we will be looking for that first win of the season.

The Gaffer

Dalworth United 1 Kingsbridge 1

Squad: Billy Stevens, Stevie Carr, Nick Sheppard, Billy Belafonte, Brian Haugh, Alex Hayes, Adam Morley, Aidan Hayes, Bobby Webster, Jimmy Smith © Luke Pilbeam, Danny Hall, Johnny Day, Ben Padgham, Charlie Fisher. **Scorer**: Pilbeam. **Man of the Match**: Webster

Tuesday 26th September

The balls are out, hooray! However the reason they are out is so the boys can chase them in a number of gut bursting sprint drills which appear to cover the length and breadth of the Rec. It's a larger than usual area that Gaffer was quick to claim much to the disgust of the rest of the teams who appear to be training on a postage stamp of an area. "First come, first served" is The Gaffers reply to his fellow managers who aren't happy. Gaffer really has spread his wings but on this occasion it's the boys who are flying. It is a really demanding session which takes its toll leaving Luke Pilbeam, Adam Morley and Johnny Day sidelined, Luke pulled a muscle, Adam turned his ankle and Johnny couldn't breathe due to his asthma.

Friday 29th September Dalworth News

Dalworth United **Under 15**s 1 Kingsbridge 1: Dalworth **Under 15**s picked up their first point of the season when Luke Pilbeam grabbed an equaliser after Jeremy Ross had given Kingsbridge an early lead

Saturday 30th September

Gaffer is on the phone. We've lost Adam Morley for tomorrow due to the ankle injury he sustained on Tuesday, the ankle apparently ballooned after training. We've also lost Johnny Day who has been off school all week and who ended up in hospital Tuesday night due to an asthma attack. Gaffer, however, is focused solely on the game and is going for a 3-4-2-1 formation tomorrow. "We'll turn it around tomorrow you watch, first win of the season"

I bloody hope so.

CHAPTER FOUR

OCTOBER

"If you can't beat em, kick em"

Sunday 1st October - Dalworth United vs Leighbridge Lions

Gaffer rings early on Sunday morning. "Charlie Fisher is out, sickness bug, I'm going to get there at 9am to prepare everything (I know what comes next). Fail to prepare, prepare to fail."

I manage an "OK Gaffer" before the line goes dead.

Dalworth United vs Leighbridge Lions:

It's a very sparse changing room with a few gaps but to be fair Adam and Johnny are still there, albeit as spectators. The gloomy atmosphere is momentarily enlightened by a tracksuit-less Adam Morley. The tracksuit, which apparently is still in the wash, has been replaced with a bright yellow body warmer, which he has combined with a red t-shirt and white cut off shorts and sandals. Gaffer uses the absentees as a means of geeing the others up.

"Yes we've only got 12 players but I wouldn't swap any of you for any of them. We are still the better team and I know you are the better players."

No ranting, just clear and concise motivation. Gaffer opts for a 3-4-2-1 formation with the players available to him, but he is right it's still a team more than capable of taking all three points.

Starting Line Up:

Billy Stevens

Stevie Carr   Nick Sheppard   Billy Belafonte

Brian Haugh   Alex Hayes   Aidan Hayes   Bobby Webster

Ben Padgham   Luke Pilbeam

Jimmy Smith ©

Sub: Danny Hall,

The boys are quickly changed and whizz through the warm up. It is 100 miles a hour and the pace of the keep ball at the end is ridiculous, hardly a pass is strung together as the boys fly into tackles. Gaffer doesn't try to curb the boys' enthusiasm instead he uses it as an opportunity to fire the boys up.

The frenetic pace of the warm up is carried over to the start of the match as the boys seem as keen as The Gaffer to register their first win of the season and they are flying out the traps early doors. In the first ten minutes Jimmy has missed three good chances. With twenty minutes gone he has also missed a penalty after Bobby is brought down in the area and a tap-in from five yards. Luke makes his feelings known:
"F**k sake Jim, you've got to put one away."

It wasn't meant maliciously, more out of frustration, but Luke is right we could be 3/4/5-0 up. There is an air of inevitability when Jimmy gives the ball away up front and three passes later the ball is nestling in our net. Gaffer's optimism that was so prevalent in the changing room has all but vanished and he lets rip at the boys:
"For f**k sake can't we defend."
"Does anyone know how to tackle?"
"Where's your bite?"

The boys to a man all look at The Gaffer with an air of astonishment, then look at each other for reassurance that they aren't going mad. However Gaffer's instructions are like a call to arms for the twins and Alex turns to his twin and shouts "F**k this!"

The next two tackles that follow from Alex would carry an x-certificate. They are purposeful, brutal and later than a one legged man running the Marathon. The first tackle, a side on sliding assault, leaves the Leighbridge Captain limping. Alex is very fortunate only to receive a lecture from the ref. The second tackle on the same player, a two footed effort from behind, which takes man and ball and in that order, sees the Leighbridge Captain hobbling off aided by his angry manager who scowls at The Gaffer and on passing gives him his thoughts on the matter:

"You f**king happy with your players making that kind of tackle?"

Gaffer just stands arms crossed with a look of disdain on his face and mutters: "Well that's football for you".

The referee has no alternative to act but is still lenient in showing the yellow card to Alex when maybe a red card was justified. Alex is now treading the proverbial tightrope. The booking, rather than suggesting The Gaffer calm things down simply antagonises him who turns his attention to the referee and launches a tirade of abuse:
"Ref, it's a man's game", "Ref what do you expect? It's a contact sport."

The Gaffer doesn't improve Dalworth/Leighbridge relations by applauding each tackle, fair or not. Just to clarify his viewpoint he adds inflammatory comments such as "That's more like it", "Great tackle" all of which merely fuels the twins' bloodlust and, not wanting to be left out or be outdone by his twin, Aidan gets in on the act and his contribution is a studs up, full impact, knee buster which leads to another Leighbridge playing leaving the field. Gaffer shows no remorse for his players' actions and instead applauds his midfielder's challenge which further infuriates the Leighbridge manager who is going mad.

The referee, sensing the game is boiling over, calms matters by the only means available to him and shows Aidan a straight red card. Aidan however is unaware of the card being dangled in front of him as he has the full attention of the Leighbridge team in his face who are berating and jostling him. A space soon clears as twin Alex barges past him and into the melee of players in front of him to drag the Leighbridge centre forward to the floor. Once again the referee calms proceedings by the only means at his disposal by issuing a red card to Alex and the twins go off the pitch side by side, their own personal mission accomplished.

The Gaffer, rather than berating the twins, applauds and sympathises with them and then begins a ferocious tirade of abuse at the ref:
"Nice one ref, why not hand the game on a plate to them?"
"If you can't tackle what's the point"
"Oh ref, for f**ks sake"

The last volley of abuse happens just as our old friend the dog walker passes with his Labrador. The man can't help but respond to The Gaffer' foul language and offers him some advice:
"Why don't you moderate your language? There are young people around."

Gaffer responds in a way that befits his current mood and manner:
"Oh, why don't you f**k off?"
"How dare you talk to me like that" replies the startled dog walker
"Oh piss off"

When The Gaffer turns to face the pitch he is met with the referee brandishing a yellow card.
"What the..."

I manage to grab The Gaffer and drag him away from the referee before he unleashes another barrage of abuse. Gaffer then turns his attentions to the Leighbridge management and says:
"Your boys started that free-for-all how comes they didn't get sent off?"

The Leighbridge management to their credit aren't interested in another argument and ignore The Gaffer which in turn leaves him still irate but with no one to argue with.

While The Gaffer is involved in a full blown argument off the pitch with our friendly dog walker, the ref and the Leighbridge management team, Ben is trying to sort things out on the pitch and has manoeuvred the remaining 9 players into a 3-2-2-1 formation courtesy of his footballing insight. He is frantically shouting instructions trying to get the attention of his teammates whose attentions are split between the game and The Gaffer's antics.

Billy Stevens

Danny Hall   Nick Sheppard   Billy Belafonte

Brian Haugh   Bobby Webster

Ben Padgham   Luke Pilbeam

Jimmy Smith ©

The impact of which is soon felt by Leighbridge as the 9 men manage to produce an equaliser of real quality. Nick feeds the ball to Bobby who exchanges passes with Brian and then plays the ball to Jimmy who lays the ball off to Luke who makes a cross field run but then plays a reverse pass to Ben who lobs the keeper from 20 yards.

It is a goal of real quality. The Gaffer, who has returned to a semi-state of normality and remembered there is a game going on, doesn't seem to appreciate the beauty of the goal and is too busy trying to provoke the opposition with an over the top, over exuberant celebration which ends with him on his knees and goading the Leighbridge management.

When he gets up he bleats out "Keep it tight until half time." On the stroke of half-time Jimmy has a glorious chance to give us the lead but somehow cannot connect with Ben's inviting cross. The Gaffer doesn't bat an eyelid at the miss and remains statuesque, arms folded but quietly fuming.

Half time and The Gaffer keeps his team talk short, sharp and sweet: "I'll settle for a point now lads, so we are going 5-2-1."

Ben suggests that we stick to the 3-2-2-1 formation as "It offers an attacking option" but Gaffer shoots it down with "I want a point". Gaffer has quickly jotted down the second half line up. Luke makes way for Stevie much to everyone's disgust.

Second Half line up:

Billy Stevens
Danny Hall   Stevie Carr   Nick Sheppard   Billy Belafonte   Bobby
Webster
Ben Padgham   Brian Haugh
Jimmy Smith ©

Ben is willing to 'discuss' matters:
"OK, where's the outlet Gaffer?"
Gaffer: "Jimmy."
Ben: "Where's his support?"
Gaffer: "You and Brian."
Ben: "Do the full backs push up?"
Gaffer: "No they stay."
Ben: "Where's our attacking options then?"
Gaffer: "The front three."
Ben: "There's a lot of space in front of the back five."
Gaffer: "That's why we defend deep they've got to get past us."
Ben: "But they are going to be right on top of us if we drop right off.
We've got to give them something to think about."
Gaffer: "OK we'll go long ball and play 5-1-2. Ben, you take a rest."

Ben throws his arms up and he looks to the skies for divine intervention.
He trudges to the technical area and parks himself down for what I can
imagine is going to be a very long half. Gaffer actually looks smug thinking
he has quashed the mutiny and proved to all concerned that he is in charge.

Revised Second Half line up:
Billy Stevens
Danny Hall   Stevie Carr   Nick Sheppard   Billy Belafonte   Bobby
Webster
Brian Haugh
Jimmy Smith ©Luke Pilbeam

The boys try hard but are overrun in the second half. Luke and Jimmy
keep dropping off but Gaffer tells them to stay up top for the long ball. The
Gaffer's second half instructions are limited to: "Stay back", "Get stuck
in" and "Do you want to play for this team?"

This is his sole response to any grumbles of discontent. Well that and
substitutions. Brian is cutting a lone figure in midfield, especially when
Gaffer tells his forwards to stay forward and full backs to stay put.

"Any chance of some support Gaffer?" shouts a desperate Brian. Gaffer summons Ben and Brian smiles. Well he smiles for all of three seconds, which is the length of time it takes for Gaffer to shout: "Brian you're off."

It's only a show of brilliance from my Man of the Match Billy Stevens that prevents a cricket score but Leighbridge manage three goals in the last ten minutes as the boys literally run out of steam and the inevitable capitulation follows. 4-1 really doesn't do the boys justice for the effort and work they put into both halves. The final whistle puts us out of our misery and our boys wearily offer handshakes to the victors until The Gaffer again spreads more bad feeling by refusing to shake hands with our counterparts and then summons the boys to the middle of the pitch.

I try to redeem things by offering a hand to the Leighbridge manager who somewhat reluctantly accepts. I go one step further by offering a "Sorry" before Gaffer shouts "Si" at me and I make my way to join the others.

The Gaffer sits the boys in the semi-circle and the Hayes twins open proceedings to apologise to their team mates for their lack of discipline and The Gaffer astonishes all by praising them for their commitment and fight. He then goes into a full-on fifteen minute rant barely pausing for breath and no one escapes, well except for Jimmy - who I don't think touched the ball in the second half - and the twins both escape a bollocking.

The boys took it on the chin but you can tell they feel it is unwarranted. By the time The Gaffer finishes, our opponents are tucking into their sandwiches and the parents are back in the pavilion checking watches and waiting for their sons. The Gaffer marches the boys back to the changing rooms and the boys change and go without troubling the plate of cheese and ham sandwiches, crisps or orange juice.

Even the ever hungry Billy B swerves the food. The atmosphere is awful and not something I've witnessed before. The Gaffer doesn't even speak to me, just grabs everything and is gone.

Walking back to the car I notice Grandad Hayes is telling his Grandsons off and telling them that he "doesn't expect to see that level of thuggery on the pitch and that any fines will be coming out of their pocket money"

The twins stand, hands behind their backs and heads bowed. Occasionally lifting their heads to let out a sorrowful "Sorry Grandad".

After Gaffer's rant, Grandad Hayes marches the twins firstly to the Leighbridge manager to apologise and secondly to the Referee's changing room to apologise to him.

The Leighbridge manager thanked the twins for their apology although he did pass a comment to Grandad Hayes that "It would have been nice if the Dalworth manager had shown the same levels of remorse." Point taken.

Sunday 1st October
Dalworth United 1 - 4 Leighbridge Lions
Dunstable Colts 2 - 2 Tamworth United

Team	P	W	D	L	F	A	GD	Pts
1 Leighbridge Lions	3	3	0	0	14	4	10	9
2 Tamworth United	3	2	1	0	11	6	5	7
3 Dunstable Colts	4	2	1	1	9	7	2	7
4 Parkfield	3	2	0	1	9	7	2	6
5 Kingsbridge	3	1	1	1	5	6	-1	4
6 Phoenix Rovers	2	1	0	1	3	3	0	3
7 Oak Town Rangers	2	0	1	1	2	5	-3	1
8 Dalworth United	3	0	1	2	5	10	-5	1
9 Redbridge Sports	3	0	1	2	5	12	-7	1
10 Langton Reds	2	0	0	2	2	5	-3	0

Smith Says:
Today was a disappointing defeat and what makes it so disappointing is that last year we would have won this game comfortably. So why did we lose? Well the boys have to look at themselves because the blame lies with them. Today they were tactically inept and were wanting to do things their own way and they were second best all game. I always demand full commitment but today indiscipline replaced commitment and that decided the result.

Last year we were a well drilled and tight unit under Michael but this year the boys are all over the place to the point we've picked up more red cards than points. The boys have to accept that Michael has moved on and if they cannot operate under new management then maybe it's time they moved on. The way we capitulated today was totally embarrassing and something I will not accept. I am the manager and the buck stops with me and I will work hard to turn things round but the boys need to put in the hard work too.

Harsh words were spoken afterwards but even harsher is the reality of how poor we have been. I was proud to accept the managers position but I'm not proud of the performances that have been served up so far. There is no blame culture but we all have a responsibility to produce the standards I expect, no demand. I will not accept second best.
The Gaffer

Dalworth United 1 Leighbridge Lions 4
Squad: Billy Stevens, Stevie Carr, Nick Sheppard, Billy Belafonte, Brian Haugh, Alex Hayes, Aidan Hayes, Bobby Webster, Ben Padgham, Luke Pilbeam, Jimmy Smith © Danny Hall,
Scorer: Padgham. **Man of the Match**: Not awarded

That night, breaking with tradition, I ring The Gaffer.

"Your column on the website was a bit harsh Gaffer."
"It's the truth Si, the boys played for Michael, they aren't playing for me."
"They are playing for you but it's becoming an internal war of wills."
"I'm The Gaffer Si, they need to accept it."
"No one is disputing the fact."
"Well the boys seem to be, they can't follow instructions."
"They are though."
"Well why did we lose the game then?"
"Because we only had nine players on the pitch!"
"Yeah, well they didn't follow my instructions with eleven or nine players on the pitch."

I can see that no amount of words is going the change Gaffer's mindset so I gracefully retreat.

"Fair enough, see you Tuesday Gaffer."
"OK Si, see you Tuesday"

Nick has been on the phone to the others, notably Ben who he is on the phone for over an hour. This is not a happy squad and Gaffer is going to have to work hard to turn things round.

Tuesday 3rd October
Training isn't great tonight. Everyone is working hard but nothing is coming off. Passes are misplaced. Tackles are missed. Crosses are overhit. Shots are off target and most important of all communication is non-existent. The boys aren't talking to each other and The Gaffer isn't talking to anyone just barking out instructions. The boys are going through the motions and it's a totally non-productive session. You can almost sense a Mexican stand-off between The Gaffer and the boys and no one is in the mood to offer an olive branch. It's a horrible environment to work in and as soon as training is finished Gaffer says: "9:30 here on Sunday." and within five minutes everyone is gone and the Rec is as empty as the Dalworth team spirit. Before Gaffer goes he thrusts a letter into my hand. It is his fine from the Cheltenham FA.

Misconduct Charge Notification

Dear Participant

Participant: Vinny Smith (XXXXXXXX)

Charge: FA Rule E3 - Improper Conduct - Not acting in the best interests of the game

The details of the charge are as follows:

You are hereby charged with a Breach of FA Rule E3 in respect of improper conduct which took place during the game Dalworth United vs Kingsbridge at Dalworth Rec on 21st Sept 2017

The Referees report is as follows:

In the 89th minute of the game after I awarded a free kick to Dalworth and the ball had gone out of play. I was struck by the ball, deliberately kicked by Mr Smith, while lining up the wall. I issued a Yellow Card for deliberate foul play.

It is another reminder of everything that is going wrong at the moment.

Thursday 5th October
No managers' meeting tonight which is a blessing as I've got a ton of marking to work my way through.

Friday 6th October Dalworth News - Dalworth Struggle Continues
The all-conquering Dalworth United have become a distant shadow of their once invincible self as three games in they have already lost more games than they did all of last season. Leighbridge Lions were the latest side to take advantage of Dalworth's current frailties as they were comfortable winners by 4-1. Manager Vinny Smith's early boasts have already fallen by the wayside as the Dalworth struggle continues. Ben Padgham hit Dalworth's consolation while on-form Lions striker Tai N'Denka hit all four of their goals. To add to their woes, both Alex & Aidan Hayes received red cards and pending three match bans.

Saturday 7th October
Gaffer rang regarding tomorrow's match and team selection. He hasn't decided on the final line up or formation but wanted my opinion on certain players. He then casually dropped into the conversation that a scout from Cheltenham Town was coming to watch Billy Stevens. At last, a bit of good news, but The Gaffer didn't sound very happy, saying:
"Can't afford to lose our keeper Si".

"Yes but you can't stand in his way Gaffer".

There was a very long and thoughtful pause and then Gaffer threw into the mix: "Mmmmm, we'll see.S ee you tomorrow Si".

I really didn't like the sound of that and I reckon The Gaffer is plotting something.

Sunday 8th October - Dalworth United vs Phoenix Rovers
I turn up for the game and, surprise surprise Billy Stevens is missing. Gaffer tells me he has a knock which he picked up from a school game on Wednesday so he has decided not to risk him and give Danny Hall a game in goal. The boys are all puzzled as some of them played in the same game and they don't remember him picking up an injury and besides he was fine in school on Thursday and Friday. The boys' suspicions are soon replaced by total astonishment as The Gaffer announces the starting line-up. I overhear Ben talking to Nick:
"Since when have we ever played a 5-2-3 and with three wingers on the bench it doesn't give a lot of scope for change does it?"

Nick nods his agreement. Luke gives me a glare and when I make eye contact he mouths: "Have a word Si".

Let's see how this pans out.

Starting line-up   5-2-3
Danny Hall
Stevie Carr   Johnny Day Nick Sheppard Aidan Hayes Billy Belafonte
Alex Hayes Adam Morley
Charlie Fisher Jimmy Smith © Luke Pilbeam
Subs: Ben Padgham, Brian Haugh, Bobby Webster

The Gaffer starts his teamtalk but it's hampered by a bombardment of reasonable questions:

Stevie: "Is that a flat back five Gaffer?"
Gaffer: "Yes."
Billy: "Do you want the full backs to push into the space in midfield Gaffer?"
Gaffer: "Yes but priority is not conceding."
Nick: "Do you want me to sweep Gaffer?"
Gaffer: "No just make sure you are the last man."
Alex: "Do we stay central Gaffer?"
Gaffer: "No hold the middle."

Adam: "Does one hold and one go or do we both push on to support the attack?"

Gaffer: "Mmmmm yes one hold and one goes."

Charlie: "Do we work the channels and get wide or do we get close to Jimmy?"

Gaffer "Work the channels AND get close to Jimmy."

There are a number of puzzled looks and it seems that there are a number of contradictions within The Gaffer's instructions, but nevertheless the boys try to take it on board.

Kick-off

The early exchanges are really cagey and the formation while making us very tight at the back seems to be nullifying any attacking potential. The fullbacks are going long as they don't have any wingers to feed, and the midfield are being swamped every time they are in possession so they are just looking to hit the front three. The long ball is working though and we are creating chances. The first of which falls to Jimmy Smith in the penalty box but he hesitates and gets tackled before he can get a shot off. Astonishingly the ref points to the spot.

The Phoenix players and management are going mental and I have to admit it is a very soft and fortunate penalty. Luke Pilbeam grabs the ball and puts it on the spot. Gaffer yells at Luke: "Jimmy's on pens".

Luke completely ignores Gaffer and Gaffer yells at Jimmy: "You take it".

Jimmy completely ignores Gaffer and gives Luke a nod of approval to take the penalty.

Luke calmly strokes the penalty home sending the keeper the wrong way to make it 1-0 to Dalworth. With the celebrations going on, Gaffer then stuns the whole team by immediately calling Brian Haugh and Bobby Webster to the touchline and substituting Jimmy and Luke. Jimmy hands Nick Sheppard the Captains armband on his exit and Luke just goes and sits outside the technical area. Ben consoles the goalscorer while The Gaffer turns on Jimmy:

Gaffer "If you can't follow instructions then you ain't playing."
Jimmy "I didn't want to take it, I gave it to Luke."
Gaffer "Luke isn't the penalty taker, you are!"
Jimmy "Luke scored. I've missed every one I've taken."
Gaffer "If I say you are on pens, then you are on pens."
Jimmy "Yeah, well I want what's best for the team."

Gaffer "I decide what's best for the team not you."
Jimmy "Fair enough."

With that Jimmy calmly gets up and asks for the key to the changing rooms, strolls off to get changed and goes home.

While Jimmy is getting changed, Johnny Day heads home a Bobby Webster corner to make it 2-0. The Gaffer didn't even celebrate the goal, in fact he hardly said a word for the remainder of the half except for arguing with, I'm guessing, Jimmy on the phone.

Half time and The Gaffer is as subdued as the boys are excited with their first half performance.

Ben says to The Gaffer:
"Am I coming on Gaffer?"
"Erm, yes come on for Charlie Fisher."
"What centre forward?"
"Yes why not."
"OK."

There is a long uncomfortable silence as the boys await their next instructions.

Nick as Captain breaks the silence.
"What are the second half instructions Gaffer?"
"Well it seems to be do what you want at the moment."
"What?"
"Just do what you are doing."

The Gaffer delivers the last line in a 'I don't really care' manner as opposed to a 'Well done lads just keep doing what you are doing'.

The lads are totally deflated. They lead 2-0 but might as well be losing. Luke Pilbeam looks at The Gaffer. Pride dictates that he will not ask Gaffer if he can go back on. Gaffer makes the first move.

"Do you want to go back on?"
"Yeah" says Luke jumping up.
"Take Adz place."
"What in midfield?"
"Do you want to go back on?" snaps The Gaffer.

Luke trudges out onto the pitch shaking his head.

Second half line up   5-2-3

Danny Hall

Stevie Carr   Johnny Day Nick Sheppard Aidan Hayes Billy Belafonte

Alex Hayes Luke Pilbeam

Ben Padgham, Brian Haugh, Bobby Webster

I would like to say that we registered our first win of the season but I can't because we fell apart second half. We weren't outplayed or outclassed or outfought we simply threw the towel in. The boys didn't look interested but then neither did The Gaffer, who spent most of the second half arguing with Jimmy on his phone. Phoenix scored four times and all four goals could have been prevented. To be fair it could have been more but there's no point apportioning blame because in the end, no one gave a damn.

So another defeat and The Gaffer launched into the players calling them a disgrace and questioned their desire. He even went as far as to say that the boys wanted him sacked. He then slammed the changing room doors, threw kit around the changing rooms, kicked water bottles and turned the air blue.

The boys just sat silently, gazing into space and trying not to make eye contact. They took all that The Gaffer threw at them, not because they feared his wrath but simply because they couldn't care less. The Gaffer was on a roll now and continued his tirade of abuse while I just stood in the corner of the changing room, near the door, feeling both embarrassed and uncomfortable in equal portions.

"You threw the towel in. You gave up. Where's your heart? Where's your passion? Where's the spirit you showed Michael last year?"

Ben was the only player that spoke and all he said was:
"Gaffer can we discuss this at training on Tuesday, when we've all calmed down?"

This seemed to stop The Gaffer in his tracks and the boys got changed and grabbed their sandwiches and crisps. The juice remained largely untouched, to be consumed from the less intimidating atmosphere of the car on the journey home.

So there you have it. Another defeat, but no arguments, no discussions, nothing. The Gaffer vented his anger and the boys displayed their contempt.

The atmosphere matched the display today: Soulless and if there is a rock bottom then I think we have hit it.

Billy S rings Nick that evening and Nick tells me that The Gaffer had rang Billy to say that he wanted to give Danny Hall a game in goal this week. Billy said he understood and had offered to come along as sub but Gaffer said: "No that's alright, it might put pressure on Dan." so Billy S spent the morning playing on his X-Box.

Results from Sunday 8th October

Dalworth United   2 - 4   Phoenix Rovers

Team	P	W	D	L	F	A	GD	Pts
1 Leighbridge Lions	3	3	0	0	14	4	10	9
2 Tamworth United	3	2	1	0	11	6	5	7
3 Dunstable Colts	4	2	1	1	9	7	2	7
4 Phoenix Rovers	3	2	0	1	7	5	2	7
5 Parkfield	3	2	0	1	9	7	2	6
6 Kingsbridge	3	1	1	1	5	6	-1	4
7 Oak Town Rangers	2	0	1	1	2	5	-3	1
8 Dalworth United	4	0	1	3	7	14	-7	1
9 Redbridge Sports	3	0	1	2	5	12	-7	1
10 Langton Reds	2	0	0	2	2	5	-3	0

Smith Says
Dalworth United 2 Phoenix Rovers 4
Squad: Danny Hall, Stevie Carr, Johnny Day, Nick Sheppard, Aidan Hayes, Billy Belafonte, Alex Hayes, Adam Morley, Charlie Fisher, Jimmy Smith © Luke Pilbeam, Ben Padgham, Brian Haugh, Bobby Webster
Scorers: Pilbeam (p) Day **Man of the Match:** Not awarded

Just in case you are wondering, I haven't left out The Gaffer's views because there weren't any, as he "couldn't be bothered".

Apathy is the new king for the day.

Tuesday 10th October
There are no discussions tonight as there is no training as Gaffer has to attend a meeting with the Dalworth United committee. He has asked me to support him and on the way to the venue/pub he hands me a letter:

The Parks Commission
Dalworth County Council
The Old Town Hall
Dalworth
DT62 1XX
Mr cccccccccccccccccccc
Dalworth United FC Chairman
XXXXXXXXXXXXXX
XXXXXXXX
XXXXXXXXX

Wednesday 1st October
Re: Official Complaint – Mr Vinny Smith

It has been brought to our attention that the above named, one of your junior team managers, has been reported to the Dalworth Council on two separate occasions. The following incidents both occurred at Dalworth Recreation Ground.
1. Showing disregard for a member of the public walking their dog and using abusive language to said member of the public.
2. The use of excessive abusive language in a public area and when challenged was both rude and aggressive towards the complainant.
We must remind your club that this is a public area and any further misconduct by the above fore mentioned person may result in a ban from the Dalworth Rec.
We hope you will treat this warning with due consideration and we hope that you will support our decision on this occasion.

Yours Sincerely
Roger Flintxxxxxx
Roger Flint
Parks Commissioner

The Gaffer accepts the charge of improper conduct as per The Dalworth United Code of Conduct and he receives an official written warning from the Committee. He looks almost tearful after the meeting. He hardly says a word on the return trip home except for when he drops me off:
"Thanks for your support Si."
"That's OK Gaffer."
"See you Sunday"

Friday 13th October
Gaffer rings (day earlier than usual) and straight away I can sense the sadness in his voice, the fact that he doesn't even say anything after the initial "Hi Si", so it's left to me.
"You OK Gaffer?"
"It's our Jimmy, he's gone."
"What do you mean gone?"
"Yeah he's left Dalworth."
"For f**k's sake Vinny, I thought you meant he was dead!"
"No he's jacked the football in."

It takes me a few seconds to regain my composure.

"Oh OK, I'm sure he'll be back."
"I'm not so sure; I'll ring you tomorrow with the team Si."
"Yeah OK."
 I put the phone down and I feel quite numb inside.
"You OK hun?" says my concerned wife.
"It's only a bloody game."
"Of course it is dear, glass of wine?"
"F**k it I'll have the bottle."

Saturday 14th October
The Gaffer, true to his word is back on the phone but again it's a pretty soulless conversation:

 "I'm taking all 14 players tomorrow and I'll pick the team at the ground."

I try to inject a bit of enthusiasm into the conversation.
"Who's getting the armband tomorrow?"
"I might let the players decide."
"What formation we going with?"
"Depends on the starting line-up."
"A good cup run will change our fortunes."
"We'll see."
"A win tomorrow could kick start our season."
"Yeah any win would be good."
"The boys'll be up for it tomorrow."
"Do you reckon?"

I tried but failed miserably.

"See you tomorrow Gaffer."
"Yeah"

Sunday 15th October - Dalworth United vs Diddlecott Ravens
David Dudley Challenge Cup

I was first to the Rec with Nick and then slowly but surely the others started turning up. Gaffer was last one there cutting a lone figure with no Jimmy. I went to his car with him to collect the kit and equipment. I tried to make conversation but quickly gave up as The Gaffer's one word answers gave me nothing to work with. The Gaffer pinned the starting line up on the changing room wall.

"There's only 12 players Gaffer"
"Oh yeah, Danny has gone away this weekend and Charlie has got a heavy cold."

Starting line-up   4-3-3

Billy Stevens
Stevie Carr   Johnny Day Nick Sheppard Billy Belafonte
Alex Hayes Adam Morley   Aidan Hayes
Ben Padgham© Luke Pilbeam Bobby Webster
Sub: Brian Haugh

Diddlecott Ravens play in the same village league as Plumpley Colts so this should be the first win of the season, however the mood in the changing room is more befitting of a wake so who knows what will happen and victory is certainly not guaranteed. The Gaffer isn't helping matters and he delivers the shortest team talk of the season:

"Teams on the board. We're going 4-3-3. Ben, you've got the armband."

And that's it, three short sentences. Then The Gaffer leaves the changing room saying he has to make a few work phone calls. After he leaves, the changing room the mood lightens a little and the boys finally start to talk. Billy B adds a touch of class to proceedings and shares last night's Chicken Madras, albeit second hand. His contribution is both loud and it stinks. Alex and Aidan pinch Adam's new Armani cap and start playing frisbee with it. Ben and Nick are deep in conversation regarding today's game. Johnny then delivers a team talk courtesy of Jose Mourinho which is surprisingly good and has the changing room rocking with laughter. The mood soon changes when the contents of Billy B's bowels see the light of day. Well the toilet bowl sees it up close and personal, the rest is left to the imagination, but the smell leaves us in no doubt that now would be a good time for the warm-up.

Ben Padgham takes the warm-up under the watchful eye of The Gaffer. It's a high tempo session and the boys look as though they are up for it.

On paper this seemed an easy game and so it proved to be, ending 16-0. Eight goals in each half and the boys did what was required. Luke even handed the ball to Billy S when we won a penalty and he duly blasted the ball home. In fact Stevie was the only player who didn't score on the day. It was still a very strange game. I would say it had the feeling of a pre-season game or one of those end of season nothing-to-play-for games, although at this level every game matters.

This was a game that needed winning and that's what happened. The boys goal celebrations were muted, even Billy S's penalty, and it's fair to say that the boys didn't even touch second gear. Each goal was met with a polite hand clap from The Gaffer which was better than no response.

The Gaffer got the boys together at the end and simply said:
"See you at training Tuesday"

Results from Sunday 15th October
Oak Town Rangers 2 - 1 Leighbridge Lions
Tamworth United 1 - 4 Langton Reds
Phoenix Rovers 9 - 0 Redbridge Sports
David Dudley Challenge Cup
Dalworth United 16 - 0 Diddlecott Ravens

Team	P	W	D	L	F	A	GD	Pts
1 Phoenix Rovers	4	3	0	1	16	5	11	9
2 Leighbridge Lions	4	3	0	1	15	6	9	9
3 Tamworth United	4	2	1	1	12	10	2	7
4 Dunstable Colts	4	2	1	1	9	7	2	7
5 Parkfield	3	2	0	1	9	7	2	6
6 Kingsbridge	3	1	1	1	5	6	-1	4
7 Oak Town Rangers	3	1	1	1	4	6	-2	4
8 Langton Reds	3	1	0	2	6	6	0	3
9 Dalworth United	4	0	1	3	7	14	-7	1
10 Redbridge Sports	4	0	1	3	5	21	-16	1

Smith Says
The boys did all that was asked of them and we comfortably move into the next round of the Challenge Cup where we will face Ardley Reds. We have another cup game next week when we face Dunstable Colts in the League Cup.

We now sit in 9th place in the league 8 points behind the leaders. It does look like it's going to be an open league this year as after four games no-one is unbeaten.

All we can do is try to get as many points on the board as possible but we have at last registered a win so hopefully we can get back to winning ways in the league.

Dalworth United 16 Diddlecott Ravens 0
Squad: Billy Stevens, Stevie Carr, Johnny Day, Nick Sheppard, Billy Belafonte, Alex Hayes, Adam Morley, Aidan Hayes, Ben Padgham©️ Luke Pilbeam, Bobby Webster, Brian Haugh
Scorers: Pilbeam 3, Webster 2, Padgham 2, Haugh 2, Alex Hayes, Morley, Aidan Hayes, Belafonte, Stevens (p) Sheppard, Day
Man of the Match: Ben Padgham

Tuesday 17th October
The Gaffer is already stressing about Sunday's game, which is a good sign because he is focused again. The Hayes twins both start 21 day bans this weekend and with Jimmy's departure it means we are down to bare bones. Gaffer therefore puts on a 'light' training session and there is still no mention of the Phoenix game.

Training is all very low-key except for Adam's oversized Neon Green sleeveless training top and Billy B's controlled explosions which he is letting off at will. It soon becomes a competition between Billy and Johnny who it seems has mastered the art of burping on demand. Every break in training becomes a personal duel between Johnny's mouth and Billy's arse. It's Dalworth's very own version of Dick & Dom's juvenile 'bogies' game. Just as Gaffer is setting up for a small-sided game, Johnny unleashes the loudest and vilest burp. All eyes quickly turn to Billy as everyone awaits his response with baited breath. Billy assumes the position and squeezes out a loud and vile fart. The boys are so impressed that they break out into a round of applause as Billy continues to squeeze out the fart from Hell. Billy's face quickly turns from one of smugness to one of concern because, as the fart peters out it is followed by an unmistakable squelching noise. The round of applause is quickly replaced with howls of disgust as everyone realises that Billy has paid the price for his show-stopper.
 "What's that smell?" asks Gaffer as he enters the scene of the crime.
"Billy's shit himself"
"What?"
"Billy's shit his pants"

Gaffer then catches sight of Billy who is crouched looking like he should be fielding at first slip but it's fair to say that Billy is not waiting for a tickle or a faint edge because he has already caught the googly and it is nestling in his distressed underwear.

"Oh my god, what the..." Gaffer looks to the heavens, what he is searching for I do not know.

Help? Divine inspiration? A spare pair of untarnished underwear? The reality of it is he has to find a solution to Billy's shitty pants. In the end the only option is a phone call home for Billy to be collected early. Thankfully the toilets are nearby and Billy can clean up before going home and avoid taking the putrid stench he has created at the Rec home with him. I do however feel pity for the poor cleaner who will stumble upon Billy's soiled and stained pants in the bin.

The remainder of the session just peters out unlike Billy's fart which I swear is still lingering in the air. Gaffer is less impressed and leaves the players with his thoughts at the end of the session:

"Maybe a bit more focus on the football and less on farting and we might start winning some bloody games."

Dalworth register first success of the season - Dalworth News
Dalworth **Under 15**s broke their duck for the season when they defeated village side Diddlecott Ravens in the first round of the David Dudley Challenge Cup. Goals from Pilbeam 3, Webster 2, Padgham 2, Haugh 2, Alex Hayes, Morley, Aidan Hayes, Belafonte, Stevens, Sheppard and Day saw them comfortably through to the next round.

Saturday 21st October
Gaffer is on the phone and I can immediately detect concern in his voice.
"Do you think we need to sign more players Si?"
"We should be OK Gaffer, the Hayes twins will be back in three games, we just need to get through until then."
"OK Si, we are down to twelve players tomorrow."
"We'll be fine Gaffer."

I hope The Gaffer didn't sense the concern in my voice because we are down to bare bones.

Sunday 22nd October - Dalworth United vs Dunstable Colts - U15s League Cup
The phone ringing at 7am brings the Sheppard household to life. Nick is the first one to get to it and the rest of us wait in trepidation as we all fear the bad news that an early morning phone call usually brings. Nick soon alleviates everyone's fears.

"Dad, it's Gaffer"

I quickly check my mobile phone and realise I have a missed call from him. I trundle down to the hallway bleary eyed and yawning.

"Wotcha Gaffer, everything OK?"
"We've got eleven players today."
"What?"
"Yeah we've only got eleven players, Johnny's got 'flu."
"Oh no, OK Gaffer I'll see you at the ground."

I realise it's pointless going back to bed so the Sunday morning routine kicks in. I walk the dog and then settle down with a newspaper, pot of coffee and a bacon sandwich. We've got the resurgent Dunstable Colts in the cup today and this was always going to be a tough game but it's about to get tougher with only eleven players.

It's a typical autumnal day at the Rec, not cold but there's a nip in the air. The trees are starting to shed their leaves and everyone is putting more layers on. Adam is wearing a bright blue puffa jacket over his tracksuit with Adidas sandals. The Hayes twins, although not available for selection, are still in attendance and on a major wind-up as discovered by everyone on their return to the after the warm up. They find their clothes and gear has been dispersed around the changing room. While everyone is shuffling around relocating their stuff, Billy B does his best to vacate the changing room with a post chilli con carne guff.

The boys are trying their hardest to get the changing room going but The Gaffer is very low key. He delivers a quick team talk and then says to the boys: "I'll see you outside".

Dalworth United vs Dunstable Colts
Starting line-up: 4-4-2:
Billy Stevens
Danny Hall   Stevie Carr Nick Sheppard   Billy Belafonte
Ben Padgham   © Adam Morley Brian Haugh Bobby Webster
Charlie Fisher Luke Pilbeam

Ben does his huddle before kick-off and the boys come out flying. The first ten minutes is played in the Dunstable half and the boys are well on top without scoring. We are dominating proceedings and controlling the game. Charlie and Luke force good saves from the Dunstable 'keeper then Billy B strikes the crossbar from a direct free kick. Billy S is virtually a passenger until Stevie tracking backwards gets a faint touch to a long ball but it's a touch that sends the ball past Billy to give Dunstable the lead. Gaffer who has been silent for most of the game makes his feelings known:

"They haven't had a shot on target and they are in the lead, f**king typical. Shame we can't do that at their end."

The boys hear the comments but they fall on deaf ears as they go looking for an equaliser.

With half time approaching, Ben plays a sublime crossfield ball to Bobby who takes off down the line and leaves two players trailing. He then plays a deep cross to the back post and Charlie hits a first time volley in off the post. Everyone goes wild except The Gaffer. Even the opposition spectators begrudgingly applaud. It was the type of goal that if it had been scored in the Premiership it would have been replayed a hundred times. The boys come off buoyant but their spirits are soon dashed as Gaffer launches into them.

"We should be 5-0 up!"
"What happened with their goal? Shoddy defending"
"How many chances do we need?"
"Last year we would have been out of sight."

It's all too much for Ben.

"Gaffer, we are well on top and the goal wasn't anyone's fault, it was just one of those things, but we're back in the game."
"Last season the game would have been won already." Gaffer sarcastically replies.
"What are you trying to say?" Ben isn't going to let this lie.
"Last season you was unbeatable, this season you can't win a game and the only change is the manager."
Ben sees where this is going: "So you saying we aren't playing for you?"
"Well let's face it you ain't winning for me."
"We are giving our all, we want to win."
"Doesn't seem like it."

At this point Ben gives up and makes his way to the pitch earlier than required. The rest of his team mates get up and silently troop to the pitch in a show of support for their newly-appointed captain. Gaffer just stands arms crossed as he watches his mutinous charges walk out.

Ben forms another huddle much to Gaffers annoyance and after a few words the boys break out of the huddle looking ready to take the game to their opponents. The second half follows the pattern of the first and we lay siege to the Dunstable goal but their keeper is having a blinder and pulls off three good saves in the first 15 minutes. We then think we have taken the lead when Luke Pilbeam controls a Bobby Webster cross and slots home but the referee adjudges him to have handled the cross. The boys surround the ref but in vain and the goal doesn't stand. I find myself vociferously questioning the decision but The Gaffer remains unmoved.

Unfortunately all it does is rile the ref who gives me a warning. The ref isn't the only aggrieved person on the pitch and the boys press for a winner. From a Billy B inswinging corner Nick powers home a header to give us the lead. Gaffer at last shows some emotion and manages to celebrate the goal. The boys aren't sitting back and they go looking for a third. Then an innocuous challenge between Adam Morley and Dunstable's captain leaves Adam clutching his right ankle and in agony. He tries valiantly to carry on but you can see he is in too much discomfort so he hobbles off and we are down to ten players. Ben shouts at The Gaffer:

"What do you want us to do?"
Gaffer shoots him down with a "You're the captain, you sort it out."

Ben glares at The Gaffer and then quickly shouts "4-3-2" to his teammates and backs it up by displaying the formation through finger gestures.

Billy Stevens
Danny Hall Stevie Carr Nick Sheppard   Billy Belafonte
Brian Haugh Ben Padgham ©Bobby Webster
Charlie Fisher Luke Pilbeam

The boys try to adapt but effectively we are missing all three of our central midfielders which means we have three wingers in the middle. The boys still look comfortable and it looks like we are going to hold on until three minutes from time. A cross flies directly into the back of the net. No one is to blame, it's a pure fluke, but it means extra time beckons and with ten tiring players and no subs it is going to be tough.

Gaffer isn't showing any emotion though and when the full time whistle goes he simply gathers them in and with the boys dead on their feet and with another 20 minutes beckoning he delivers a moral bursting team talk:
"We need to work harder and we need to make the chances count."
"We need 110% effort from everyone."
"No one goes hiding, we stand up and be counted."

Noone says a word, they just haul their tiring bodies up and make their way to the pitch.

Extra time begins and five minutes in Brian goes down with cramp. He bravely soldiers on but is a virtual passenger for the remaining 15 minutes. Ben pushes him up top and Charlie takes his place in midfield. The first half of extra time finishes with the score still 2-2 and we change round for the second half. Charlie nearly wins it with a 20 yard lob but it hits the cross bar. Then just as penalties loom Dunstable win a penalty after Stevie misjudges a long ball and it bounces up and hits his hand. It's a harsh call especially on Stevie but if it had been the other way I would have been screaming for the penalty. Dunstable put the penalty away and that's it, they are through to the next round.

The boys troop wearily off having given their all but The Gaffer isn't happy and his "Would have walked that last year" comment, as the boys pass him on their way to the changing room just makes matters worse.

The Dunstable manager is the complete opposite and shakes hands with every one of our boys at the final whistle offering them sincere commiserations. Gaffer says a few words as the boys get changed in silence.
"We can discuss this at training on Tuesday for what it's worth."

The boys look at Gaffer and carry on changing.
"I need to do some serious thinking about where we go next."

Still no response from the players and they grab a few sandwiches out of respect for the mums who made them and then they are gone, leaving a second plate of sandwiches and crisps for the victorious Dunstable players.

I try to reason with The Gaffer.
"They gave their all today."
"Yeah but they lost."
"A couple of flukey goals and a penalty that could have gone either way. Finishing the game with ten men and not having any subs. Everything went against us today."
"But it's happening week after week."
"Talk to them Gaffer they are good lads."
"Yeah but I don't want 'good lads' I want winners."
"Please Vinny (I never call him Vinny) talk to them."
"We'll see."
"Thanks."

Nothing else is said and I have to admit I can't wait to get out of this place.

Results from Sunday 22nd October
Redbridge Sports 0 - 4 Langton Reds

League Cup
Dalworth United 2 - 3 Dunstable Colts (AET)

Team	P	W	D	L	F	A	GD	Pts
1 Phoenix Rovers	4	3	0	1	16	5	11	9
2 Leighbridge Lions	4	3	0	1	15	6	9	9
3 Tamworth United	4	2	1	1	12	10	2	7
4 Dunstable Colts	4	2	1	1	9	7	2	7
5 Langton Reds	4	2	0	2	10	6	4	6
6 Parkfield	3	2	0	1	9	7	2	6
7 Kingsbridge	3	1	1	1	5	6	-1	4
8 Oak Town Rangers	3	1	1	1	4	6	-2	4
9 Dalworth United	4	0	1	3	7	14	-7	1
10 Redbridge Sports	5	0	1	4	5	25	-20	1

Smith Says
Another game, another defeat and the boys threw the towel in too easily for my liking. Last season they would have won this game 4/5-0 but this season the determination and desire is missing. Last season they would have run through brick walls for the previous manager but not this season.

This campaign the drive and the spark is missing. I have never been a quitter and I'm not starting now. I will turn things round and if the players can't do it my way then I will find players who can. I don't want excuses I want solutions and more importantly I want results.

There will be no training this week but we will meet as a team at the Rec at the usual time.

Dalworth United 2 Dunstable Colts 3 (AET)
Squad: Billy Stevens, Danny Hall, Stevie Carr, Nick Sheppard, Billy Belafonte, Ben Padgham, © Adam Morley, Brian Haugh, Bobby Webster, Charlie Fisher, Luke Pilbeam.
Scorers: Fisher, Sheppard
Man of the Match: Webster

Monday 23rd October
Gaffer rings and it's short and sweet.

"I've mulled things over and I know what I'm going to do and say tomorrow." and before I can reply he says "See you tomorrow Si."

Tuesday 24th October
Not a football in sight tonight and I must admit I don't know what to

expect as Gaffer is keeping his cards close to his chest.

Everyone is on time and soon sharing their own views and thoughts, mulling around in small groups and talking in whispered tones. Nick had been on the phone to the others earlier and the boys have been talking at school. They've all got their own ideas of what might happen but it is all assumptions some of which are:

    1. Gaffer is going to resign.
    2. The club have asked Gaffer to resign.
    3. Gaffer is going to get new players in.

Gaffer is the last to arrive making a grand entrance, last to arrive, first to speak:

"I've got us all here tonight to have a clear the air talk and try to work out how we go forward. I'll have my say first and then let everyone else have a say."

Everyone is listening intently.

"I think you lot would rather still have Michael in charge. I know you enjoyed playing for Michael but he's gone and I've tried my hardest to carry on the success but I don't think you are playing for me. Jimmy left because he felt no one wanted him in the team."

This comment receives a number of puzzled looks and on this occasion I'm with the boys.

"You've argued with my decisions and I don't think you've given them a chance. Ben I know you've been my biggest critic. What do you think?"

If anyone was going to be the boys spokesman it was always going to be Ben and he is happy to take the mantle.

"Gaffer, if I'm honest I was glad you were taking over because you knew us and I thought if anyone was going to continue the success it was you. But you tried to change too much too soon when it didn't need changing. Formations, tactics, positions. It was all there for you and all you had to do was carry it on."

"I was gutted when Jimmy left but you made him captain and he hated it. Then you played him up top and he hated it. You put him on pens and he hated that. Jim is a really good centre back so why not play him there? You've left players out and not given them much game time but Gaffer, more than anything, it's not enjoyable anymore. Look at the Leighbridge game. We gave it our all, even with nine men we had one goal and that was to win the game."

Gaffer looked taken back at first but then nodded and said:

"I wanted to stamp my own authority on the team. I didn't want people saying 'yeah he's done well but it's Michael's team'. As for Jimmy I wanted to boost his confidence."

Adam piped up "If you wanted to boost Jim's confidence you should have played him in the right position and given him game time at the back."

Gaffer nodded. "Fair enough, Adz"

Then Aidan piped up:
"Gaffer, when we got sent off we was giving everything to win a game of football."

Alex continued:
"Yeah, we went over the top but we did it for you."

Gaffer again nodded in agreement. Nick then took over:
"Do you think we are happy, Gaffer? Every defeat hurts us, we hate losing."

Gaffer again nodded and then he turned to me and said: "Are they right Si?"
I felt like I had been put on the spot but replied.

"Yes they are right Gaffer, but it's not just you. I've got to hold my hands up because you have made mistakes but I've just let you crack on. I should have been in your ear and I should have been more hands on. Ben is right about one thing though, no one is enjoying this and we've all forgotten why we do it. We do always play to win but we also play to enjoy it."

Gaffer nodded in agreement and you could feel the tension rapidly disappearing. Everyone had their say and it wasn't malicious, it was just constructive and not overly critical. Slowly the smiles were reappearing on faces and everyone began laughing and joking. We must have spoken for a full 90 minutes and after everyone had their say it was left to Gaffer to wrap up proceedings.

"Thank you for your honesty. I know I've made mistakes but at least I know now that we are all in this together. Let's not worry about winning titles or cups let's take each game a game at a time and let's have some fun. See you Sunday boys."

And that was it, the tension was gone and more importantly we were a group again. Would this be the season defining moment and would we start winning games again? Noone knew but at least everyone was willing to give it a try. Gaffer was happier though:

"Right let's get things back on track Si."

I couldn't help feeling that surely that wasn't the magic solution. Was that all that was required, a 90 minute chat? I have my reservations but only time will tell.

Friday 27th October - Dalworth News - Valiant Dalworth exit cup
A depleted Dalworth United **Under 15**s exited the League Cup at the first hurdle after losing to Dunstable City after extra time. Goals from Charlie Fisher and Nick Sheppard were not enough as a brace from Barry Dawson and Elijah Domesk saw Dunstable through against a valiant Dalworth who due to injuries started the game with a bare 11 and finished the game with ten men.

Saturday 28th October
Gaffer is on the phone but somethings not right he sounds really down.
"Alright Si, I've got some good news and bad news."
"What's up?"
"I've been sacked."
"What? Why? That's out of order. What's the good news?"
"That was the good news you twat, the bad news is I've been given the England job."
"What the...!"
"Only joking, see you tomorrow, everyone's available except Alex and Aidan."
"See you tomorrow mate."
If this is an indication of the new Gaffer I think I preferred the old one. Not sure if I like the all-new Gaffer. Twat!

Sunday 29th October - Dalworth United vs Oak Town Rangers
This is our seventh game of the season and seventh home game in a row but hopefully today will produce our first league win of the season. The Hayes twins are still suspended but are in attendance and going round the changing room trying to gee everyone up. We only have twelve players available for selection but looking around the changing room I know they are capable of winning the game and registering our first three points in the league. Gaffer has a quiet chat with the boys and the mood, unlike recent weeks, is relaxed among the players. It's a good warm-up too and

the intensity and focus is spot on. Gaffer opts for a solid and dependable 4-4-2 with Johnny cutting a lonely figure in the technical area.

Starting Line Up:

Billy Stevens
Danny Hall Stevie Carr Nick Sheppard Billy Belafonte
Ben Padgham © Adam Morley Brian Haugh Bobby Webster
Charlie Fisher Luke Pilbeam
Sub: Johnny Day

Ben wins the toss and as the boys line up you can see the determination and desire is back and what follows is the complete performance. More importantly, it is a performance devoid of the individual errors, poor decision making, indiscipline and bad luck that littered the previous games. The boys controlled the game from start to finish and the result never looked in doubt from first whistle to the last. Goals from Charlie, Luke, Ben and a sublime 25 yarder from Billy B secured all three points. It could have been more but it didn't matter because it was a masterclass from the boys and the quality of their passing and play was superb. Gaffer used the roll on, roll off system for the subs but it never disrupted play and this was the Dalworth from last season. The boys received a round of applause from the parents at the end and it was gratefully received and they repaid the compliment to their parents.

Gaffer was full of praise and it was all positive feedback after the game. The whole atmosphere was good and everyone was smiling. Gaffer reserved special praise for Ben Padgham for his leadership skills.

"Padg, I reckon you've got a career as England Manager or a Sky pundit."
"Cheers Gaffer so what you're saying is I'd make a great manager or pundit but a crap footballer?"
"No, no, I didn't mean that, I….."
Gaffer pauses as he sees the smirk spread across Ben's smug face.
"You git, Padg!"
"Gotcha Gaffer!"
"Oh Padg by the way I like your idea, we will discuss the game at training on a Tuesday. It gives everyone time to have a think about it and we can discuss with clear heads. Great shout Padg."

The boys change quickly and they are off to eat while we tidy the kit away.

"Give us a hand with this lot Si." Gaffer points to the kit.
"Yeah sure Gaffer." I grab the kit bag and we trundle off to the car.

"That's more like it Si."

"It was definitely more enjoyable Gaffer."

"I think I was so desperate to put my stamp on things that I forgot that these boys can play football."

"Today we saw what they do best."

"Yeah, I think I learnt today that all we need to do is be facilitators and the boys will do the rest."

"We learnt today that it can and should be a pleasure to be involved with this team."

"Yeah alright Si, I think we need to stop now otherwise it's going to get emotional."

"Fair enough you tosser."

"Ok you w**ker."

Results from Sunday 29th October

Leighbridge Lions 1 - 2 Dunstable Colts

Dalworth United 4 - 0 Oak Town Rangers

Phoenix Rovers 2 - 3 Tamworth United

Team	P	W	D	L	F	A	GD	Pts
1 Tamworth United	5	3	1	1	15	12	3	10
2 Dunstable Colts	5	3	1	1	11	8	3	10
3 Phoenix Rovers	5	3	0	2	18	8	10	9
4 Leighbridge Lions	5	3	0	2	16	8	8	9
5 Langton Reds	4	2	0	2	10	6	4	6
6 Parkfield	3	2	0	1	9	7	2	6
7 Kingsbridge	3	1	1	1	5	6	-1	4
8 Dalworth United	5	1	1	3	11	14	-3	4
9 Oak Town Rangers	4	1	1	2	4	10	-6	4
10 Redbridge Sports	5	0	1	4	5	25	-20	1

Smith Says

It was a fantastic performance from the boys today. In fact it was the complete performance and there was only going to be one winner from the first whistle. We scored four superb goals including an absolute wonder strike from Billy B and kept a clean sheet too. We aren't going to get carried away though as it's only one game and we are still looking up rather than down. It has however shown that we are capable of reaching the standards that we set at the start of the season. Now we need to build on our win and start to climb the table.

Next Sunday we have an early chance to avenge our defeat against Leighbridge Lions and look to record back to back wins.

Dalworth United 4 Oak Town Rangers 0
Squad: Billy Stevens, Danny Hall, Stevie Carr, Nick Sheppard, Billy Belafonte, Ben Padgham © Adam Morley, Brian Haugh, Bobby Webster, Charlie Fisher Luke Pilbeam,
Johnny Day
Scorers: Fisher, Pilbeam, Padgham, Belafonte
Man of the Match: Padgham

Tuesday 31st October
Training has a surprisingly competitive edge tonight courtesy of the currently suspended Alex & Aidan who are doing everything at 100 miles a hour and giving their all and an extra 10%. They leave everyone trailing in the running drills and are on fire during the passing drills. We finish the session with keep-ball and a small-sided game. The keep-ball consists of the Hayes twin hunting the ball in a pair when not in possession and winning it by literally forcing mistakes or tiring the opposing team out. Then when they win it back they are working like crazy to keep the ball. All you can hear is Alex and Aidan shouting out commands and instructions: "Show him left", "Press, press", "Nick it off him", "On his touch", "Man on", "Give and go".

The Gaffer is absolutely drooling at their efforts and becomes a virtual spectator at The Hayes Twins Show. I feel dizzy watching them and then Gaffer calls a halt to the keep-ball and sets up a pitch for the small-sided game but rather than take on fluids and have a five minute rest the boys use the break as an opportunity to play their own keep-ball and they split into two groups of seven and have six in a circle and one piggy in the middle. The piggy has to win the ball or make a player misplace possession. The piggy then swops and they go again. The player who loses possession also has to take six flicks on the ear from the others, which is OK but if you are Billy B, who tonight, has the touch of an elephant, then you end up with painfully glowing red ears. Gaffer is intrigued by this and lets the boys carry on for an extra ten minutes because 1) The quality of the play is very good (with the exception of Billy B) and 2) The boys are having a bit of fun (again with the exception of Billy B). Gaffer eventually calls a halt to the game much to the relief of Billy B's ears.

The Gaffer has set up a 7 v 7 two touch game. He tries to make it fair by splitting the twins but it totally nullifies the game and neither team can string two passes together such is the intensity of the game. The Gaffer then changes it to free play (as many touches as you want) and it's still competitive but the ball-players come into play and it's a joy to just sit back and watch. The communication is excellent and all the boys are vocally active.

I catch The Gaffer's attention: "I'm tired just watching them."
Gaffer is looking pensive "We could still do it you know."
I'm puzzled "Do what?"
"Win the league."
"Do you reckon?"
"Yes, now that would be a fantastic achievement."
I smile "Well, let's do it!"

This brings about a spontaneous high-five causing the 7-a-side to draw to a temporary halt as the boys check out this moment of managerial bonding and it certainly draws lots of strange looks from the players.

From the doom and gloom of previous sessions this one is absolutely exploding with positivity and I think this season is just about to get very interesting.

CHAPTER FIVE

NOVEMBER

"Are we out of the title race? Of course not! It's a marathon, not a sprint."

Thursday 2nd November

The mood of tonight's managers' meeting takes everyone by surprise. Item number two on the agenda is discipline. Apparently the committee are concerned at the number of cautions the club have picked up, and every manager has to feedback on their own team. Of course, the Dalworth team with the worst discipline is us and The Gaffer is one of those to have contributed to the cautions we have received. It's painful watching The Gaffer address the committee, who in turn leave him under no doubt that there must be a vast improvement. To make matters worse, Michael Harris catches Gaffer afterwards and asks how it's going and then offers him some advice. It's not intended to be patronising but Gaffer isn't in the mood for advice and he is in a foul mood by the time we leave the pub.

It's an awkward journey home and I stick Paul Weller's Stanley Road on shuffle to fill the uncomfortable silence. I can see that Gaffer is stewing and just as we get to opening bars of 'Out of the Sinking' Gaffer opens up:

"They think I'm an idiot don't they?"

"Don't be stupid of course they don't."

"Michael couldn't wait to stick his oar in."

"He wasn't being patronising, he was genuinely trying to help."

"They still think I'm an idiot."

"No they don't."

"I know I've made mistakes but I'm trying to turn it round."

"You have turned it around" I can see the self-doubt come creeping back.

"Yeah but I'm still no Michael."

"For f**ks sake you need to stop thinking like that, I know you can turn things round so stop f**king worrying about what others think and put all your f**king efforts into showing everyone what you can do."

Gaffer is startled by my response and to be honest I startled myself. Gaffer doesn't respond until I drop him off.

"OK, you with me on this?" I just nod at him.

"Right then, let's do this." It's quite ironic that this is played out to a backdrop of 'Changing Man' and all we've got to do now is wait for the bang.

Friday 3rd November - Dalworth News - Dalworth register first league win

Dalworth United **Under 15**s 4 Oak Town Rangers **Under 15**s 0: Dalworth finally registered their first league win of the season with a comprehensive 4-0 win over Oak Town Rangers. Goals from Charlie Fisher, Luke Pilbeam, Ben Padgham and Billy Belafonte saw Dalworth take all three points.

Saturday 4th November

Gaffer is on the phone.

"We've got twelve players tomorrow Si, it's the twins last game suspended so we've got to get through this one. It's going to be tough but we can do this."

"It would be nice to turn them over after last time."

"We are still short in midfield so I'm going to go 4-1-3-2 with Adz in the holding role and we'll give it a go. Nothing ventured, nothing gained."

"So true Gaffer."

"See you tomorrow Si."

"See you tomorrow Gaffer."

Sunday 5th November - Leighbridge Lions vs Dalworth United

This could be the turning point in our season, five weeks ago we suffered a demoralising defeat against today's opponents, had both twins sent off and team morale hit rock bottom. Fast forward five weeks later and we have finally registered our first win of the season. Another defeat today and our season could be over before its began, a win and we could get our season back on track.

Our 15-man squad is looking threadbare with Jimmy gone and the twins suspended but we've still got a twelve man squad capable of winning the game. The twins might be suspended but they are again in the changing room and geeing the players up in their own unique manner, not that the boys need it.

Gaffer is remarkably calm considering the importance of the game and sticks the team up on the changing room door for the boys to digest before delivering his team talk.

Starting Line Up:

Billy Stevens

Danny Hall Johnny Day Nick Sheppard   Billy Belafonte

Adam Morley

Brian Haugh Ben Padgham © Bobby Webster

Charlie Fisher Luke Pilbeam

Sub: Stevie Carr

"I know it's a new formation but it's based on a defensive unit and an attacking unit which effectively gives us 5 defenders and 5 attackers but that's not to say attackers neglect their defensive duties and defenders their attacking duties."

The boys are listening intently and there are no burning questions or disapproving looks, just nods of approval.

"Last game against Leighbridge I tried to defend with nine men on the pitch and gave us no attacking options. I got it seriously wrong and we got hammered. Today we take the game to them and play the game in their half. I want us to get the ball forward quickly but not route one. I want the fullbacks to push up alongside Adam when we attack effectively giving us a 2-3-3-2 and then we play from there."

Short, concise, clear and understood instructions. It's left for the Hayes twins to provide the fist pumping, high fiving, chest bumping, head butting acts of encouragement and it works because the boys are fired up and ready to go.

They dive into the kit bag and Charlie asks:
"Gaffer what colour do Leighbridge play in?"

"Red." He looks puzzled. "Why's that?".

He isn't left in suspense for long though because Charlie is holding up a red shirt. Gaffer closes his eyes and shakes his head. "Oh shit. I've picked up the wrong f**king kit!"

Gaffer is momentarily speechless until a barrage of questions and comments hit him.

"Where's the white kit Gaffer?"
"At home."
"Schoolboy error Gaffer."
"Really?"

"Shall we play in skins Gaffer?"
Ben throws in: "We could put bibs over our shirts."

Gaffer pauses and then shoots out of the changing room. Two minutes later he is back.

"Stick the red kit on I'll be back in a minute."

The boys start to get changed and moments later Gaffer is back, red face and out of breath, he is carrying a large bag full of a variety of coloured bibs. He starts frantically emptying the bag scattering bibs all around the changing room and then starts chucking yellow bibs at the boys.

"Put these over the red kit."

Once all the boys have a yellow bib on Gaffer shoots off again. Literally seconds later Gaffer returns with the ref in tow. The ref looks around the dressing room and nods his head

"Yeah I'm OK with that" and the ref is off.

Gaffer gives us the thumbs up and he shoots next door to tell Leighbridge we are good to go and then he's back again. As I edge towards him he slumps onto the bench and holds his hand up to signal he needs a minute, or two. I decide to leave him to recover and put the various coloured bibs that are strewn across the dressing room floor back in the bag.

So as The Gaffer said, we are good to go, and it's Leighbridge Lions in all red vs Dalworth United in all red with yellow bibs.

The addition of bibs to our match day kits causes much moaning amongst the boys.

'This is unprofessional."
"This is bloody uncomfortable."
"This bib's too tight."

Billy checks the size: "It's a bloody small, someone swop with me."

Ben jumps in "Stop bloody moaning we've got a game to win"

The boys moan all the way through the warm-up and they spend half the of it adjusting and readjusting their bibs and when Gaffer tells half the boys to take off their bibs for the keep ball it's a race who can get them off the fastest. Billy S is remarkably smug throughout due to the fact that his blue goalkeepers top clashes with no one.

Gaffer gives his last instructions and an apology: "Look I'm sorry I picked up the wrong bag"

Ben is quick to respond: "I don't care what kit we are in, we're here to win a game. "

Kick-off

Leighbridge, buoyed by the last result seem to have the same idea as us and come out full of confidence and all guns blazing. This seems to negate both teams attacking play and the game becomes bogged down in a midfield battle. Then the boys take the lead with the first chance of the game and it's a goal of real quality. Billy S collects a long throughball and rolls it out to Billy B who exchanges a one-two with Adam, who has dropped off deep, and then picks out Bobby. Bobby drops a shoulder and goes past his marker but as the Leighbridge defence drop off he turns and plays a sublime crossfield ball to Brian on the opposite wing. Brian takes a touch and then spots the run of Charlie who peels out to the right at the same time as Luke makes a diagonal run in to the space vacated by Charlie. The whole Leighbridge defence follows the two strikers runs, leaving a gap for Ben to exploit and Brian finds Ben who from a full 25 yards out hits the ball into the top right hand corner to give Dalworth a 1-0 lead.

It really is a magnificent team effort and it changes the complexion of the game as Leighbridge, realising this is the not the Dalworth they played last time, drop deep. This plays into our hands and the lead is doubled five minutes later when Billy B finds the corner from a free kick after Bobby is fouled on the edge of the box. It's all Dalworth now and The Gaffer is a picture of composure as he offers tactical observations and instructions in a calm and collected manner.

Occasionally he will lean over and run something by me but he has a clear head and is well ahead in the mind games stakes. Then against the run of play Leighbridge grab a goal out of nothing. A long upfield punt is misjudged by Nick who gets under the ball. Billy S tries to atone for the error but the striker gets there first and lobs the ball over Billy S who is stuck in no man's land. Billy is soon in action again and saves at the same striker's feet and gets a kick to his right hand which requires a bit of treatment but he is soon up and carries on. With half time approaching Billy comes to collect a cross but drops it, he goes to reclaim the ball at the same time as the Leighbridge striker lines up for a shot and takes the full impact of the shot on the same right hand. The loose ball falls to a Leighbridge player who strikes the ball into the unguarded net.

This sees The Gaffer display his first bit of emotion all day but he doesn't apportion any blame just bemoans our luck. Billy S is in some discomfort now and it's obvious he can't continue, so Danny takes the gloves and Stevie slots in at right back and once again we are down to bare bones and eleven players.

Half- Time Leighbridge Lions 2 Dalworth United 2

The Gaffer is reflective and surprisingly upbeat.

"OK boys we go again. Same formation as it worked for most of the half and I'm sure that if we keep doing what we were doing in the first half we can get our noses in front again. Let's just watch the long ball, Johnny. Nick, hold the back line and if one attacks the ball the other drops in behind. Our attacking play was superb so let's get the ball in their half and the chances will come."

Once again there are lots of nods of approval and everyone is ready to go. Billy S has changed his top and grabbed an outfield player's shirt. Gaffer gives him a puzzled look.

"Better a one handed sub than ten players Gaffer."

Gaffer smiles at him and Billy S makes his way to the technical area in the case of an emergency.

The Hayes twin are now going around firing everyone up and have added a full on skull crunching head butt to rouse the players. Ouch!

Second half line up

Danny Hall

Stevie Carr Johnny Day Nick Sheppard Billy Belafonte

Adam Morley

Brian Haugh Ben Padgham© Bobby Webster

Charlie Fisher Luke Pilbeam

If the first half was anything to go by, the second half would have played out with us as the better team but Leighbridge stealing the points with a disputed penalty. However what happened was ten minutes into the second half Charlie was poleaxed in the penalty area and couldn't continue due to his right ankle swelling and the Fisher family was soon off to join the Stevens family in Dalworth's A&E for the afternoon.

This was due to Billy's right hand alarmingly swelling up within five minutes of the re-start and the young keeper rushing off to hospital. Thankfully Luke put the penalty away but although we had the lead we now had to play the rest of the game with ten players. The Gaffer didn't change a thing other than the formation and it worked a treat. Rather than set up defensively and change the mind set we went 4-1-3-1 and carried on attacking.

Danny Hall
Stevie Carr Johnny Day Nick Sheppard Billy Belafonte
Adam Morley
Brian Haugh Ben Padgham© Bobby Webster
Luke Pilbeam

Losing Charlie galvanised the team spirit and while we lost one forward we still had another and that was all we needed. All the boys played their part but Ben and Luke were unplayable. Luke scored another three goals and all were assisted by Ben. At one point I counted the Leighbridge players because it seemed as though we had the numerical advantage. They couldn't get the ball off Ben he was everywhere and every time Luke got the ball he looked like scoring.

Gaffer was looking smug but on this occasion who could blame him. He called it right and got everything spot on. Having said that we did have two twelfth men, well two eleventh men in the Hayes twins who were racing up and down the touchline, screaming and hollering words of encouragement and celebrating each goal like it was the winning goal in the FA Cup, Champions League and World Cup final all rolled up together.

Leighbridge were shellshocked and their manager was less than complimentary to his players: "There's only ten of them", "Where's the bloody effort gone?", "Any chance of someone putting a shift in?"

Gaffer nudged me and laughed "Remind you of anyone?"
"Not anyone I know now." I winked back at him.
"We've won this Si, when the manager loses it like that there's no coming back."

He was right and we ran out 6-2 winners against a team that, five weeks ago, we lost 4-1 to. Gaffer shook hands with the Leighbridge manager and even apologised for his behaviour during the last game. The Leighbridge manager accepted the apology and even offered a "Good luck for the rest of the season."

"Nice touch Gaffer."
"Yeah well I was a bit of a pr**k last game Si."
"Yeah you was!"

Gaffer gathered everyone together at the end and shook each of the boys' hands, he even gave the Hayes twins praise:
"You two were outstanding today, epitomises everything that is good about this team."

The twins were beaming ear to ear but still managed to make me wince when they did their celebratory head butt.

Gaffer finished off with a "Thank you boys, we've got our Dalworth back." and that was it.

Results from Sunday 5th November
Leighbridge Lions 2 – 6 Dalworth United
Oak Town Rangers 1 – 3 Redbridge Sports

Team	P	W	D	L	F	A	GD	Pts
1 Tamworth United	5	3	1	1	15	12	3	10
2 Dunstable Colts	5	3	1	1	11	8	3	10
3 Phoenix Rovers	5	3	0	2	18	8	10	9
4 Leighbridge Lions	6	3	0	3	18	14	4	9
5 Dalworth United	6	2	1	3	17	16	1	7
6 Langton Reds	4	2	0	2	10	6	4	6
7 Parkfield	3	2	0	1	9	7	2	6
8 Kingsbridge	3	1	1	1	5	6	-1	4
9 Oak Town Rangers	5	1	1	3	5	13	-8	4
10 Redbridge Sports	6	1	1	4	8	26	-18	4

Smith Says
That was the best performance to date since taking over. Luke Pilbeam and Ben Padgham will take the plaudits with a four goal haul and three assists and a goal but it was a real team effort today and special mention must go to Danny Hall who did an outstanding job taking over from Billy S in goal.

The table is beginning to look more promising after two wins on the bounce and we have put ourselves back in the mix. Fifth place and three points behind top place is certainly a more positive place to be after our poor start. There is still a long way to go and there are a lot of points to play for but for now we have to concentrate on one game at a time. Everyone in the camp wish Charlie Fisher and Billy Stevens a speedy recovery and I will keep everyone updated regarding their injuries.
The Gaffer

Leighbridge Lions 2 Dalworth United 6
Squad: Billy Stevens, Danny Hall, Johnny Day, Nick Sheppard, Billy Belafonte, Adam Morley, Brian Haugh, Ben Padgham© Bobby Webster, Charlie Fisher, Luke Pilbeam, Stevie Carr
Scorers: Pilbeam 4(1p), Padgham, Belafonte
Man of the Match: Pilbeam & Padgham.

Tuesday 7th November
Training is absolutely buzzing tonight. The boys are in an excellent mood as is The Gaffer. Charlie is a spectator but Billy is playing on pitch with his hand strapped for protection (and loving the opportunity to show his peers what he has in his 'top drawer'). It is high spirits and high intensity training tonight. Gaffer puts on keep-ball and line-ball games as we have only one goalkeeper. We have no game this weekend much to the disgust of Alex and Aidan, who are available again. The boys also incorporate their own game within a game: 'megnuts'. Putting the ball through an opponent's legs and shouting 'MEGNUTS!'. The highlight of the game is Alex getting Aidan, who in turn responds with a double 'megnuts' on his brother. Aidan compounds his brother's embarrassment by whooping around the pitch shouting 'megnuts' high fiving all and sundry while imitating riding on a horse. While everyone is anticipating a 'messy' response from Alex he shocks us all by simply applauding his brother.

We have just witnessed a miracle.

Friday 10th November - Dalworth News - Dalworth hit Leighbridge for Six
Leighbridge Lions 2 Dalworth United 6: Dalworth are well and truly back to winning ways as they avenged their early season defeat to the Lions. Goals from from Luke Pilbeam, Ben Padgham and Billy Belafonte ensured that all three points went to Dalworth.

Sunday 12th November
No game and no training.

A break in routine today and a treasured lie-in, well, it doesn't quite happen as planned. I haven't set the alarm but the imaginary alarm clock in my head still goes off at 7am and as soon as I stir, my Staffie-Boxer cross Faith decides it's business as usual and she reminds me it's time for walkies. OK then, a change of plan. Walk the dog and grab the papers and then go back to bed for a few extra valuable hours of sleep. Dog walked, papers bought and back home, I suppose I could give Faith her breakfast. Scrambled eggs, cheese and chicken, so that I don't have to do it later. I start scouring the sports pages of the papers and then decide to make a quick cup of tea to take back to bed with the papers. I then decide to opt for a pot of coffee to save a return trip to the kitchen if I want another cup. The boiling kettle seems to trigger something in my subconscious and I'm starting to feel hungry. No point in going to bed hungry so a bit of toast, a small bowl of cereal. No I'm really hungry so I reach for the bacon. Do I fancy a quick bacon sandwich? What about an egg and bacon sandwich or sausages? Before I know it the bacon's on, so are the eggs and the sausages and the beans and the tomatoes and the mushrooms and the toast. The fry-up is on and the first cup of coffee is going down nicely and I'm totally engrossed in an article on Premiership spending this season so I don't notice that Nick is also up.

"What's cooking Dad?" as if he didn't know.
"A fry up son."
"Can I have some?"
"The works?"
"Be rude not to!"
"OK" I say realising that more food is required.
"Oh Mum said could she have a cup of tea and a bacon sandwich and Katie (my daughter) said could she have whatever's going and a cup of coffee."

And there you have it. I realise the tea and toast option would have been the safer and less time-consuming choice. But the result of my hunger pangs have stirred the rest of the Sheppard clan with the smells of a fry-up and coffee wafting round the house and awakening them from deep slumber. Fortunately, they don't have to move as Cafe Dad is in full swing and Nick has been sent with breakfast requests, leaving me to slave over the proverbial hot stove. Cafe Dad has extended it's opening hours. With the requests, the thoughts of a lie-in disappear, which are but a distant memory, as I'm left preparing breakfast for the five thousand.

"Will that be the seven, eight, nine or ten-item breakfast?"

The breakfast that was intended for my own consumption has been dispatched to the four corners of the house and Nick's attempts to take his fry-up back to bed are soon squashed as I hold his breakfast to ransom until he has hand waited on his mum and sister. Once the needs of the family have been met I can finally sit down. I distance myself as far as possible away from the kitchen and the family by settling in the conservatory. The pot of coffee has been replaced by a cup of tea, I'm on my third cup now and I sit down with tea, fry-up, minus mushrooms which Nick had the last of, and newspapers. Funnily my appetite has gone due to all the cooking but I've cooked it and I'm certainly going to eat it and proceed to polish it all off. Mid-sentence of an article about Brexit I glance at the clock. It's now 9am and any thoughts of a lie-in have long-gone. I'm now wondering how I'm going to fill a day devoid of Football.

My wife, who has decided to rise, soon takes away any lingering doubts that I may have:
"The grass could do with a cut."
"Yes dear."
"The cars are grubby too."
"OK I'll do them."
"You can help me with shopping too."
"Really?" I hate shopping.
"I'll treat you to a pub lunch."
"OK darling."
"Then we can pop into my Mum's."
"F**k".
I realise I've said this aloud and not in my head as it was intended to be said. Thankfully my wife didn't hear it. Nick did and he is sniggering.
"Don't worry about the cars, Nick can do them."
"OK darling" It's me sniggering now and Nick is the one uttering: "F**k".

Twenty minutes later I'm cutting the grass and Nick is washing the cars.

Roll on next Sunday and Global Sports away in the cup.

Results from Sunday 12th November
Oak Town Rangers 1 - 7 Kingsbridge
Tamworth United 6 - 1 Leighbridge Lions
Phoenix Rovers 5 - 2 Langton Reds

Team	P	W	D	L	F	A	GD	Pts
1 Tamworth United	6	4	1	1	21	13	8	13
2 Phoenix Rovers	6	4	0	2	23	10	13	12
3 Dunstable Colts	5	3	1	1	11	8	3	10
4 Leighbridge Lions	7	3	0	4	19	20	-1	9
5 Kingsbridge	4	2	1	1	12	7	5	7
6 Dalworth United	6	2	1	3	17	16	1	7
7 Parkfield	3	2	0	1	9	7	2	6
8 Langton Reds	5	2	0	3	12	11	1	6
9 Oak Town Rangers	6	1	1	4	6	20	-14	4
10 Redbridge Sports	6	1	1	4	8	26	-18	4

Tuesday 14th November
Charlie is back training. He has decided to wear two pairs of socks inside

an older and softer pair of Puma boots. He is a bit apprehensive with his first few touches but grows in confidence as he has no adverse reaction to any contact with his foot and the ball. Gaffer is happy as it looked like we would get Alex & Aidan back but lose Charlie and Billy. Billy still has strapping on his hand but is training. Gaffer has said we can stick Danny in goal and use Billy on pitch if we need to.

The twins are desperate to play and have been checking the weather forecast such is their desperation. They are giving it their all in training and it will be good to see them back. Gaffer is trying to keep things non-contact as he doesn't need any more injuries and he is struggling to contain the enthusiastic Hayes twins so the entire session consists of no contact drills. It works as we appear to have a clean bill of health at the end.

Friday 17th November
Smith Says
Sunday we travel to Global Sports for the second round of the David Dudley Challenge Cup. We have the twins back from suspension and Charlie and Billy S back from injury so we have a strong squad available. We are meeting at Dalworth Rec at 9am where I will give out maps. If anyone is stuck for transport please let me or Simon know asap.
The Gaffer

Saturday 18th November
Gaffer rings and sounds relieved/happy that we have a squad of 14 to choose from. He tells me he is going to put Danny in goal and keep Billy S as back up and Billy is happy with that.
"Big game Si, I fancy a good cup run and the boys are firing."
"I've got every faith in them Gaffer."
"Going to have to keep a leash on Alex and Aidan."
"I'd rather have ten Dobermans on a leash than those two."
"Point taken Si, See you tomorrow."

Sunday 19th November -Global Sports v Dalworth United - David Dudley Challenge Cup
We meet at Dalworth Rec at 9am for the 10:30 kick-off. Gaffer reckons it'll take about 40 minutes to get to the ground. The directions are all handed out and after a quick headcount all are present and correct. Danny Hall and Stevie Carr are travelling with the Hayes twins and all I can say is the twins' Grandad is a brave man to have that lot in one car.
It's a surprisingly mild day for November and it's not a bad journey to the ground. Global Sports play at a privately owned sports complex and their facilities are one of the best in the county so it's a treat to play there.

One by one the players turn up but we are missing Alex, Aidan, Danny and Stevie leaving us with ten players and no fit goalkeeper. The Gaffer and me are panicking.

Game Set and Match – The Hayes Twins.

I will explain what happened next in chronological order to give you the full story:

9:45 – The Gaffer receives a text message from Alex: "Soz Gaffer b there in 5 mins had 2 stop 4 petrol"

9:50 – Another text from Alex: "Soz Gaffer the traffic is really slow moving. B there asap"

9:51 - The Gaffer immediately texts back: "Where are you?"

9:53 – Alex replies: "Hadley"

9:53 – I can immediately see The Gaffer's face change as he takes on board the text. "Hadley is about 20 f**king mins away!"

9:54 – Gaffer receives another text this time from Aidan: "Yeah we are on the by-pass and there has been an accident. We r crawling"

"Oh s**t, they ain't gonna make kick off"

9:55 – Gaffer grabs a bit of paper and is furiously scribbling away.
"Fish didn't you play in goal at school?"
"Yeah Gaffer I did."
"Good, you're in goal"

He sticks up a hastily written team sheet and it looks like we might have a one handed keeper up front.

Charlie Fisher
Johnny Day Nick Sheppard Billy Belafonte
Adam Morley
Brian Haugh Ben Padgham© Bobby Webster
Luke Pilbeam Billy Stevens

9:56 – Gaffers phone is beeping and it's Danny: "Gaffer we r moving, b there asap, leave the kit out"

9:55– Gaffer responds straight away: "Keep me posted" while Charlie is trying to fit his small and wiry frame in Billy's goalkeeper top and gloves.

9:57 - Gaffer is now in full on panic mode and pacing the dressing room shouting out instructions. "Give Fish as much protection as possible", "Bill just be a nuisance up top and keep feeding Luke", "Keep it tight until the others get there."

He turns to me. "I hope they get here asap."

9:58 – Gaffers phone is going and this time it's Stevie: "Gaffer don't think we were in Hadley"
9:58 – "Where the f**k are you then?"
9:58 – "Not quite sure Gaffer"
9:58 – "Let me know asap" Gaffer is sat down, phone in hand and eyes firmly fixed on the screen. He probably doesn't realise, but he is tapping his foot in anticipation of the next text.
10:00 – Gaffer's phone beeps and he leaps out of the seat
"Think we know where we r"
10:00 – "WHERE THE F**K ARE YOU" Gaffer is almost shaking with anticipation and the boys have stopped getting changed while they look at The Gaffer's descent into insanity.
10:01 - While The Gaffer stares at his phone waiting for an update Alex, Aidan, Danny & Stevie calmly stroll in without saying a word and sit down. Gaffer notices them and is rendered speechless. Silence falls over the changing room and then the whole room dissolves into fits of laughter as The Gaffer realises he has been well and truly stitched up.

"You f**king little shits!"
"Sorry Gaffer, couldn't resist it!"

The Gaffer has tears rolling down his cheeks but thankfully they are tears of laughter. He looks at Alex, Aidan, Danny and Stevie shakes his head and then produces the biggest smile I think I have ever seen him give. The Gaffer rips up his hastily written team sheet and retrieves his original one.

Charlie, despite being relegated to the bench, gladly gives up the keepers top to Danny. "You're welcome to it Dan"

Starting Line Up:

Danny Hall
Stevie Carr Johnny Day Nick Sheppard Billy Belafonte
Alex Hayes, Aidan Hayes
Ben Padgham © Adam Morley Bobby Webster
Luke Pilbeam
Subs: Billy Stevens Brian Haugh Charlie Fisher

The boys, and Gaffer, and me too for that matter, chuckle our way through the entire warm-up. There are lots of references to 'players going missing' 'players hiding' and 'passes going astray' but it's all in good humour and Gaffer has the final word by telling Alex and Aidan they will be playing "Right and leftback in the changing room today"

Global Sports are a good side and their pitch is one of the largest we will play on this season. The game starts in a really cagey fashion with both teams feeling each other out. Both sides are happy to keep the ball and try to work openings but both defences are on top and the Hayes twins are providing an effective shield for the back four and turning over lots of possession. Chances are at a premium but Danny pulls off an excellent double save and then Billy B hits the bar with a long range effort. The majority of the play is in midfield and when Alex is the victim of a late challenge that leaves him in poleaxed, Aidan goes charging over. I turn to The Gaffer and I can see the apprehension on his face as we wait with baited breath at the response. Aidan goes straight over to his brother and helps him up as the ref brandishes a yellow card. We both let out a sigh of relief and the first half finishes with no score.

Gaffer tells the boys to keep doing what they are doing and that the chances will come. Bobby makes way for Brian with Gaffer keeping the partially fit Charlie in reserve.

The second half carries on in the same fashion and Danny tips a long range shot over the bar before Luke stings the Sports' goalkeeper with a rasping drive. Then Sports take the lead when a low drive which Danny has covered takes a deflection off of the Sports number nine and he can do nothing to stop the ball going into the net. No panic though and Gaffer tells the boys to keep pressing. Slowly but surely they start to impose themselves.

It is funny how sometimes a team is more content on holding a lead than increasing it and this is the case with Global Sports as their manager gets them to drop deeper and deeper. While we are finding it hard to break them down, there is space in front of their penalty area and when you have someone like Billy B you can exploit it and when Billy hits one of his trademark thunderbolts it looks like parity is restored. The Gaffer and I are already celebrating until the Sports 'keeper throws an arm out and somehow tips the ball onto the bar. I almost feel sorry for the keeper because after such an amazing save he can only watch as Luke is the first to react and he heads home the equaliser. But my sympathy for the 'keeper is soon replaced with full on celebrations as the equaliser puts us back in the game. Whereas Global seemed content to hold on to their short-lived lead, our boys now search for a winner and we have the momentum going into the last ten minutes. First Ben and then Adam go close but the Sports 'keeper is having a blinder. With the last kick of the game Luke hits the post and extra time beckons.

Having lost in extra time to Dunstable Colts Gaffer senses an air of 'here we go again' and reassures the boys that the game is theirs if they carry on knocking on the door. He makes a couple of changes with Bobby back on for Adam Morley. This is the only change as Gaffer is still reluctant to use Charlie.

The first half of extra time is a really dour affair as both teams are struggling to make headway and the half finishes 1-1.

Bobby and Stevie are struggling with cramp so Aidan slots in at right back and Adam goes in alongside Alex and Charlie is reluctantly slotted into midfield.

Danny Hall

Aidan Hayes Johnny Day Nick Sheppard Billy Belafonte

Alex Hayes, Adam Morley

Ben Padgham © Charlie Fisher Brian Haugh

Luke Pilbeam

The game is virtually walking pace now with neither team wanting to make a mistake and neither having the energy to break down the other. It's the freshest player on the pitch Charlie who has the best chance of the half when he heads a Ben Padgham cross over the bar and then Danny Hall tips a low shot round the post and the referees whistle signals the dreaded penalty shoot-out.

Penalties are nobody's favourite way to finish a game, unless of course you are German. What doesn't help is the penalties will be taken by tired legs.

Let the lottery begin.

Gaffer hands the ref his list of 5 penalty takers:

    1 Charlie
    2 Luke
    3 Billy B
    4 Ben
    5 Danny

The first three all pick themselves and Ben steps forward as captain but Danny is a surprise volunteer.

Ben wins the toss and decides to go first.

Gaffer wishes all the boys good luck and says he is proud of them whatever happens, which is a really nice touch.

Charlie steps up and sees his penalty brilliantly saved by the 'keeper. 0-0
The first Sports taker hits it low to Danny's left. 0-1
Luke is his usual calm self as he sends the 'keeper the wrong way. 1-1
Sports' number seven hits the ball straight down the middle. 1-2
Billy smashes the ball home. 2-2
Sports' third taker sends the ball in off the post just past Danny's right hand. 2-3
Ben hits a low kick into the left corner. 3-3
Danny pulls off a great save low to his left. 3-3
Danny then steps up and smashes the ball into the top right corner. 4-3
Danny tips the last kick onto the crossbar and we have won 4-3.

The team race to Danny and all the disappointments of October are forgotten as the lottery of penalties has gone in our favour. Losing on penalties is a horrible feeling but winning on them is a mixture of relief and joy and ultimately elation. In a true sporting gesture and in keeping with a manner we are accustomed to, Ben is the first person to offer commiserations to the Sports player who missed the final penalty. This is the true mark of a great captain and leader. Ben is closely followed by The Gaffer who shakes every one of the opposition players' hands.

The Gaffer doesn't say much to our boys and just goes round and shakes their hands, letting them enjoy the victory. He then offers me his hand to shake. He doesn't say anything but it's a very heartfelt gesture and I gratefully replicate the sentiment without making a sound.

Sunday 19th November
David Dudley Challenge Cup 2nd round
Global Sports 1-1 Dalworth United (Dalworth won 4-3 on pens)

Smith Says
What a rollercoaster ride of a game that was. The boys gave their all and I was so pleased that their efforts were rewarded with a win. It was probably the closest game we have had all season and at the end of the day we had enough quality, class and determination to progress to the next round. All the boys played their part but a special mention goes to Danny Hall who

not only saved two penalties but had the 'kahunas' to step up and take the decisive kick. I was really proud of all the boys and it is a testimony to their spirit that they have turned things around.
The Gaffer

Global Sports 1 Dalworth United 1 (Dalworth win 4-3 on pens)
Squad: Danny Hall, Stevie Carr, Johnny Day, Nick Sheppard, Billy Belafonte, Alex Hayes, Aidan Hayes, Ben Padgham © Adam Morley, Bobby Webster, Luke Pilbeam, Billy Stevens, Brian Haugh, Charlie Fisher
Scorer: Belafonte
Man of the Match: Hall

Tuesday 21st November
Training is a pleasure to participate in and once again the boys are firing on all cylinders. Gaffer is doing some conditional small-sided games and Billy Stevens is back in goal but the boys are giving him real stick every time he lets one in or makes a mistake.

"Danny would have stopped that one."
"Danny would have caught that."

Billy pulls off a stunning save to tip a Billy Belafonte pile driver round the post only to be 'mugged off' by Stevie Carr who says "Danny would have held on to that one" Billy's "F**k off" is a worthy response and there's smiles all round.

Gaffer finishes off with a small sided 7v7 game and the quality is there for all to see. He does have to remind Alex and Aidan that although there is no game this weekend he would rather no one got injured and the rest of the session passes off pretty trouble free.

Gaffer finishes the session with an announcement:

"Right boys, Sunday all round mine for the Huddersfield v City game on Sky"

Dare I dream of a lie-in on Sunday?

Friday 24th November - Dalworth News
Dalworth **Under 15**s move into next round - Global Sports 1 Dalworth United **Under 15**s 1 (AET: Dalworth win 4-3 on pens) Dalworth progressed through to the next round of the cup with a hard fought victory over Global Sports. A Billy Belafonte equaliser took the game to extra time before Dalworth edged past their opponents with a 4-3 win in the penalty shoot-out.

Saturday 25th November

I'm not expecting a phone call from Gaffer but he's ringing anyway.

"Alright Si, still ok for tomorrow?"

"Yeah of course Gaffer it'll be a nice team bonding exercise."

"Yeah and I'm hoping that Jimmy gets the bug again."

Strange how our turn of fortunes has almost made Jimmy Smith the forgotten man of Dalworth United.

"He'll be back when he's ready."

"Yeah hope so, see you tomorrow Si."

"Yeah see you tomorrow Gaffer."

Sunday 26th November

Gaffer has gone all out to impress, not that he needs to because the first thing that strikes you is The Gaffers Gaff. It is a five bed detached mock Georgian home and it's obvious the building trade has been good to him. Equally impressive is the spread that's been laid on and I felt guilty for having had lunch, not to mention another fry up this morning. The display of food is like a miniature scale version of the Dalworth presentation buffet. It is soon polished off by the ravenous collection of footballers aka Dalworth **Under 15**s.

"Here get that down your neck Si."

I take a sip

"That's got a kick!"

"Yeah it's a single malt whisky."

We are joined by a couple of interlopers.

"What year is it Gaffer?"

"Is it Irish or Scottish Gaffer?"

"Coke is over on the table boys."

"Can't we try a drop Gaffer?"

"No you f**king can't"

Gaffer ushers Alex & Aidan to the soft drinks.

"They are a couple of chancers them two."

"Yeah but I wouldn't swop them for anyone Si."

"No I know what you mean Gaffer."

"Another one Si?"

"Be rude not to!"

It's good to see Jimmy mixing with the boys again and he is soon involved in the 'bants' as they call them. Bants is short for banter but Bants is also apparently lifted from the Inbetweeners TV programme and involves naming anything that involves the word bants. To give you some idea of what it involves here are some of the better ones:

"The Archbishop of Banterbury"
"The Bant of England"
"Bant Holiday"
"Gordon Bants" That was my contribution although only Gaffer got it.
"The Banterbury Tales" Gaffer's contribution and yes only I got it.
"Underbants"
"Banthom of the Opera"
"Bant and Dec"
"Eric Bantona"
"Bantomime"

Although the best one as voted by the boys comes courtesy of Adam Morley

"Adam and the Bants"

Alex and Aidan as usual have to take the Inbetweeners thing too far and it's poor old Stevie who ends up in The Gaffer's bushes in his garden after Alex 'nudges' him and Stevie and his drink end up in the bush. While the boys are creasing up Aidan sends Alex flying. Billy B decides to join in on the fun but his intended target Ben anticipates him and side steps a second before impact and Billy ends up taking out one of The Gaffer's garden gnomes. Gaffer at this points steps in: "No more nudges."

The boys are still laughing and joking and Jimmy is very much part of it. Gaffer keeps looking over to monitor the situation and he is looking hopeful. You really get a sense of camaraderie amongst the boys and there are no outsiders or cliques, just a collective group of people. They genuinely enjoy each other's company and although it is football that binds the group it is a genuine friendship that motivates them to succeed.

The game has just started and some watch it, some keep flicking back to it and some just talk but the conversation flows. I'm having an in depth conversation with Ben about sustainability of form and how some teams can dominate matches, seasons, decades. I sometimes have to remind myself that Ben has just turned 15 as his mastery and knowledge of the tactical side of the game belies his young years.

It is a very pleasant afternoon and it gets me out of marking for a few hours, not that I could do any marking after several large whiskeys. Everyone is saying their goodbyes at the end when Ben puts his arm round Jimmy and says "When you're ready Jim, we'd have you back tomorrow." I seriously thought The Gaffer was going to cry especially when Jimmy said "OK skipper."

Result from Sunday 26th November
Leighbridge Lions 4 - 3 Langton Reds

Team	P	W	D	L	F	A	GD	Pts
1 Tamworth United	6	4	1	1	21	13	8	13
2 Phoenix Rovers	6	4	0	2	23	10	13	12
3 Leighbridge Lions	8	4	0	4	23	23	0	12
4 Dunstable Colts	5	3	1	1	11	8	3	10
5 Kingsbridge	4	2	1	1	12	7	5	7
6 Dalworth United	6	2	1	3	17	16	1	7
7 Parkfield	3	2	0	1	9	7	2	6
8 Langton Reds	6	2	0	4	15	15	0	6
9 Oak Town Rangers	6	1	1	4	6	20	-14	4
10 Redbridge Sports	6	1	1	4	8	26	-18	4

Tuesday 28th November
An absolute downpour during the day leaves the Rec waterlogged and the club calls off training at the request of the council. Gaffer has the right hump as he has to send text messages to the players. It's funny how the Premier League clubs have recently requested a winter break. Well at grassroots level you don't need to request a winter break as they inevitably happen. Games usually fall by the wayside as do training sessions and everyone is left twiddling their thumbs. Once Gaffer has sent all his text messages and received all the notifications back that players have received them he rings me:

"I had a bloody good session planned too."

"It'll keep Gaffer besides the weather is f**king awful."

"I hate not training before a game."

"I wouldn't worry, the game'll be off if it carries on like this."

"F**K me Si you're like the prophet of doom tonight!"

"Yeah, well you try teaching Shakespearian sonnets to Year Eleven!"

"Fair point my liege, ring you Saturday."

"Ooh listen to the bard!" we both start laughing at this point.

"See you Saturday Gaffer."

"See you Si."

CHAPTER SIX

DECEMBER

"A cold Sunday morning at the Dalworth Rec will soon sort out the men from the boys..."

Friday 1st December
Gaffer Says
We lost our first training session of the season to the elements and I'm hoping that Sunday's game doesn't also fall foul of the conditions. This Sunday, weather permitting, we are away to Langton Reds in the league and I'm hoping that we can take another upward step and keep this good run going. The plan for Sunday is to meet at Dalworth Rec at 9:15am. I will let everyone know asap if the game is called off
The Gaffer

Saturday 2nd December
Gaffer rings and it's another one of his quick calls:
"It's looking good for tomorrow Si."
"That's good."
"See you tomorrow morning."
"See you tomorrow."

I must check with Gaffer tomorrow to see if he has discovered the art of sending a text message.

Sunday 3rd December – Langton Reds v Dalworth United
It's a freezing cold morning at Dalworth Rec. It must be cold because Adam Morley is wearing a Ski jacket and the tallest beanie hat you will ever see. Imagine Marge Simpson's hair for scale. It's so big that it droops halfway down the back of his jacket. He is also wearing bright blue dungarees which are more befitting of a children's presenter on CBeebies. The boys would have been in tracksuits but it's too cold for that and they have been granted the equivalent of a Dalworth United tag day, without having to pay a pound though. The Gallagher twins, I mean the Hayes twins are both in matching white parkas. That is the only resemblance because they certainly swear more and definitely fight more than Liam and Noel. The glove wearers amongst the group are first in line for a 'jolly good ribbing'

even ahead of the outlandish Adam. "Wearing gloves? You pussy!", "Man up and lose the gloves you w**ker!".

The Gaffer is in good spirits though and although it's perishing his only concerns on our arrival to the Rec are the huge black clouds floating menacingly above our destination the Langton ports pavilion.

"Game on, come on let's get going!" he claps his hands together and we are off.

He has a beaming smile in-keeping with the seasonal feel and he is the grateful recipient of an early Christmas present in the shape of a game against Langton Reds.

A quick 15-minute journey and we are at our destination and despite the close proximity it feels colder in this neck of the woods. The rain clouds still hang ominously overhead but I'm wondering if a quick downpour would take the temperature up.

The changing rooms are of the portakabin variety and are even colder than outside. The toilets look like they are in danger of being condemned and they are wet underfoot. The showers are covered in mould as are the window frames. The carpet looks Persian, Persian age that is, not Persian quality. The only thing that appears to be keeping it together is the grime and filth that covers the entire surface. The boys get changed quickly as various items of clothing are placed around the changing room as the boys try their hardest not to make contact with the freezing floor. The glove wearers at this point are looking rather smug until those who were mocking them begin to reveal their own carefully hidden gloves.

"Who's a pussy now you w**ker?"
"Where's the string that attaches them? Is it tucked through your arms?"
"F**k me are they your Dad's driving gloves"
"Oi Harry Potter you got the scarf to go with those gloves?"

The boys don't hang around, getting changed in record time and this is despite the additional layers they add to their usual match day wear. Under armour shirts and shorts, extra t-shirts, gloves, two pairs of socks. The boys are starting to resemble sumo wrestlers as layer after layer is added. The winner of course is Adam Morley who warms up, I say this with a touch of irony because no one is warm, wearing a beanie hat and a snood.

The warm-up is high intensity, in a futile attempt to create body heat, and shorter than usual. The rain looks like it might hold off but the wind is really picking up and when Billy Stevens tries a few goal kicks in his warm-up routine they aren't travelling very far. Once back in the changing room, Gaffer gives his last instructions while the boys are blowing in their hands and stamping their feet, desperately trying to generate heat to keep warm. I'm beginning to think we are going to have to prise Adam's beanie and snood off him.

Starting Line-Up

Billy Stevens

Johnny Day Nick Sheppard Billy Belafonte

Alex Hayes, Aidan Hayes

Ben Padgham © Adam Morley Bobby Webster

Luke Pilbeam Charlie Fisher

Subs: Brian Haugh Danny Hall Stevie Carr

It looks like a 3-2-3-2 formation but is more 3-5-2 with the Hayes twins holding. Ben loses the toss and it looks like we are going to be up against a vicious high wind first half.

Any way the wind blows...

The ref's initial blast on his whistle not only signals the start of the game but also seems to summon Njord the Norse God of the sea and winds. One almighty gust rips across the pitch, either that or Billy B had a curry last night. I think I would prefer the latter as the heat from one of Billy's 'blasts' might at least warm the place up. The wind is causing chaos and a cross field ball from Johnny Day not only flies out of touch but also seems to travel at least 20 meters backwards. From the resulting throw in, Langton take it quick from just inside our half and the Reds' right back launches the ball in the direction of our penalty area. Billy Stevens has his eye on the ball and watches it all the way as it sails right over his head and into an unguarded net. Barely a minute played and we are 0-1 down.

Gaffer looks at me in stunned disbelief and I just shrug my shoulders and raise my arms. The boys kick off and any attempts at a long pass are pointless. At one point Billy B attempts one down the channel to Charlie and has to clear his own pass from danger as it comes hurtling back towards him. The message from The Gaffer is simple: "Keep the ball down", which is fair enough, but the entire team is dropping deeper and deeper to receive the ball and to support the player on it. This is in complete contrast to Langton who are putting their foot through the ball at every opportunity. In fact they appear to be playing a 5-0-5 formation with the back five simply launching the ball forward to the front five and hoping something happens.

Gaffer has all but given up hope of getting anything from this half and changes to a defensive 5-4-1 formation.

Billy Stevens
Stevie Carr Johnny Day Nick Sheppard Aidan Hayes Billy Belafonte
Ben Padgham © Alex Hayes, Adam Morley Bobby Webster
Luke Pilbeam

The unlucky Charlie makes way for Stevie in order to combat the onslaught from Langton and while it strengthens the defence it virtually nullifies any attacking threat and Luke is a virtual spectator for the remainder of the half.

Just as it seems as though we have squashed Langton's attacking threat they grab a second as a punted clearance from their 'keeper has Billy S scrambling backwards. He somehow manages to claw the ball from under the crossbar, but his efforts are in vain as he merely puts it on a plate for the Langton centre forward who taps the ball home. 2-0 Langton. The next ten minutes are an onslaught and Billy is like a man possessed saving shots with his arms, legs and even his head at one point. He can do nothing with Langton's third as a corner flies straight in. That's the last kick of the half and the boys can't wait to get in and a) warm up b) change ends.
Gaffer changes things around and reveals via his tactic board a revolutionary new formation.

Ladies and Gentlemen introducing the 1-3-4-2

Second half line-Up
Billy Stevens
Nick Sheppard
Danny Hall Alex Hayes Aidan Hayes
Stevie Carr Ben Padgham © Brian Haugh Billy Belafonte
Luke Pilbeam Charlie Fisher

Johnny, Adam and Bobby make way for Danny, Brian and Charlie and Gaffer's instructions are simple "Get the ball forward quickly, not hit and hope, pick your passes and play through the quarters and then we play the game in their half. Nick you hold."

The boys are chomping at the bit to get back out and within five minutes of the restart Billy B has hit one of his trademark free kicks, albeit assisted by the wind. You can visibly see the panic in the Langton faces and the manager replicates that as with 40 minutes left he decides he is going to defend his lead and go all out defence.

This simply plays into our hands and the next twenty minutes resemble the Siege of Stalingrad, The Alamo, The Battle of Little Big Horn and Dunkirk all rolled into one as Langton adopt another almost revolutionary formation: a 10-0-0. In fact not one Langton player steps foot in the Dalworth penalty area during the half, even Billy Stevens spends all that time without stepping foot in his penalty box.

However try as the boys might they cannot find a way through the Langton wall of defenders, that is until Nick picks up a clearance and plays the ball back to Billy S who is occupying the halfway line. Billy drills the ball forward with a low trajectory and the ball flies straight into the Langton goal without bouncing. It takes Billy by surprise and he genuinely doesn't know how to celebrate until his teammates pile on top of him. Gaffer looks at me and simply says: "Well if you can't beat them, join them!"

Despite still trailing 2-3, Billy's goal is the catalyst for a final push and within four minutes we are on level terms, and what an equaliser it is. Billy B plays a deep crossfield ball to Stevie Carr who takes the ball on the chest and feeds it into a gap for Luke Pilbeam to run onto. Luke makes his way to the by-line and crosses the ball deep to the far post where Aidan Hayes heads the ball back into the path of the onrushing Alex Hayes who hits an unstoppable volley past a static Langton keeper.

The boys, the technical area and the parents go wild. This is a contender for goal of the decade, let alone goal of the season. It kills off Langton's resistance and seals their fate as Danny Hall heads in a Billy Belafonte corner and then Aidan Hayes bursts through three challenges to drill the ball home to cap an amazing comeback. This really was the proverbial game of two halves and it's rare for the elements to play such an active part but they did today. It was an incredible comeback and to The Gaffer's credit he never panicked at any point even when we were 0-3 down at half-time.

The boys are absolutely buzzing back in the changing room and Gaffer decides to let them enjoy the moment and to let them get changed. Within five minutes they are changed and gone. All that is left is me and The Gaffer chucking kit into the kit bag and we aren't hanging about.

"Come on Si, I could murder a cup of tea. I can't feel my bloody feet!"

 The cup of tea that awaits us in the club room hits the spot and I hold it as close as possible to my face to get the full benefit of the heat rising from the steaming cup. The boys are making light work of the sandwiches and then they are saying their goodbyes. Gaffer is still trying to warm up but manages a "Well done boys, see you Tuesday"

"You off now Si?"
"Yeah I'm in need of a bath."
"That's a good shout. I might take the whiskey in with me too!"
"That's a blinding call." and we are gone.

Results from Sunday 3rd December
Oak Town Rangers 0 – 3 Dunstable Colts
Parkfield 2 – 1 Redbridge Sports
Kingsbridge 1 – 3 Tamworth United
Langton Reds 3 – 5 Dalworth United

Team	P	W	D	L	F	A	GD	Pts
1 Tamworth United	7	5	1	1	24	14	10	16
2 Dunstable Colts	6	4	1	1	14	8	6	13
3 Phoenix Rovers	6	4	0	2	23	10	13	12
4 Leighbridge Lions	8	4	0	4	23	23	0	12
5 Dalworth United	7	3	1	3	22	19	3	10
6 Parkfield	4	3	0	1	11	8	3	9
7 Kingsbridge	5	2	1	2	13	10	3	7
8 Langton Reds	7	2	0	5	18	20	-2	6
9 Oak Town Rangers	7	1	1	5	6	23	-17	4
10 Redbridge Sports	7	1	1	5	9	28	-19	4

Smith Says
Well that was certainly an early Christmas present and what a cracker it was. The weather played its part but even at 0-3 down at half-time I was always convinced we would get something out of the game. What was interesting was that the goals were scored by our keeper, two defenders and two defensive midfielders and what goals they were. Billy Stevens' clearance was as sweet a strike as you are likely to see, well that was until Alex Hayes hit an amazing volley after great build up work from the team. Then Aidan Hayes showed great tenacity to burst through three challenges before finishing with composure. The boys thoroughly deserved the win and it goes to show you that, whatever obstacles, or elements they face, they will never give up. We now face another difficult cup tie next week away to Ardley Reds in the third round of the Challenge Cup. I'm hoping we get another two training sessions in and then that will be all until the New Year.
The Gaffer

Langton Reds 3 Dalworth United 5
Squad: Billy Stevens, Johnny Day, Nick Sheppard, Billy Belafonte, Alex Hayes, Aidan Hayes, Ben Padgham © Adam Morley, Bobby Webster, Luke Pilbeam, Charlie Fisher,
Brian Haugh, Danny Hall, Stevie Carr.
Scorers: Belafonte, Stevens, Alex Hayes, Hall, Aidan Hayes
Man of the Match: Alex Hayes (For his wonder goal)

Tuesday 5th December
The boys are still buzzing from Sunday and before the session even starts they have formed a 'Magic Ring'. A Magic Ring involves all the boys forming a circle with three balls inside. Three boys go into the circle and compete against the other two, performing tricks and the winner is the one deemed by the circle to have performed the best tricks. Gaffer is watching intently, instead of setting up and is mesmerised by a trick Adam performs which involves standing on the ball and doing a 180 degree turn with both feet on the ball neither touching the ground. Gaffer sends the boys off with Ben to do the customary warm-up of stretching and jogging round the Rec.

Gaffer is now strolling between the footballs, eyeing them up with purpose and then casually tapping them with his left foot and then his right foot. I can see he is weighing them up and he casually flicks a ball into the air with his laces and does a couple of keepy-ups. He then rolls his foot over another ball, instep to outstep, scoops it into the air and does a couple of keep-ups with his knees. I can see that there is a purpose to this and that he is building up to something, but he is very cautious in his approach and gives a glance left and right before attempting anything. He then begins to tap a ball between his insteps using both feet. He stops and steadies the ball. I'm half watching The Gaffer without him knowing while also keeping an eye on the boys who are currently doing hamstring stretches at the top of the Rec. I can see the boys are making their way back when I hear a thud and turn round to see Gaffer prone and flat out on the ground and making a very strange whistling noise which I think is his breathing.

Gaffer it appears was waiting for his moment to copy Adam's earlier trick but Gaffer, who remember is heavy of build, stepped on the ball and then performed a totally new trick as both feet leave the ball travelling in an upward motion before passing his head which is travelling in a downward motion. Despite there not being a Hayes twin in the vicinity the impact of Gaffer's 'fall to grace' is still nasty and leaves him both dazed and confused and struggling for breath as he has literally had the wind knocked out of him. While I attempt first aid on The Gaffer, mouth to mouth resuscitation is out of the question, Ben organises a keep ball session followed by a small sided game.

Gaffer is slowly but surely regaining his breath and no longer resembles a 90-year-old chain smoking asthmatic. He is however a spectator for the entire session and during the next drinks break Adam again shows off his new trick and Gaffer turns away, not in disgust but simply because it is too fresh in the mind and too painful to watch. He is still short of breath at the end of the session and even contemplating a quick (when is it ever quick?) trip to A & E. He decides against it in the end and after the boys have put everything in Gaffer's van and I've given them the details for Sunday, he just wants to get home. He did try to give the boys the details but gave up in the end because Stevie's best Darth Vader impression whilst addressing Luke Pilbeam - "I'm your manager now Luke" - left The Gaffer in more pain and the rest of us laughing.

Thursday 7th December
Tonight's managers' meeting is totally different to the last one and the Christmas cheer is flowing, especially from The Gaffer. Michael catches him before the start and his "Well done Vin, I knew you could turn it around." comment leaves Gaffer beaming from ear to ear. Gaffer has managed to cadge us both a lift from the Under 14s manager Brian so Gaffer is throwing pints at me all evening which leaves me tipsy and visiting the toilet at frequent breaks. The meeting itself is brief but the social side isn't and I'm a relieved man when Brian announces its time to go.

Friday 8th December - Dalworth News
Langton Reds **Under 15**s 3 Dalworth United **Under 15**s 5
Dalworth Under 15s made a remarkable comeback last Sunday when they overturned a 3-0 half time deficit to score five second half goals and win 5-3. Goals from Billy Belafonte, goalkeeper Billy Stevens, Alex Hayes, Danny Hall and Aidan Hayes kept Dalworth's current winning streak going after Danny Conlon, Frank Slegg and Harry Shearing gave Langton a 3-0 lead at half time.

Saturday 9th December
Gaffer didn't ring, he text instead. Hooray! He has mastered the art of texting.

Sunday 10th December - Ardley Reds v Dalworth United - David Dudley Challenge Cup
It's another early meet at Dalworth Rec although to be fair I have already

been up for three hours. I was up so early I was kicking my heels with the dog while I waited for the Newsagents to open. I still managed an egg and bacon baguette and four, yes four cups of coffee so although I was up at stupid o'clock and thus deprived myself of much needed sleep, I am well and truly wide awake due to my caffeine induced state. Gaffer on the other hand looks half asleep and not his usual buoyant self but that is down to the fact that he hasn't been sleeping due to a case of severely bruised ribs caused by his recent fall. Your secret is safe with me Gaffer.

All the boys are present and all are track-suited and booted. Adam Morley is wearing a pair of outrageous fluffy Ugg boots with his tracksuit. Gaffer gives him a disapproving look but Adz simply says "Me feet are cold Gaffer." The Gaffer conducts a quick headcount and gives out his maps and we are off.

Ardley Reds ground is about 40 minutes away. Well, as the crow flies it is, but today the crow isn't flying. There are two routes to the ground and everyone bar the Hayes twins' Grandad has taken the more conventional and quicker route. They get to the ground at 9:45 and at 9:55 Nick gets a text message from Alex: "Where the f**k r ya". Nick's reply is simple but concise: "F**k knows, where r u". "We r at the ground but no one else is". "Ok we r on our way".

We eventually get to the ground at 10:15 (kick off is 10:30) and by my reckoning we have gone through three sets of temporary traffic lights, one accident, one diversion and got stuck for three miles behind Bert and Doris, out on their weekly 20mph Sunday morning drive. Gaffer hastily arranges a 15-minute delay to the kick-off time. The boys are scrambling around for their kit while I am sticking up the team sheet and giving Gaffer's instructions, which are lost amidst the chaos of the changing room. "Where's the number seven shirt?", "Who's moved my bloody bag?", "Anyone got any tape?", "Billy have you farted?".

Starting Line Up:

Billy Stevens

Stevie Carr Johnny Day Nick Sheppard Billy Belafonte

Alex Hayes, Aidan Hayes

Ben Padgham © Adam Morley Brian Haugh

Luke Pilbeam

Subs: Danny Hall, Charlie Fisher, Bobby Webster

Ben runs the boys through the quickest warm-up ever under Gaffer's watchful eye. By my reckoning it was exactly eight minutes, and before you know it we are lining up for the quick off.

The boys are struggling to get going but our opponents can't take advantage, we are misplacing passes, missing tackles and snatching at shots. I'm positive that the reason for the slow start is due to the boys missing the keep-ball session from a warm up that just consisted of stretching and running. Anyone who doubts the effectiveness of a good warm up, take note. Ardley are top of their division so we were always expecting a tough game but despite the boys not being at their best they are comfortable. Neither side can manage to muster a shot in anger so the first half peters out into a tame stalemate.

The Gaffer tries to inject whatever has been missing via his team talk but he struggles to find anything constructive to say so just offers up "Be patient boys, don't force it and don't go chasing a game that doesn't need chasing." Gaffer reverts to a 4-4-2 and Danny, Charlie and Bobby replace Stevie, Brian and Adam as Gaffer adds some additional firepower to the forward line.

Second Half:

Billy Stevens

Danny Hall Johnny Day Nick Sheppard Billy Belafonte

Ben Padgham © Alex Hayes, Aidan Hayes Bobby Webster

Luke Pilbeam Charlie Fisher

The boys start to impose themselves at the start of the second half and both Bobby and Ben go close with long range efforts. Billy S then keeps us in the game with a brilliant double save as he parries an effort from outside the box before spreading himself to block the follow up. Gaffer is pacing up and down and scratching his chin deep in thought and looking for a way of breaking the deadlock.

"Do I change it Si?"
"I don't know Gaffer it's so tight."
"We're still on top aren't we? I'll give it another 10 minutes." So he leaves it.

If this was a game of Chess both sides would have shaken hands and agreed to a stalemate by now but there has to be a winner otherwise it'll be the dreaded penalties again. Extra time looms when Billy S and Johnny collide going for a cross, which they both miss. The loose ball is crossed back into the Dalworth penalty box into the path of an onrushing Ardley forward. He doesn't connect cleanly but still nods the ball towards the empty goal. The Ardley players, management and fans begin to celebrate when Aidan appears from nowhere and somehow throws his body in the direction of the looping ball, hooks it over his left shoulder and off the line.

I turn to Gaffer and give him my insightful and analytical thoughts on the matter: "Thank f**k for that!".

Gaffer looks at me and replies: "And breathe!".

Both sides are pressing for a winner and with minutes of normal time remaining, Bobby sees his low shot tipped round the post. Ben swings the resulting corner over and Nick makes a late run to the penalty spot and rises like the proverbial salmon powering a bullet header into the Ardley net. Everyone goes wild and The Gaffer and I are jumping up and down hugging each other that is until he lets out an "Ouch! Me f**king ribs!".

"Whoops sorry Gaffer!".

Nick has run the length of the pitch to include Billy S in the celebrations and he is soon at the bottom of a celebratory pile which contains all eleven players and the three subs. This is celebrating the Dalworth way and boy does it feel good. Ardley have three minutes to find an equaliser but there is no way the boys are letting this lead slip and the final whistle is met with huge relief and euphoric celebrations.

The Gaffer and I compose ourselves and shake hands with our opposite numbers and make our way to the changing rooms. The party is in full swing and the changing room is absolutely rocking.

The boys are hugging and high fiving and dancing and singing and you can tell just how much it means to the group. Adz is banging tunes out on his IPhone 7 via his docking station speaker and the dismal days of September and October are but a far and distant memory.

Gaffer goes round all the boys shaking their hands and giving individual praise "Great saves Bill" "Amazing clearance Aidan" "Great header Nick" and there is no necessity for a post-match debrief just a simple "Go get some grub boys you've earnt it"

While we collect the kit Gaffer leans over.
"I'm physically drained Si."
"Yeah I know what you mean but what a feeling. I prefer this winning lark to losing."
"Yeah, fancy a sesh' later?"
"What do you think?"
Guess where we went Sunday afternoon?

Results from Sunday 10th December
Leighbridge Lions 1 – 4 Oak Town Rangers
David Dudley Challenge Cup 3rd Round
Ardley Reds 0 – 1 Dalworth United

Team	P	W	D	L	F	A	GD	Pts
1 Tamworth United	7	5	1	1	24	14	10	16
2 Dunstable Colts	6	4	1	1	14	8	6	13
3 Phoenix Rovers	6	4	0	2	23	10	13	12
4 Leighbridge Lions	9	4	0	5	24	27	-3	12
5 Dalworth United	7	3	1	3	22	19	3	10
6 Parkfield	4	3	0	1	11	8	3	9
7 Kingsbridge	5	2	1	2	13	10	3	7
8 Oak Town Rangers	8	2	1	5	10	24	-14	7
9 Langton Reds	7	2	0	5	18	20	-2	6
10 Redbridge Sports	7	1	1	5	9	28	-19	4

Monday 11th December
Will I ever learn?

Mr Ross a fellow English teacher catches me before our regular Monday morning all staff briefing.
"Blimey Si, you look rough!"
"Don't ask."
"Don't let old Harris (The head) see you like that."
"F**k off! I don't look that bad do I?"
"Well by the amount of cuts on your face you look like you had a shave in the dark and the toothpaste round your face is a nice touch but the tea stains on the tie is the dead giveaway!"
"F**k it" I say rushing off to the staff toilets.
"I've got a spare tie if you need it" shouts Rossy as I speed off.

I look in the mirror and have to agree with Rossy. I've looked better but I still can't help smiling at yesterday's exploits and I do think it was all worth it. I feel a tap on my shoulder and Rossy is standing there with a hideous Green and Yellow tie.

"Unwanted present." he says as he hands it to me.
"Thanks."
"Have you checked the cover list?"
"No. Why?"
"You've got 11z2 first lesson."
"What?"
"Karma's a bitch isn't it?"

The discomfort of the hangover I'm harbouring is now an inferior second to the pain of teaching poetry to 11z2. Kill me now.

Smith Says
It was a very hard fought victory on Sunday but the boys showed huge resilience and commitment to grind out the win. It was especially pleasing to pick up a clean sheet too. The question now is can we go all the way in the cup and the answer is yes we can. We have shown vast improvement in our recent games and I expect us to keep getting better and if we do we may even make a challenge for the league title. But for now it's one game at a time and as long as we are all enjoying ourselves, and we really enjoyed ourselves Sunday, then it's all good. We have a Christmas break after Tuesday's training session and while I'd rather not stop, the boys have earned the break and I would like to take this opportunity to wish everyone A Merry Christmas and a Happy New Year.
The Gaffer

Ardley Reds 0 Dalworth United 1
Squad: Billy Stevens, Stevie Carr, Johnny Day, Nick Sheppard, Billy Belafonte, Alex Hayes, Aidan Hayes, Ben Padgham © Adam Morley, Brian Haugh, Luke Pilbeam, Danny Hall, Charlie Fisher, Bobby Webster
Scorer: Sheppard
Man of the Match: Sheppard

Tuesday 12th December
Gaffer is wearing a Santa hat for tonight's session when I get there and I'm a little premature with my judgment:
"You look a right idiot Gaffer."

At which point he smiles a sarcastic smile and tosses me an identical Santa hat and I reluctantly stick it on my head. If he thinks we are the only two spreading a little bit of Xmas cheer then he is wrong. Adam is wearing a Christmas jumper bearing a quote from Home Alone: "Merry Christmas ya filthy animal". The Hayes twins are wearing matching Rudolph jumpers (Rudolph the Red Nosed Reindeer that is and not Rudolph Hess) Stevie is wearing Father Christmas pyjama bottoms and a Star Wars 'I can feel your presents Luke' t-shirt over a red sweatshirt. He tops off his outfit with a pair of antlers which makes heading a ball interesting. For once Adam Morley is outdone by Billy B who is wearing an outfit similar to the one worn by Will Ferrell in the film Elf. Billy, of course adds a little extra colour to proceedings by letting rip with a humongous fart, exclaiming:

"Merry Christmas and good elf"

This is a really light session with the emphasis on enjoyment and Gaffer puts on lots of little fun but competitive competitions with the winner of each being thrown a bag of chocolate coins. There is a constant stream of 'bants' laughing and micky-taking throughout the session. At the end Gaffer gathers everyone together and wishes them a Merry Christmas. He hands everyone a selection box and then offers round an open packet which contains, wait for it, Chocolate Brussel sprouts, not everyone takes one which simply means there's more for Billy B who quickly devours the remainder of them and then with a devilish grin asks :
"Anyone got a lighter?"

It's a really nice gesture from The Gaffer, the selection boxes not the Chocolate Brussel sprouts, although he is not certain and says to me:
"Do you think they are too big for selection boxes Si?"
"Course not Gaffer, although Alex and Aidan would have preferred a bottle of Monkey Shoulder."

Gaffer's question is quickly answered as next comes an even bigger surprise when Ben takes out two presents from his bag and hands one to Gaffer and one to me. The boy's eyes are fixed on us as we open them to find two framed pictures of the team taken at the start of the season. There is also an engraved silver plate within the frame which reads:
"To Gaffer – Merry Xmas – The Dalworth Boys."

We are both touched by the gesture, which we were not expecting. We thank the boys and that's it for this year.

As they drift off into the distance, Gaffer taps me on the arm.
"Merry Christmas Si."
"Merry Christmas Gaffer"

Friday 15th December - Dalworth News
Ardley Reds 0 Dalworth United 1 - Dalworth **Under 15**s continued their good run of late when they knocked Ardley Reds out of the David Dudley Challenge Cup with a late goal from Nick Sheppard.

The phone rings and I look at my wife with a puzzled look. Surely not.

"Alright Si?"
"Ee, hello Gaffer."
"What you up to?"
"Erm, nothing really."
"Fancy a pint? My treat. I'm bored."
"Erm, I'll ask the wife."

I realised once I had said it how under the thumb I sounded. I shouted to my wife:

"Mind if I go out for a pint with The Gaffer?"

"Yeah sure then I can watch TV in peace."

"Charming, yeah that's fine."

"OK I'll be there with the taxi in a hour Si."

He can't resist a little dig and finishes with: "Tell her I'll get you back home safe and sound and at a reasonable time" and with that The Gaffer is gone.

A quick freshen up and sure enough the taxi and Gaffer are at mine bang on 8pm. A 20-minute journey and we are on the outskirts of Dalworth in a proper old school pub The Old Maid of Clogsworth. I've passed it several times but never been in. The first thing you notice is that they still have the hitching rail outside to tie horses to. I half expect to see a young street urchin making sure the nose bags are suitably filled for the horses while the Master has a mead or two.

When you step into the pub you feel like you've stepped through a time tunnel. Renovated kegs double up for table stems and beer barrels have been modified for chairs. The workmanship is something else. There's no jukebox or fruit machines or any other machine for that fact. There is no dart board or pool table not even bar billiards. A sprinkling of sawdust covers the carpetless stone floor, thankfully there is no spit to accompany the sawdust. The beer is served from kegs and hand pumps and you can tell by the delightfully named brews what type of pub this is: 'Old Rovers Dog Ale' sits by 'Cunning Codgers Mild' which is on top of 'Todgers Best Bitter' in fact a quick surveillance of the pub reveals that there is more facial hair than a ZZ Top concert. This is the quintessential CAMRA pub and if you don't fancy beer there's always 'Dumpy's Grumpy Scrumpy'.

I keep my wits about me in case a press gang appear looking to drag some drunk into nautical service. I observe in the corner two elderly gentlemen and notice one is blind but I can't see the presence of any black spots, phew! The landlord is also an elderly man with ferocious sideburns a bald head, a Cyrano de Bergarac nose and a waistcoat. Sadly there are no buxom serving wenches just, and I'm only assuming, the landlords' wife who is neither buxom nor young, an elderly woman with silvery grey hair and silver rimmed glasses who looks like she should be solving murders, not serving pints. The barkeeps squad is completed by Colin, a university student with bigger sideburns than the landlord and an afro that is the size of a small country accompanied by a man collecting glasses who I believe, judging by his appearance, doubles up as the village idiot during the day. He is good though and is balancing at least twenty glasses although when he throws a smile my way I realise he is carrying more glasses than he has teeth in his mouth.

After at least three trips the landlord pours him a pint and he downs it quickly before setting off on another trip. I'm frantically trying to remember the words to 'Master of the House' from Les Mis just in case the pub breaks out into an impromptu sing song and I get detected as an outsider. I then bump into a man whose facial hair covers 80% of his face and make a mental note to self: watch out for Werewolves and don't walk home alone.

My over imaginative and flamboyant thoughts are then disturbed by Gaffer who is like a kid in a sweet shop and is enthusing, nay salivating, over the chalkboard that is placed just above our table.

"You've got to try this one Si."
"You'll love this one."
"This one's got a kick Si."

The Gaffer is soon lining up pints and downing them in minutes, such is his eagerness to try the next one. I glance at my watch and realise time has sped on and its 9:30. I've had 4 pints in a hour and I'm really starting to feel it. Gaffer however is only warming up. Now seems like a good time to visit the loo. On my return Gaffer's enthusiasm hasn't waned.

"This one's a belter Si."
"I'll get us two pints of Badgers Brown Brew..." and Gaffer is off again.

I start to panic as my senses start numbing and I seek help.

"I better text my wife Gaffer"

9:35 "Hi darling, just having a couple more then I'll be home. Love you xxxxxxxxx"
My wife replies almost immediately:
9:36 "Ok love; don't forget we are going shopping tomorrow haha J. Love you too xxxxxxxx".

The next pint goes down quickly and before the last drop hits the back of my throat Gaffer is up and getting another one in. This time he puts an 'Old Gits Toffee Apple Cider' in front of me. I'm not going to lie this is a good pint, too good and a distinct and fruitier alternative to the pints of real ale that we have consumed. This one slides down too easily and against my better judgement I quickly get another couple in but not before another visit to the loo.

Now I like a drink, I'm a teacher after all and I love a good red wine but real ales or potent ciders are not my choice of poison so this is totally new territory for me although I get the feeling Gaffer has done this before. The chat for the evening is mainly football but after eight pints it could be Love Island, Brexit or the novels of Dostoyevsky. I begin to lose the conversation as everything is slowly becoming a blur and although Gaffer's lips are clearly moving I'm only catching every fourth word as my ability to process conversation is fast dwindling.

"I'm starving. Fancy a curry?"

Now I manage to hear the word 'curry' but I'm struggling to process the sentence and my head and stomach become embroiled in a battle and all I can hear is two conflicting arguments: "No, go home Si" my head is saying but my stomach counters with: "Hell yeah let's add a curry to the mix". It's a flat argument as I find myself allowing primitive instinct to take over and I mumble the fatal words: "Yeah why not."

Whoops I better text the wife again.

10:15 "Hello Love, Gaffer has ask me for a cirry and I feel rudr saying no so do you mins if I go. I really lovr you xxxxxxxx" (the spelling mistakes are exactly how I typed them as my wife saved all the messages for evidence)
10:18 (obviously took my wife a few minutes to work out what I had text)
"Ok, how many have you had? I don't mind but remember we are shopping tomorrow. Let me know when you are leaving the Indian. Lovr (sarcasm) you too xxxxxx
10:22 (It took me a while to read it)
"Yoy are one in milllion xxxxxxxxx

"Right I've ordered a taxi Si, get that down your neck and I'll get another" Gaffer pushes my unfisnihed drink towards me and I neck half a pint in one go. We down another pint of the Toffee Apple Cider, that's 3 of my 5 a day taken care of. While we are waiting for the taxi I manage not one but two more pisses and I'm now at the point where I may as well cut out the middle man and pour it straight down the loo.

The taxi arrives and as soon as my backside touches the seat of the taxi I need the loo again. It's a painful 15 minute journey to the town centre and I've lost the ability to converse as I'm concentrating on holding onto the contents of my bursting bladder. I'm even considering asking the taxi driver to stop but I hold back and as soon as we pull up outside the Indian I'm dashing off to the toilet. It's one of the best pisses I've ever had and one of the longest and most aggressive as a mixture of real ales and ciders spray the porcelain like a water cannon soacking rioting football fans.

When I've eventually finished I stumble into the restaurant searching for The Gaffer. I see him in the corner and stagger over only to discover two JD and cokes already in place. The Gaffer thrusts a menu into my hand and says "I'm starving, what you having?". Negotiating an Indian menu after having consumed nine pints of strong ale and cider is about as easy as marking 8xB's essays on *Of Mice and Men*.

Gaffer is impatient at best and starts assisting me, to which I give in and say: "I'll have what you're having".
Now I thought I knew The Gaffer fairly well but what I learnt tonight was not only can the man drink but he can also put his food away. Gaffer is munching away through poppadums and pickles while I stare blankly into space. Another two JD and Cokes and two pints of Cobra precede the food, which is being ushered in on a very full trolley. I quickly shoot off to the loo.

"Oi Si, you got a bird in the bogs?" laughs Gaffer. On my return I'm amazed at the amount of food and I start wondering when the other diners are coming. The full order consists of:
Chicken Jalfrezi x1
Meat Bhuna x1
Lamb Passanda x1
Bombay Potatoes x1
Sag Aloo x1
Sag Paneer x1
Onion Bhajis x4
Pilau Rice x1
Mushroom Pilau x1
Naan Breads x4 (1 Plain, 1 Garlic, 1 Peshwari & 1 Keema)

On top of this mountain of food follows another two JD and Cokes and two more pints of Cobra each and at the end it is fair to say I'm paralytic. The Gaffer however isn't. He is doing his impression of a human conveyor belt as an endless stream of food and drink heads towards his mouth. My own attempt at impersonating a human conveyor belt involves frequently visiting the toilet (Damn you bladder).

It is now 11:45 and I notice my phone is flashing away. When I pick it up I notice I have five missed calls, four text messages, three naan breads, two untouched JD & cokes and a 'banging headache' (sorry just keeping in with the festive season).

"Hello darling."
"Don't hello darling me, where are you?"
"The Indian in town."
"Are you slurring?"
"No (hic!)"
"Are you drunk?"
"Erm I've had a few."
"Well when will you be home then?"
"Shortly darling (belch)."
"Well don't forget we are shopping tomorrow."
"Bye darling."
"Erm!"

Thankfully Gaffer has already booked the return taxi and also finished off all the food, paid for the meal and drained any remains of anything alcoholic on the table. I, on the other hand, am starting to panic about the journey home and what awaits me on my return. My anxiety levels force me into another trip to the toilet and I'm determined to empty my bladder before the journey home and must spend about five minutes in the cubicle draining and squeezing every last drop out of my battered bladder.

The entire journey is a blur mainly because I keep dozing off but we are soon at my house and unfortunately (for me) my wife is waiting at the front door when the taxi pulls up. I get out and that's when it hits me. I can feel my legs going. The Gaffer assists me to the front door, then through it, then upstairs to the bedroom where he deposits me on the bed. I don't remember anything after that but my wife does and apparently after Gaffer went the following chain of events occurred:
1. I went to the toilet and was sick (for some reason I didn't use the ensuite which was closest but chose to use the main toilet and bounce off every wall enroute).
2. I stumbled to the spare room and collapsed on the bed face down.
3. I went to the toilet again minus my shirt, which was left on the floor, and was sick.
4. I went to our bedroom and collapsed on the floor.
5. I went to the ensuite and was retching; in between each session of involuntary gagging I told my wife a) I loved her b) I'm never drinking

again c) She was my world. My wife said what made this last sentiment really special was that it was delivered with sick dribbling down my chin. 6. I went back to the spare room, threw my trousers in a corner and went to sleep.

The next morning I am awoken by a cup of tea being slammed on the side along with two paracetamol. All that registers is a series of grunts and then the door is slammed shut for my benefit. Ten minutes later my wife returns and disturbs my deep slumber by roughly shaking my lifeless body.

"I'm going shopping now. I'm going with my sister so I'll see you tonight."
"I'll be fine. I'll come."
I moved gently towards the untouched steaming cup of tea but as soon as I moved my head the Dalworth Brass Band started playing in it and my entire body ached.
"Give me 20 minutes and I'll be fine."
"I've given you 3 hours and no you won't!"

I glanced at my watch which I was still wearing. It was 11am.

"Nick has walked Faith so I'll see you tonight."

I wasn't in a mood to argue and just slumped under the covers wishing for my head to leave my shoulders and went back to sleep for another four hours.

When I awoke I realised that the tea was stone cold and the paracetamols untouched. I crept to the loo with Faith in tow and once I had emptied both my bladder and my bowels (my stomach, I'm pleased to report was already empty). I let Faith out the back, a walk was totally out of the question. Thankfully the house was empty so I was left to my own post-hangover devices so I made a pot of coffee, some toast and slumped in front of Soccer Saturday.

Every expulsion of wind was a reminder of the night before as the smell of Indian food gently wafted under my nostrils. I wrapped a blanket round me, drank more coffee, ate more toast and then watched Manchester City demolish Spurs. Faith had to make do with frequent trips to the garden and any deposits she left will have to wait until tomorrow to be picked up.

My wife returns in good spirits and the expected backlash doesn't materialise. Thankfully the only thing to take a battering today was the bank account. I spend the rest of the evening cocooned in the blanket watching football and drinking some home-made soup my wife kindly prepared for me. Gaffer rang early evening to see if I was still alive and although I didn't feel like talking I reassured him that I had survived the night of carnage. He was pleased I had and then informed me that he was off out for a meal, the very thought of it turned my guts upside down and inside out. I slumped back into my chair, farted, gagged on the smell and then fell asleep.

I leave you with the words of Ebenezer Scrooge "I am as giddy as a drunken man. A Merry Christmas to everybody!"

Results from Sunday 17th December

Oak Town Rangers 0 - 4 Phoenix Rovers
Parkfield 0 - 3 Tamworth United
Langton Reds 8 - 3 Redbridge Sports

Team	P	W	D	L	F	A	GD	Pts
1 Tamworth United	8	6	1	1	27	14	13	19
2 Phoenix Rovers	7	5	0	2	27	10	17	15
3 Dunstable Colts	6	4	1	1	14	8	6	13
4 Leighbridge Lions	9	4	0	5	24	27	-3	12
5 Dalworth United	7	3	1	3	22	19	3	10
6 Langton Reds	8	3	0	5	26	23	3	9
7 Parkfield	5	3	0	2	11	11	0	9
8 Kingsbridge	5	2	1	2	13	10	3	7
9 Oak Town Rangers	9	2	1	6	10	28	-18	7
10 Redbridge Sports	8	1	1	6	12	36	-24	4

CHAPTER SEVEN

JANUARY

"It's a New Year with the same goals"

Result from Sunday 7th January
Leighbridge Lions 1 - 2 Phoenix Rovers

Team	P	W	D	L	F	A	GD	Pts
1 Tamworth United	8	6	1	1	27	14	13	19
2 Phoenix Rovers	8	6	0	2	29	11	18	18
3 Dunstable Colts	6	4	1	1	14	8	6	13
4 Leighbridge Lions	10	4	0	6	25	29	-4	12
5 Dalworth United	7	3	1	3	22	19	3	10
6 Langton Reds	8	3	0	5	26	23	3	9
7 Parkfield	5	3	0	2	11	11	0	9
8 Kingsbridge	5	2	1	2	13	10	3	7
9 Oak Town Rangers	9	2	1	6	10	28	-18	7
10 Redbridge Sports	8	1	1	6	12	36	-24	4

Smith Says
I can't wait to go again this Tuesday but first of all can I wish everyone a Happy New Year. As we are all aware the season didn't start too well but over our last six games we have shown huge improvements and mathematically we have forced our way back into the title race. We are also only two games from a cup final so there's all to play for in the second part of the season. We have the first of many big games this weekend against Phoenix Rovers who are second in the league in the fourth round of the Challenge Cup. It will be another tough game but I'm confident it is one that we can win. The aim is to continue our recent good run and continue our climb up the table when hopefully we can become genuine title contenders and bring home some silverware along the way.
The Gaffer

Tuesday 9th January
It's perishing tonight and I could have sworn that I passed some brass monkeys and a polar bear sitting on a iceberg on the way to training and the irony of listening to The Arctic Monkeys on the CD player wasn't lost on me either. The dark nights mean that all the Dalworth age groups are

fighting for the limited light produced by the Dalworth Rec floodlights. Approximately a quarter of it is illuminated and it is very cosy. It is beneficial being cramped together as the shared body heat combats the freezing temperatures. Fortunately for us, due to the weather, not all the teams have turned up which increases our training space. I'm soon beginning to think that they are the fortunate ones not having to train in these freezing conditions. The boys start to turn up and as usual Adam Morley turns a few heads with a catching ensemble.

From top to bottom he has a beanie hat over a balaclava with a snood. He is wearing a long sleeve Under Armour shirt with a t-shirt, sweatshirt and thermal gloves. This is matched with Under Armour leggings and two pairs of socks. The only part of Adam Morley that is visible is his eyes. The rest of the boys are wearing body warmers, tracksuit bottoms, padded gillets, coats, you name it it's being used to combat the cold. Billy B saunters over to where everyone is standing, lifts a leg and let's rip. "Happy New Year boys!".

The boys gather round the hot air that Billy has expunged hoping to recycle any heat from Billy's New Year's present in the hope of warming up, that is until the smell hits their nostrils and the stench sends everyone quickly scampering away from the area in disgust.

"Been eating cat food again Bill?"

"Nope, just a s**tload of brussels!".

Alex and Aidan are passing something round the group which some of the boys are only too eager to accept I later discover that the boys were swigging whiskey from a hip flask, just to keep warm of course.

Gaffer, as usual is oblivious to proceedings, nods at me and then leans in to whisper: "Nothing intense tonight Si, I just want the boys to get back into the swing of things."

The warm-up seems irrelevant as no amount of jogging or stretching is going to warm anyone up. The boys, against Gaffer's instructions, try their hardest to inject some intensity into everything undertaken in a futile attempt to warm up. I wouldn't say it was a bad session but it never got going due to the extremities and everyone was extremely relieved when it was over and they could go home to the comforts and warmth of their homes.

Thursday 11th January

No managers' meeting for me tonight due to a year ten parents evening. Gaffer rang me later on to say I hadn't missed much, in fact it was pretty uneventful. This is of little consolation to me because however boring the meeting was, it would have been preferable to my evening feeding back to parents on their children's visionary insight into JB Priestley's *An Inspector Calls*. There are only so many ways to say: "They hate the book and the text".

Sunday 14th January – Dalworth United vs Phoenix Rovers – Challenge Cup Fourth Round

After the freezing conditions of Tuesday night today is considerably milder but we have a major problem regarding our pitch. The referee has spotted a corner that is still frozen and is deemed a hazard to the players' safety. The sunlight is hitting 98% of the pitch bar a small section that is obscured by the trees and as a result the ref has said if it hasn't defrosted by kick-off he has no option but to postpone the game. Both teams are eager to play so the ref agrees to let Mother Nature try to work her magic for the next hour but he is adamant that if any part of the area is still frozen the game is off. Gaffer is already on the case and is talking about driving his car over to the corner and trying to defrost it with his exhaust but in the end we decide to let nature take its course.

Gaffer gives a quick team talk but the boys are preoccupied with the condition of the pitch and whether or not the game will go ahead: "What do you reckon, moulds?", "I'm going with blades".

The boys get changed quickly and make their way to the pitch for the warm up.

Pending the game going ahead Gaffer's going with a 4-2-3-1 formation:

Starting Line-Up

Billy Stevens

Danny Hall Johnny Day Nick Sheppard Billy Belafonte

Alex Hayes Aidan Hayes

Ben Padgham © Adam Morley Brian Haugh

Luke Pilbeam

Subs: Stevie Carr, Bobby Webster, Charlie Fisher

It's a weird warm-up as thoughts are still preoccupied with the pitch and it's a very luck lustre session due to everyone expecting the game to be called off. All eyes are set on this corner of the pitch and every five minutes Gaffer keeps running over to check. The good news is the area is no longer in the shade. The bad news is we only have 30 minutes before kick-off and the pitch is still frozen. The additional good news is the referee is willing to give it up until kick-off for his final inspection.

The boys are sitting in the changing room getting their final instructions that may or may not be relevant when there is a knock on the door. The ref pokes his head round the door and his smile relays the all-important decision before his words do: "Game on!". "Cheers Ref".

You can see the relief on ours and the boys' faces that today's early morning exertions haven't been a complete waste of time. Gaffer gives a few more brief instructions then we are ready to go.

Phoenix Rovers are a big strong physical side and early on it's a real physical battle. The Hayes twins love the physical element and are winning the midfield contest but we as a team are struggling to play any football as our opponents are harrying, chasing and pressing us every time we are in possession. The first real chance falls to Phoenix and Nick does well to block a low shot that is goalbound but gives away a corner as a result. As both sides line up for the corner the height advantage is clear for all to see and pays dividends as the six foot-plus centre back for Phoenix heads home despite Johnny's best efforts to get a challenge in. Gaffer is looking worried, in fact I'm sure if I were to look in a mirror I would have the same look on my own face.

"They are killing us in the air Si."
"Yeah we need to keep the ball on the deck."
"They are also very direct and they are winning a lot of first and second ball."
"As long as we are competing for everything."
"We are competing for everything, but they are winning it."

The boys are battling for every scrap and then just when it is needed comes the first bit of luck for the team. Billy B has the ball in the left channel and plays a one-two with Brian and on the return hits a sublime ball to Ben on the right wing. Ben controls the ball and spots Luke peel off at the back post and hits a deep cross Luke's connection isn't great but he guides it back to penalty spot where Alex Hayes is making a run into the box and he guides the ball in via his knee. It's a scrappy finish and Gaffer shrugs his shoulders, letting out a sigh of good fortune but it's the break we needed and we are back in the game.

Just as we get back into the game Phoenix put us under intense pressure when Johnny nods a long ball narrowly over his own bar. From the corner the same Phoenix centre back crashes a header off of the cross bar. Then another long ball causes panic in the defence until Johnny smashes the ball clear for a throw. The rest of the half follows the same pattern with us trying to play football but due to Phoenix's pressure we are misplacing passes or getting caught in possession and Phoenix are immediately launching a long ball which is keeping us penned back. On the stroke of half time we have another close escape as a long ball is flicked on and the Phoenix forward races clear and lobs the ball over Billy S but thankfully the ball lands on the top of the net.

Half Time: Dalworth United 1 Phoenix Rovers 1
Gaffer makes major changes to personnel and formation as Danny, Adam and Brian make way for Stevie, Bobby and Charlie. Aidan drops into defence to give us a back three and Stevie drops in alongside Alex in the centre of midfield while Billy B moves into midfield and in a bold move Gaffer goes with a front three of Charlie, Luke and Bobby in a very attacking 3-4-3 formation.

Second half Line-Up
Billy Stevens
Johnny Day Nick Sheppard Aidan Hayes
Ben Padgham © Stevie Carr Alex Hayes, Billy Belafonte
Charlie Fisher Luke Pilbeam Bobby Webster

"Nick you sweep and let Johnny and Aidan attack the ball, you concentrate on the second ball."

This seems to work better and Phoenix can't get the ball behind our back three anymore and they start to overhit the long ball with Billy S picking everything up. The front three are seeing more of the ball and Bobby is causing their right back problems with his direct running. It is Bobby's direct running that gives us the lead as he takes off down the left and skins the full back and with everyone expecting a cross Bobby pulls the ball back into the path of Billy B who unleashes a shot that curls into the near post to give us the lead.

To The Gaffer's testament his changes are working whereas Phoenix's route one approach is now being comfortably dealt with by our back three. Nick is superbly marshalling the defence and the long ball is no longer troubling us. Our attacking play however is causing them untold problems and as soon as we are in possession the movement is superb. Alex and Stevie, more known for their tackling abilities than passing, are keeping it simple but are constantly finding a red shirt and the front three are too hot to handle. Phoenix however come back and score a disputed equaliser when there's a scramble in the box and Billy S gets his hands to the loose ball but appears to get kicked on the hand and the loose ball is tapped into the empty net. The referee after much deliberation and protests allows the goal to stand. More worryingly is the injury sustained by Billy who already has bruising around his right wrist. Danny takes over in goal as a precaution and immediately makes a stunning save low to his left. The corner is swung over and Danny punches it clear. Charlie clears it from just outside the box and Luke chases it down and looks up to see Bobby making a run down the centre. Luke hits a ball for Bobby to chase, he collects it and is gone. Before you know it he has rounded the keeper and we are 3-2 up.

This completely knocks the stuffing out of Phoenix and ten minutes later it's game over as Luke picks up the ball on the half way line and hits a ball into the left hand channel and Bobby is off again, this time he waits until the 'keeper commits himself and chips the ball over the his head to make it 4-2. Bobby runs to the technical area and is followed by his team mates as all eleven players, subs and management celebrate in unison.

It's a touching moment and in that moment you realise how much it can all mean and why the game of football can unite people and give so much joy. The final whistle signals the end of the game and it means that we are in the semi-finals.

The changing room is electric at the end of the game and there are smiles all round, lots of hugs and high fives. I think back to the start of the season and The Gaffer's request for 'Invincibles'. Well we may not go through the season unbeaten but today we were unbeatable and the side are replicating the football they played last year.

The one thing that really strikes me today is the belief in the side. When we were losing at the start of the season the boys' attitude was: "Oh well, we'll get it right next time' and they kept plugging away. I'm positive that they were convinced they were always going to turn around their fortunes. Gaffer thought it was him, but it never was, and it was inevitable things were going to change. He was always going to be the manager of a successful side and all he had to do was be patient and let the boys do their thing.

Gaffer offers Bobby his hand. "Match-winning performance today Bob." "Don't forget the others Gaffer, we all put in a match winning performance today."

That one statement sums it all up "We win together, we lose together, we remain together."

Gaffer slaps me on the back and as I turn around he is beaming from ear to ear.

"Fancy a semi-final Si?"
"Yeah why not!"
"We've still got a chance of rescuing this season."
"We always had a chance Gaffer, we just didn't know it..." I point to the boys. "...but they did."

Results from Sunday 14th January
Redbridge Sports 0 – 1 Kingsbridge
Parkfield 0 – 1 Leighbridge Lions
Tamworth United 6 – 2 Oak Town Rangers
David Dudley Challenge Cup 4th Round
Dalworth United 4 – 2 Phoenix Rovers

Team	P	W	D	L	F	A	GD	Pts
1 Tamworth United	9	7	1	1	33	16	17	22
2 Phoenix Rovers	8	6	0	2	29	11	18	18
3 Leighbridge Lions	11	5	0	6	26	29	-3	15
4 Dunstable Colts	6	4	1	1	14	8	6	13
5 Kingsbridge	6	3	1	2	14	10	4	10
6 Dalworth United	7	3	1	3	22	19	3	10
7 Langton Reds	8	3	0	5	26	23	3	9
8 Parkfield	6	3	0	3	11	12	-1	9
9 Oak Town Rangers	10	2	1	7	12	34	-22	7
10 Redbridge Sports	9	1	1	7	12	37	-25	4

Smith Says
The winning run goes on and the early season despair has made way for mid-season elation as we climb the table and look forward to a Challenge Cup semi-final. Today's success was based on teamwork, spirit, an excellent work ethic and quality. The boys were superb from start to finish against a very strong, physical and direct outfit. We battled when we needed to battle and once we won those battles, our quality shone through and Phoenix had no answer once we negated their physical side. At the start of the season I made lots of predictions which fell at the first hurdle. Well now I'm saying we will be trying our hardest to win as many games as possible in the league and we will see what happens. We are now one game away from a cup final and we will be trying to go as far as we can in the cup, but more importantly we aim to play every game with a smile on our face and enjoy each one.
The Gaffer

Dalworth United 4 Phoenix Rovers 2
Squad: Billy Stevens, Danny Hall, Johnny Day, Nick Sheppard, Billy
Belafonte, Alex Hayes, Aidan Hayes, Ben Padgham © Adam Morley,
Brian Haugh, Luke Pilbeam, Stevie Carr, Bobby Webster, Charlie Fisher
Scorers: Webster 2, Alex Hayes, Belafonte
Man of the Match: Webster

Tuesday 16th January
Billy Stevens is resting as a precaution and Danny Hall has got, as Stevie
Carr calls it: "The two bob bits and is s**ting through the eye of a needle".
I personally thank young Stevie for the vivid image he has left with me. So
tonight's training session is without any goalkeepers, or so I thought. It's
a really chilled atmosphere but the boys are all working as hard as usual.
The desired intensity is present in every drill and there is a real sense of
contentment in everything we do. Ben takes the now customary warm-up
or as Johnny has renamed it "The Dalworth Rec sightseeing tour".

With no 'keepers present it's all about the ballwork and there's lots of
keep-ball games which gives the show oaters a chance to show off. Gaffer
then says: "Shall we have a 7v7 game to finish off?" Cue puzzled looks.
"But there are only 12 of us?"
"Me and Si will go in goal."

Gaffer digs into his bag and throws me an old pair of keepers' gloves.

"Really, is it a good idea?"
"Yeah come on, where's your sense of adventure?"
"Well I'm not diving, the grounds still hard."
"Leave it out you tart and get in goal!"

Well just for the record I don't think it's a good idea and my sense of
adventure is going on Stealth at Thorpe Park or mountain-climbing up
Ben Nevis or even playing Dodgeball with 11xc. Going in goal with our
lot smashing shots at me on hard ground does not stimulate my sense of
adventure.

"Come on Si, just a quick game to finish the session."
"It'll go wrong."

I plead with The Gaffer but he's having none of it and he picks two sides.
Gaffers side: Johnny Day, Billy Belafonte, Ben Padgham © Alex Hayes,
Aidan Hayes, Luke Pilbeam.
My side: Nick Sheppard, Adam Morley, Brian Haugh, Stevie Carr, Bobby
Webster, Charlie Fisher.

I quickly assess the dangers.

Billy = Owner of a fearsome and deadly left peg which packs both accuracy and of more concern power.

Alex & Aidan = An ability to wipe out any opponent, including opposition keepers, at will.

Luke = The ability to humiliate you when he is banging shots past you for fun.

Gaffer = 'Bants' if his side wins".

What starts off as a supposedly light-hearted game quickly gets competitive and when Nick plays a short back pass to me I realise I need to clear the ball before Luke can nick it off of me. Luke slides in as I clear the ball and catches my ankle. I collapse in a heap and in pain and then receive a torrent of abuse from the opposition.

Luke: "Ref that's a dive!" (No it isn't and besides there's no ref).

Johnny: "A perfect ten from the Russian judge" (Bit harsh).

Ben : "Auditions for Swan Lake are next week Si" (A cultured insult).

Aidan : "Get up you tart" (Plain hurtful).

Alex : "There's more where that came from Si" (Intimidation).

Gaffer doesn't say a word but I can see him smirking and trying to contain his amusement at my misfortune. I slowly get up, ankle throbbing, but carry on to keep my reputation and more importantly my pride intact. I hear in the distance a "Come on Si, it was only a tap" from Gaffer who has given up trying to conceal his amusement and who openly laughing from the other end of the makeshift pitch. He is really enjoying my predicament that is until he lets a shot from Charlie squirm through his fingers and it is then his turn to be bombarded with abuse.

Stevie: "Are you part Scottish Gaffer" (A racial slur).

Bobby: "Couldn't catch a cold Gaffer" (Cutting).

Adam: "I'd check those gloves for holes" (Hurtful).

Alex - his own team mate: "For f**ks sake Gaffer save the bloody shot" (Blunt and to the point).

There is soon a pattern developing: One team shoots and they score. I'm virtually hobbling between the sticks now but I finally manage to save a shot from Luke. The problem is it's a point blank save and it's with my legs, in particular, my rapidly swelling left ankle. To add insult to injury the rebound falls to Luke who calmly taps the ball into the vacated net. A net vacated by my injured and prone self.

"Next goal wins" shouts Gaffer looking to put both of us out of our misery. "Thank f**k for that" I mutter under my breath.

The first shot in anger is from Bobby, who hits a sweet volley, top bins. Out of nowhere The Gaffer has flung his portly frame in the direction of the ball and pulls off an absolutely amazing fingertip save which draws applause from all 13 remaining players on the pitch. Gaffer bounces straight up in a manner not dissimilar to Del Boy when he fell through the bar of the wine bar. He also shakes his body, seemingly clearing the cobwebs before pulling his glove off. He turns away from his outstretched hand before presenting it for inspection to everyone. It looks perfectly OK until close examination of the little finger on his left hand reveals that the tip of said little finger sits at a 45 degree angle to the rest.

The silence is broken by Aidan when he announces that which is painfully obvious: "That's f**king broken, I'm telling you that's f**king f**ked." Alex confirms his brother's medical diagnosis: "Yep its f**ked." And that Ladies and Gentlemen is confirmation that training is over.

Gaffer spent four hours at A&E having the tip of his finger put back into place. He said there was a young girl opposite him who had suffered a similar injury but who, unlike Gaffer, was absolutely dreading the corrective surgery that was required to put it back into place. The Doctor had explained the procedure step-by-step but the scared young patient wasn't prepared to let the Doctor perform the necessary corrective surgery due to the anticipated levels of pain. The Gaffer being The Gaffer suggested that the young girl watch the Doctor perform the procedure on him in order to reassure her. The Gaffer did reassure her but also nearly passed out due to the jolt of pain that raced round his body. "Thank you Mister", "Mmmmm". The Gaffer wasn't being rude he was just rendered speechless due to the jolts of pain that were coursing round his body.

I was more fortunate and I simply went home had a large glass of Red Wine, wrapped an ice compress round my ankle, finished off the bottle of red and then opened another while watching my elevated ankle turn various shades of Blue, Black and Purple.

Wednesday 17th January
I'm off work today due to a severely bruised ankle. So I'm frantically emailing my cover work to the school at stupid o'clock in the morning. The Gaffer is also on light duties due to a broken finger so he is frantically ringing round his labourers dishing out orders and instructions.

Thursday 18th January
I'm back to work today but my swollen ankle is still very painful and I walk into a barrage of abuse from pupils and staff alike although Rossy's "Here comes Simple Simon" is particularly spiteful.

Friday 19th January - The Dalworth News

Dalworth United 4 Phoenix Rovers 2: Dalworth progressed to the semi-finals of the Challenge Cup after knocking out Phoenix Rovers at Dalworth Rec. Phoenix took the lead through Adam Shearing but Dalworth equalised through Alex Hayes before half-time. Billy Belafonte gave Dalworth the lead before Declan Hall equalised again for Phoenix. A fine brace from Bobby Webster ensured that it was Dalworth who would be contesting the semi-final in three weeks' time.

Saturday 20th January

Well I know The Gaffer and I are doubtful for tomorrow (if only) but Billy S is 50/50 and Gaffer says he won't risk him if he isn't right. Thankfully Danny is no longer suffering from the 'two bob bits' and is available for selection so we will have a recognised keeper. Equally worrying we are going to be without top scorer Luke who is away this weekend at a 50th surprise birthday party for his Uncle George. Going into a difficult game with Dunstable Colts without your top scorer and goalkeeper isn't ideal preparations but we are on a six game unbeaten run and we owe Dunstable one for the defeat in the first round of League Cup.

Gaffer is still upbeat when he makes his customary pre-match call:
"Just a bit of tweaking and we'll be fine. No Luke but we've got goals all over the team."
"I agree we've got nothing to fear."
"How's your ankle Si?"
"Still sore, how's your finger?"
"Still broken, so is my pride!" he laughs.
"Will we ever learn?"
"Of course not, see you tomorrow Si."
"See you tomorrow Gaffer."

Sunday 21st January - Dalworth United vs Dunstable Colts

The first person I see at Dalworth Rec is Billy S but although he is kitted out in his tracksuit this is the only kit he has got.

"Alright Si"
"How is it Bill?"
"Still painful, but doesn't matter, we've got Dan in goal" says Billy nodding at Dan.

Dan acknowledges Billy's compliment by nodding back.

The changing room has got a few gaps in it but it just means Billy B can put his selection of pre-match snacks of Jaffa Cakes and Haribo beside

him to munch on while he gets changed. Stevie is sitting beside Billy and every time Billy turns away from his snacks Stevie nicks a Jaffa Cake or a handful of Haribo. It takes Billy a while to realise his stock of refreshments are fast disappearing. Billy looks at Stevie who is munching on something.
"You nicking my f**king sweets?"
Stevie carries on munching and simply nods no.
"You f**king sure?"
"I f**king haven't" says Stevie spraying half-chewed Haribo all over Billy.
"You f**king w**ker" says Billy before bursting out laughing.

The whole changing room joins in and any tensions that may have been present have evaporated into laughter and smiles. Gaffer brings the laughter to an end as he addresses the team and brings them back to task.

"Right boys here's the line-up" he says, taping the team sheet to the changing room wall.

Gaffers opted for our favoured 4-2-3-1 with Charlie as a lone striker. The team virtually picks itself and despite only having one sub we can virtually cover every position, with the exception of Goalkeeper.

Starting Line-Up
Danny Hall
Stevie Carr Johnny Day Nick Sheppard Billy Belafonte
Alex Hayes, Aidan Hayes
Ben Padgham © Adam Morley Bobby Webster,
Charlie Fisher
Sub, Brian Haugh

The boys are in a confident mood and why shouldn't they be. Gaffer gives out his last instructions, the main one being no one get injured. Then it's just a case of reinforcing what we've been doing in our previous games, be patient, keep the ball, work for each other, don't be afraid to take a player on or have a shot, take risks and enjoy yourselves out there. The instructions are short, sweet and concise and more importantly understood.

Kick-off:
It's a very cagey affair early on with both sides struggling to impose their own game on their opponents. Dunstable are up for a battle and the boys are willing to stand toe to toe with them. It's a typical case of two very good teams nullifying each other but both still managed to hit the woodwork. Charlie is very unlucky to see his header strike a post after an excellent cross from Bobby. On the stroke of half time Dunstable work the ball

down the left and a low cross is met by a Dunstable central midfielder who doesn't get a clean connection on his shot and Danny has got it covered until Nick deflects the shot away from Danny and into the path of the Dunstable number nine.

With Danny stranded the forward has an empty goal to aim at and as he picks his spot Johnny launches himself at the ball and just manages to get a touch, diverting it away from the Dunstable forward, who then strikes Johnny's foot and the sickening noise that follows leaves everyone's hearts in their mouths. The seriousness of the collision is confirmed by Johnny's sobbing moans and the look on the now upright Danny who is screaming "AMBULANCE!" at us. I'm straight on the phone as Gaffer rushes to examine Johnny's foot and even from a distance I can see him physically wince and turn away as he does the whirling circular arm motion that signals Johnny isn't going to be able to carry on.

The next problem is the length of time we are likely to wait for an ambulance and our call to the emergency services confirms this could be in excess of a hour. Johnny's parents decide they can't wait and we agree that as it is Johnny's foot and not his leg that we can safely move him to the car so they can take Johnny to hospital. Johnny's dad brings the car to the pitch and we manage to manoeuvre him in and he is off to hospital. The referee, with both managers in agreement, blows for half-time and both teams shuffle off to try to regain some form of composure. Dunstable's number nine is distraught beyond consoling and plays no further part in the game. The boys are physically and mentally shaken up and we try to firstly reassure them that Johnny will be ok. Ben is the one to bring everyone back to task when he says: "We win this for Johnny."

So the 'Noone get injured' quote has come back to haunt us and once again Gaffer has to reshuffle the pack. Aidan drops back into defence and Gaffer sets up a 4-1-4-1 formation.

Second Half:

Danny Hall

Stevie Carr Nick Sheppard Aidan Hayes Billy Belafonte

Alex Hayes,

Brian Haugh Ben Padgham © Adam Morley Bobby Webster

Charlie Fisher

It's a very attacking line up but the boys start slowly and it's no wonder with the image of Johnny's nasty injury still fresh in their minds, the football has become secondary to Johnny's welfare. Just like the first half there are few chances and the first decent one falls to Dunstable but Danny is again equal to the goal bound shot. With ten minutes to go Dunstable win a corner and the taker curls the cross directly into the net as the ball somehow evades everyone. Game over? You would have thought so, but this seems to be the wakeup call the boys needed. Gaffer makes a slight change to the formation and we go again.

Danny Hall
Stevie Carr Nick Sheppard Billy Belafonte
Alex Hayes Aidan Hayes
Brian Haugh Adam Morley Bobby Webster
Ben Padgham © Charlie Fisher

Gaffer tells the boys to get the ball forward quickly and speed up the play, not going route one but working the ball through the quarters quickly. With five minutes to go Brian and Ben work an opportunity for Charlie who beats the goalkeeper with a low shot only for it to be hacked off the line. The clearance clears the area, bounces once and then is smashed into the back of the net courtesy of a sensational strike from Adam. Surprisingly there's no celebrations only from Gaffer and I. Charlie grabs the ball from the back of the net and Ben is waving the players back to the centre circle.

This is a team on a mission and as soon as Dunstable kick off the boys are chasing and harassing every touch. Dunstable are desperately trying to play the game in our half but there's no let up and we are breathing down their necks. The boys are pressing now with wave after wave of attack being cleared by a desperate Dunstable defence. With extra time looming Bobby breaks down the left and hits a low and hard cross into the near post. Charlie adjusts his position but somehow manages to completely miss the ball. The Dunstable leftback is covering and clears the ball but smashes it straight at Ben who was sprinting into the box. The ball hits him on the leg and gently loops over the keeper and nestles into the back of the net.

If the boys didn't celebrate the first goal they made up for it with the second and somewhere under a pile of red shirts is Ben. Lady Luck is certainly shining on Dalworth today. The referee starts the game and before Dunstable can mount a meaningful attack blows the full time whistle. We shake hands with the Dunstable management who wish us all the best in our forthcoming semi-final and ask us to send their best wishes to Johnny. I have and still retain the utmost respect for the Dunstable Colts players and their management who are different class and a credit to their club and I wish them all the best for the rest of the season.

In the changing room there are no celebrations as everyone is concerned about Johnny. The latest update is he is still in A&E waiting to be assessed. Gaffer tells everyone he'll give feedback about todays game on Tuesday and all are in agreement as everyone just wants to go home or visit Johnny.

That night Gaffer rings me to say Johnny has broken his ankle and that it is likely to be about two months before he can even train. It's another major setback and it leaves us with just 13 players.

"We need one or two more players Si."

"It's going to be difficult because they have to be of a decent standard."

"I'll ask the boys if they know anyone at training."

"See you Tuesday Si."

"Yeah thanks for ringing Gaffer."

Results from Sunday 21st January

Oak Town Rangers 2 - 3 Parkfield
Dalworth United 2 - 1 Dunstable Colts
Tamworth United 0 - 2 Kingsbridge
Langton Reds 4 - 2 Phoenix Rovers

Team	P	W	D	L	F	A	GD	Pts
1 Tamworth United	10	7	1	2	33	18	15	22
2 Phoenix Rovers	9	6	0	3	31	15	16	18
3 Leighbridge Lions	11	5	0	6	26	29	-3	15
4 Kingsbridge	7	4	1	2	16	10	6	13
5 Dunstable Colts	7	4	1	2	15	10	5	13
6 Dalworth United	8	4	1	3	24	20	4	13
7 Langton Reds	9	4	0	5	30	25	5	12
8 Parkfield	7	4	0	3	14	14	0	12
9 Oak Town Rangers	11	2	1	8	14	37	-23	7
10 Redbridge Sports	9	1	1	7	12	37	-25	4

Monday 22nd January
Smith Says

The win on Sunday was overshadowed by the injury to Johnny Day who suffered a broken ankle. Johnny is going to be out for at least 3 months and everyone at the club would like to wish Johnny a speedy recovery. With regards to Sunday's game I was pleased that we got the win we deserved and the players showed great determination and tenacity after witnessing such a nasty injury to one of their own. We are continuing to put as many points as possible on the board and we keep climbing the table. While the top two have a bit of daylight between us they both lost today so I think there will be a few more twists before the end of the season and we certainly haven't thrown the towel in yet.

The Gaffer

Squad: Danny Hall, Stevie Carr, Johnny Day, Nick Sheppard, Billy Belafonte, Alex Hayes, Aidan Hayes, Ben Padgham © Adam Morley, Bobby Webster, Charlie Fisher, Brian Haugh
Scorers: Morley, Padgham
Man of the Match: Fisher

Tuesday 23rd January
It's a very subdued atmosphere at training that is until Johnny turns up on crutches and the mood immediately changes. The 'bants' are soon coming thick and fast and all the defenders are contributing.

"That'll teach you to put in half-hearted tackles." (Nick)
"Well someone had to cover you." (Johnny)
"At least we can tighten up the defence now." (Stevie)
"I could play with a broken ankle and still be more effective than you." (Johnny)
"One less liability to worry about." (Billy B)
"Yeah but you're still playing Bill." (Johnny)
"Gaffer doesn't have to worry about upsetting your feelings by leaving you out now John." (Danny)
"At least you'll spend less time on the bench and get a few more minutes now Dan." (Johnny)
"Stop bitching bitches." Ben, the voice of reason, interrupts the 'bants' .

The injury may have affected Johnny's playing abilities but it hasn't dimmed his razor-sharp wit. Gaffer however is concerned and knows we are looking very light in numbers. He gets the boys together and has a chat about adding to the squad.

"My mate might be interested."
"My mate hasn't got a club."
"My mate plays in the school team but doesn't play for a club."

Ben chips in: "Trouble is, are they as good as us? Anyone who comes in has to be on a par with us ability-wise otherwise he is just going to make up the numbers and that's not fair."

Gaffer has the final word "OK if anyone wants to try out for us that's fine but I won't sign anyone just to make up the numbers."

The training session is a good one and everyone is still putting the effort in but the lack of bodies is having an effect. Gaffer is well aware of the situation but knows all the players will be working hard not to let things slip and we are all confident that we can keep the winning run going.

"No game this weekend boys so enjoy the weekend and I'll see you next Tuesday."

Friday 26th January - Dalworth News
Dalworth United **Under 15**s 2 Dunstable Colts 1
Dalworth United came back from a goal down to take all three points with a last minute winner from Ben Padgham after Danny Carr had given Dunstable the lead and Adam Morley scored Dalworth's equaliser.

Sunday 28th January
Oak Town Rangers 2 – 1 Langton Reds
Kingsbridge 3 – 0 Redbridge Sports

Team	P	W	D	L	F	A	GD	Pts
1 Tamworth United	10	7	1	2	33	18	15	22
2 Phoenix Rovers	9	6	0	3	31	15	16	18
3 Kingsbridge	8	5	1	2	19	10	9	16
4 Leighbridge Lions	11	5	0	6	26	29	-3	15
5 Dunstable Colts	7	4	1	2	15	10	5	13
6 Dalworth United	8	4	1	3	24	20	4	13
7 Langton Reds	10	4	0	6	31	27	4	12
8 Parkfield	7	4	0	3	14	14	0	12
9 Oak Town Rangers	12	3	1	8	16	38	-22	10
10 Redbridge Sports	10	1	1	8	12	40	-28	4

Tuesday 30th January
There are a few new faces at training tonight which is weird because it feels like mid-season trials.

Stevie Carr has brought along a mate named Ryan, he plays right back for his school and he is a typical old school 'don't cross the half way line, kick anything that moves and hoof everything' rightback.

Adam Morley's mate Trevor or as he likes to be called 'Tre' is a stocky centre back who plays in the village league.

The last of the trialists is a midfielder called Gary who Danny has brought along. Gary hasn't kicked a ball in anger this year.

Gaffer is watching their every move like a hawk and has the signing on forms to hand just in case. Fifteen minutes into the session during a keep-ball session Gaffer catches Ben's attention
"What do you think Ben?"
Ben, ever the realist, doesn't even stop the game to deliver his thoughts:
"Uncultured, unfit and useless!"

Gaffer tried to be optimistic but sadly has to agree with Ben.
"Yep you're right."

Gaffer has a small-sided game and pairs Stevie and then Aidan with Nick in a defensive pairing and is satisfied that both will do a job. By the end of the session Ryan is nursing an injured left leg, Tre is sitting out blowing out of his arse and Gary disappeared on his bike for his tea before the small sided game.

Gaffer thanked the two boys for coming and they nodded and left quickly under no illusion that they were totally out of their depth. Gaffer then called Stevie, Adam and Danny over.
"Thanks for bringing your mates over, but they weren't quite up to scratch, sorry boys." Gaffer was trying his hardest to be diplomatic but Stevie put him out of his misery.

"Don't worry Gaffer, they were s**t"
"Well I wouldn't say that."
"Yeah they were c**p."

Ben as usual is the voice of reason and adds his thoughts.
"Gaffer, we've still got 13 very good players, so don't worry we've got enough in the locker."
"I don't disagree Ben, I'm happy with the squad, just worried about the depth."

Gaffer turns to me "Can't afford anymore injuries though Si."

He's right and while we do have 13 reliable and capable players you can tell that it is playing on the others' minds. The numbers game throws up lots of little scenarios.

"What if Nick gets injured? That's all our centre backs out."
"We are down to two subs per game."
"We are really short in certain positions so that means players playing out of position."

One of the worst things is training sessions with small numbers, it affects what drills you can put on and small-sided games become five-a-sides. It puts a downer on proceedings and you worry it will impact on matches too. Gaffer puts a positive spin on it though: "Whenever we are against the odds we always seem to pull it out the bag and adversity seems to be a great motivator for us"

The Gaffer is right but it's still a very precarious situation at the moment.

CHAPTER 8

FEBRUARY

"What is more important to us the cup or league? The double of course!"

Saturday 3rd February

Gaffer rings to say all thirteen fit players available and that he is going to go with a centre back pairing of Nick and Stevie in a 4-2-3-1 formation. It's a good shout in my opinion and I have every confidence that we can win the game. It's going to be a tough one but we've had a few difficult games recently and come out on top, besides we are one win from a cup final which, in light of the way things started this season, would be a major achievement.

Sunday 4th February - Amley vs Dalworth United - David Dudley Challenge Cup Semi-Final

It's an early meet at the Rec, 8:45 as it is a good 45 minute journey to Amley. I've been up since 6am and was again kicking my heels waiting for the newsagents to open. Back at the rec all the boys are on time and everyone is quickly ferried to the fleet of transport destined for Amley. Gaffer's only concern is Billy B, who for once isn't carrying a McDonalds bag full to the brim. Today, due to him oversleeping, he is carrying a tin foil package which contains a hastily prepared double bacon sandwich.

The issue is not the sandwich itself but the tomato ketchup, which he has somehow managed to get down his tracksuit during the preparation of his mammoth sandwich, leaving a very distinct stain down his it. In the scheme of things this could be construed as being a trivial matter, however, Gaffer's ever increasing anxiety levels have just gone up an extra notch or two. Thankfully help is at hand as someone produces several sheets of baby wipes from an emergency tournament kit that has been left in the boot of a car.

A quick mop up job and within minutes Billy and tracksuit are both presentable and Gaffer is happy again. Billy, however, is less than happy when Gaffer gives him two minutes to eat his bacon sandwich and Billy is positively mortified when he has to chuck the uneaten portion in the bin two minutes later.

Thankfully it's a stress-free journey to Amley, devoid of traffic jams, wind ups or Sunday drivers and everyone arrives at roughly the same time. All the boys are tracksuited and booted today, even Johnny who has ditched his bottoms in favour of black shorts but he still looks the part as do his teammates. Even the freshly laundered Billy B. Adam as usual has got his beats by Dr Dre headphones on and is immersed in his music which today is Macklemore and Ryan Lewis. In fact most of the boys have got headphones on and their choice of music is interesting. The Twins are listening to Oasis and singing along at the top of their voices, sadly they are listening to different songs and the changing room is treated to a Roll with It/Supersonic mash up which is an assault on the aural senses to those of us without headphones. Stevie is conducting his own aural assault listening to Slipknot although that is still preferable to the Hayes twins Oasis karaoke. Nick is quietly rapping along to Stormzy. Billy B is listening to a dance compilation and Ben is neither singing along nor tapping his toes. My curiosity gets the better of me and I catch Ben's attention and question him on his choice of listening.

"What you listening to Ben?"
"Mozart's fifth symphony."
"Really?"
"No you pillock, I'm listening to a Talksport podcast."
"Of course you are!"

The boys all seem to be in their own zones and you would almost be able to hear a pin drop if it wasn't for Alex & Aidan's rendition of 'Wonderwall' Yes at last they are synched but Alex is about 15 seconds in front of Aidan so it's an annoyingly out of tune, out of synch acappella version. It's funny how quiet our changing room can be because most teams want their changing room to be loud and buzzing but ours is a changing room of quiet reflection but one that will be ready when the whistle blows. Gaffer addresses the boys and headphones are respectfully removed and music turned off. This is match time now and Gaffer requires full attention. Gaffer sticks up the starting line-up.

Starting Line-Up
Billy Stevens
Danny Hall Stevie Carr Nick Sheppard Billy Belafonte
Alex Hayes, Aidan Hayes
Ben Padgham © Adam Morley Brian Haugh,
Charlie Fisher
Sub, Luke Pilbeam, Bobby Webster

It's the now familiar 4-2-3-1 formation and Gaffer appears to be keeping Bobby and Luke in reserve, a brave shout. Gaffer's instructions are also familiar: "Be patient, don't force things, keep the ball, press high." Gaffer asks me if I want to add anything and my response is also a now familiar "Don't get injured and enjoy it."

The boys are ready to go and they start to gee each other up. It's not aggressive and there's no shouting, just lots of hugs and handshakes. Ben as usual has the last word and it's a simple: "It's our day today boys."

Kick-off

We are expecting a really tough contest as would befit a cup semi-final, but early doors we are looking good and controlling the game. The boys are carving out chance after chance but the Amley defence are standing firm especially their keeper who pulls off save after save. The trouble with dominating a game is you have to take your chances when the opportunity arises and we haven't. Amley look dangerous on the counter-attack due to their right winger who is lightening and is keeping Billy pegged back and depriving us of his deadly left foot. The boys are still on top when a loose pass from Stevie is intercepted by Amley's winger who sails past Billy and charges into the box. Stevie tries to make up for his error and just as the winger gets ready to shoot Stevie manages to block the shot and in doing so let's out a loud yelp and that's the signal for the end of Stevie's participation in this contest with a dead leg and 'The Curse of the Dalworth Defence' continues.

I look towards Gaffer who it seems is searching for divine inspiration as he holds his arms up and looks to the sky. He then spoils the moment by shouting "For f**ks sake!" and any possible connection with the Lord Almighty is instantly gone. Reality kicks in as he shouts to Bobby: "You're on Bob." A quick shuffle of the pack with Aidan dropping into the back four and Ben taking his place in the defensive midfield role and we are lining up as follows:

Billy Stevens
Danny Hall Nick Sheppard Aidan Hayes Billy Belafonte
Ben Padgham © Alex Hayes,
Bobby Webster Adam Morley Brian Haugh,
Charlie Fisher

Gaffer is holding Luke back but again we are top heavy with attackers and one injury away from having two recognised defenders. The boys to be fair don't let it get to them and Bobby and Brian both see shots flash past the post before half time. The ref blows the whistle for half time and Gaffer and I are both scratching our heads in amazement that we are not already in the final.

"Don't panic boys, this game is still ours to win and I believe in you. Keep doing what you are doing and the goals and victory will come."

Gaffer makes one change and Charlie makes way for Luke. The boys make their way to the pitch and Gaffer pulls Billy B to one side. "Watch that winger Bill, he is their only danger."

He then has a quick word with Aidan but I can't catch what he says. I do see Aidan smile after Gaffer's quick word and he trots off to the pitch.

Gaffer is right and the first chance of the half falls to Amley as their winger again skins Billy B and fires a shot against the post. Billy S then makes a superb double save as first he saves from the winger and then somehow tips the rebound over the bar. Gaffer is deep in thought and then unveils his master plan.

He signals to Billy B and Aidan "Switch" and Billy goes centre back and Aidan leftback. Aidan nods and shouts "It's sorted" to Gaffer.

Amley are now feeding their winger at every opportunity but while he has been running riot against Billy B he has a new challenge now and the next time he receives the ball he is met with a little 'taster' from Aidan in the shape of a firm but fair block tackle which leaves the winger visibly shaken, much to Aidan's delight. The next encounter sees Aidan and the winger chasing a long ball and while the winger is first to the ball his first touch is uncertain and his second touch is met with another Aidan tackle which this time leaves the winger in a heap. It's another fair but firm challenge but it's also Aidan's way of stamping his authority on matters.

Whereas Billy B was wary every time the winger got the ball, now it's the winger who is unsue and Aidan has well and truly got him in his pocket. With Amley's danger man out of the game, literally, as he is subbed five minutes later after he signals an injury to the Amley bench, the boys pile the pressure on. This now becomes a personal battle between Luke and their 'keeper with the Amley custodian on top form as he saves three good strikes from Luke.

With ten minutes on the clock we are piling forward and cometh the hour, cometh the man. Some strikers are confidence players and once they start missing chances it goes, but such is Luke's belief in his own abilities he will keep plugging away in the belief that he will eventually score. So when he receives the ball on the halfway line he has one thing on his mind and it's not passing.

His first touch takes the ball past the first defender and as he races away he leaves a second for dead. The Amley leftback tries to make a recovery run but is left on his backside by Luke's change of direction and pace. He is now left one on one with the 'keeper who races out to block him. He feigns to shoot and the goalkeeper commits himself. Then Luke calmly chips the ball over the diving 'keeper and into the net.

We've scored some great team goals this campaign, but this is individual brilliance and a contender for the goal of the season. Luke turns to face his onrushing team mates. He stands upright and simply nods his head a gesture that almost suggests: "Who doubted me?" Gaffer looks at me and doesn't say anything but makes a face that I instantly read as "Whoa, what a goal!" and without speaking I just nod and he immediately understands my reply.

Amley throw their winger back on and Aidan licks his lips in anticipation. If that is intimidating then it worked because our friend didn't touch the ball in his ten minute cameo role and, as they say: "That's all folks." Dalworth United Under 15s are in the final.

We shake hands with the Amley management who now have the unenviable job of consoling and lifting their players. Yes for every winner there is always a loser and where there is elation there is dejection. I cast an eye over the Amley boys and I spot a few tears. I genuinely feel for our opponents. Losing a semi-final is such a painful experience in football, if you lose a final you still get to experience the occasion and you receive acknowledgement of your achievements in the form of a losers' medal. Lose a semi-final and there is no consolation whatsoever, no celebrating making a final or receiving a medal, be it winners or losers.

I have every sympathy for our opponents but I wouldn't swap places because today is our day and it's us going to the final. As soon as we have spoken to the Amley management we are faced with 14 ecstatic Dalworth boys. Stevie is hopping about on one leg and Johnny is dancing on his crutches. The other boys are celebrating on adrenaline and are absolutely knackered, but nothing is going to take this moment away and like a fine wine you want the full experience and to savour every last drop.

Once the celebrations, high fives, hugs and dodgy dances fade The Gaffer takes centre stage.

"Absolutely A-f**king-mazing. I'm proud of every single one of you. When I took over I imagined winning leagues and cup finals but I stupidly thought it was all about what I did. But it's not. It's all about what we do as a group. Today I feel that we as a group have hit the heights I had hoped for and for that I can't thank you enough."

"I believe that together we can achieve anything we want and we will continue to grow as a group. Today is all about the team but I would like to single out Stevie for one of the bravest tackles I have ever seen. Luke for that amazing goal and for my Man of the Match Aidan who totally transformed the game."

The whole team roar their approval and twin Alex slaps him on the back (a little too hard in my opinion) and gives him a 'top game bro' compliment. Gaffer finishes with his usual "See you Tuesday boys" and they leg it to the food, but not without a comment from Charlie:

"Oi Bill that's the quickest you've moved all day" and then Luke:
"If only their winger was a Bacon Sandwich, Billy would have caught him all day long."

Billy has the last word, well if you can count a long and loud fart as a word. Gaffer catches me as the boys disappear.

"Did you see Stevie's leg? It didn't look good, massive bloody bruise. If we lose him we are going to struggle next week. Can't afford anymore injuries Si."

Results from Sunday 4th February
Redbridge Sports 0 – 3 Parkfield
David Dudley Challenge Cup Semi-Final
Amley 0 – 1 Dalworth United

Team	P	W	D	L	F	A	GD	Pts
1 Tamworth United	10	7	1	2	33	18	15	22
2 Phoenix Rovers	9	6	0	3	31	15	16	18
3 Kingsbridge	8	5	1	2	19	10	9	16
4 Parkfield	8	5	0	3	17	14	3	15
5 Leighbridge Lions	11	5	0	6	26	29	-3	15
6 Dunstable Colts	7	4	1	2	15	10	5	13
7 Dalworth United	8	4	1	3	24	20	4	13
8 Langton Reds	10	4	0	6	31	27	4	12
9 Oak Town Rangers	12	3	1	8	16	38	-22	10
10 Redbridge Sports	11	1	1	9	12	43	-31	4

Smith Says

Put Sunday 8th April in your diary because we are in the cup final against Bridgham at Petersfield Park home of Cheltenham Saracens FC. Today's performance was nothing short of brilliant and we thoroughly deserved our win against a very good side that pushed us all the way. Luke's goal was one of the best I have ever seen at any level and reminded me of Michael Owen's in the World Cup against Argentina. I must however give special praise to my man of the match Aidan Hayes who put in a real gutsy match winning performance. He started off in his favoured central midfield position and then switched to centre back when Stevie got injured and then when asked to mark Amley's dangerman he did a totally professional job and took him out of the game, figuratively speaking, not literally. Stevie Carr sadly picked up an injury to his right leg making what was a brave match-saving tackle. We are hoping it is just bruising and everyone hopes he makes a very speedy recovery. We are still sticking to our philosophy of one game at a time but we are pleased to add a cup final to our plans and we will be giving our all in the league until it is mathematically impossible.
The Gaffer

Amley 0 Dalworth United 1 – David Dudley Challenge Cup Semi-Final
Squad: Billy Stevens, Danny Hall, Stevie Carr, Nick Sheppard, Billy Belafonte, Alex Hayes, Aidan Hayes, Ben Padgham © Adam Morley, Brian Haugh, Charlie Fisher, Luke Pilbeam, Bobby Webster
Scorer: Pilbeam
Man of the Match: Aidan Hayes

Monday 5th February

Gaffer rings. Stevie has got soft tissue damage and has been told to rest for about ten days so he should be back in time for our next game but he is definitely going to miss the next two training sessions. In fact everyone is going to miss tomorrow's training session because it's Dalworth Grammar School's Year 10 Parents evening which takes out six of our remaining twelve players. So no training which is probably just as well because after Sunday's exertions the boys could do with a rest. Gaffer brings the call to an end but then pauses and like an embarrassed schoolboy asking his first girlfriend out finishes with a "What you up to tomorrow Si?"

"Mmmmm nothing."

"Fancy a pint?"

"Mmmmmmmm."

Gaffer senses the panic in my voice and follows up with:

"Just a couple in the pub near you and I promise you, no curries!"
"Mmmmmm OK,"
"Alright see you at eight tomorrow I'll come and knock for you."
A mental image pops into my head as I see Gaffer knocking on the door:
"Mrs Sheppard, can Si come out and play?"
"No he can't he's been a very naughty boy!"
"OK. Sorry Mrs Sheppard."

Tuesday 6th February
True to his word Gaffer is knocking on the door at 8pm and I quickly scurry out the front door having signed an imaginary contract which contains the following clauses:
1. Do not get drunk
2. Home by 11pm
3. NO CURRIES

No Badger's Old Peculiar ale tonight just a simple pint of Fosters. Three pints last two hours and I'm home by 10:10 which earns me bonus brownie points. Gaffer is not up for a 'sesh' tonight as all his thoughts and concerns evolve around the team and he is worried about numbers.

"I don't want to be turning up for games with eleven players Si."
"We should be OK Gaffer."
"Do we look to poach a few players, what about that Amley winger, he was tasty?"
"But was he better than Ben, Bobby or Brian?"
"Fair enough. What about that Phoenix centre back?"
"Seriously Gaffer, let's go with what we've got, the boys have got us this far"

Gaffer nods his head and the rest of the evening is taken up with small talk about our remaining fixtures, the pending cup final and presentation evening.

Thursday 8th February
"Cup final anyone?" It looks like a lot of the managers will be attending our cup final including Michael Harris. Gaffer is the recipient of a fair few pats on the back and even makes the agenda Item seven: Cup final. "Well done to the Under 15s for making the Challenge Cup final, let's make sure they receive as much support as possible".

It's a typical mid-season meeting with talk of the presentation night surfacing and the U12s begging for new kit, which they receive due to the Under 13s generous offer of their third kit. 'Third kit?'

Friday 9th February - Dalworth News

Dalworth book finals date - Amley 0 Dalworth United **Under 15**s 1
Dalworth United will face Bridgeham in the David Dudley Challenge Cup
Final at Petersfield Park home of Cheltenham Saracens FC on Sunday the
8th April. A close encounter was settled by a solitary strike from Luke
Pilbeam which ensured Dalworth will be contesting the same trophy they
won last season.

Results from Sunday 11th February

Leighbridge Lions 0 – 2 Kingsbridge
Parkfield 1 – 2 Phoenix Rovers
Tamworth United 4 – 1 Redbridge Sports
Dunstable Colts 2 – 0 Oak Town Rangers

Tuesday 13th February

Thank god for mobile phones because 30 minutes into the session tonight
the heavens open. The session had started so well with a quick five minute
chat and then Ben did a quick warm-up. Then Gaffer moved onto a keep-
ball session, two touch, three teams of four, four vs eight and the team that
loses possession to the defending team becomes the defending team. It was
all going so well and then a few drops of rain fell and that was followed by
torrential downpour which had everyone rushing to find cover under trees,
in the toilets and in cars. Ten minutes later the downpour turned to drizzle
but it didn't stop and 15 minutes after the initial torrent Gaffer asked the
boys to ring parents to get picked up. Once we had quickly gathered in all
the equipment everyone was ready to go home for a hot bath and a change
of clothes. To be fair a lot of the parents had anticipated our predicament
and were at the Rec five minutes after the initial phone calls. Ten minutes
later the Rec was a sodden mass of empty pitches.

Gaffer rang me once he, like me, had had a hot bath.
"Stevie's Dad rang. He isn't going to be available on Sunday, his leg still
isn't right."
"Oh no that's not good. Aidan at Centre Back then?"
"He'll do a job there but more importantly that leaves us with twelve
players."
"We'll get by, we always do."
"Hope so Si, I bloody hope so."

Saturday 17th February

Gaffer rings late evening while I'm polishing off a delicious bottle of
Cabernet Sauvignon and nodding off while watching the film Dunkirk.

"Fancy a pint and a curry?"
Long pause.
"Only joking, all sorted for tomorrow. Twelve players and we are playing Redbridge Sports so we should be OK."
"We'll be fine, night Gaffer."

Sunday 18th February - Redbridge Sports vs Dalworth United
Gaffer is ringing at an ungodly hour.
"Everything OK?"
"No it isn't The Hayes twins have got the two bob bits."

The Hayes twins bring a lot to the table. They bring double trouble, double intimidation, double energy and on this occasion double 'two bob bits'. To their credit they both wanted to play but the image of two Tasmanian Devils rampaging through the midfield trailing streams of shit and fire was too much to take, even for a team with only ten fit players.

"So we are down to ten players?"
"Yep. We should still have enough about us to take three points, but it's going to be tough."
"We can do this."
"Yeah see you at the Rec at 9am."

Nick and I are the first ones at the Rec with Ben who we picked up on the way. Gaffer is the next one to arrive and he's not alone. He throws the door of his Merc open and strides over with his passenger in tow.

"Meet our new centre back."

Jimmy Smith is standing their tracksuited and booted and looking the part.
"Jimmy, it's great to see you back, especially today."

I turn towards Nick who strides past me and offers his hand to Jim "Nice one Jim, glad you took up our offer."

I question Nick before Gaffer can.

"You organised this?"
"Yep, we knew Alex and Aidan were out so we text Jim."

The boys are all turning up now and Jimmy is the centre of attention. The full story is Ben spoke to all the boys and they ALL asked Jimmy to come back thankfully he chose today to make his return. To be fair we couldn't care less how it happened and who organised it. We've got eleven players today and that's all that matters.

Gaffer sticks his hastily scribbled team sheet up and while we have no subs, we do have a full team.

Starting Line-Up:

Billy Stevens
Danny Hall Jimmy Smith Nick Sheppard Billy Belafonte
Ben Padgham © Adam Morley Brian Haugh,
Charlie Fisher Luke Pilbeam, Bobby Webster

Gaffer opts for a 4-3-3 formation which is a line-up oozing in attacking creativity but is lacking in good old fashioned grit.

On paper this should have been an easy three points but several factors came into play.
1) Jimmy's lack of match fitness.
2) Being overrun in the midfield.
3) Not putting our chances away.

As soon as the midfield get the ball Redbridge are chasing, harrying and forcing errors. Redbridge are playing a 4-5-1 and while they are offering little threat in attack they are proving difficult to break down. Gaffer tells Danny and Billy to push on but neither have the pace to trouble Redbridge and they offer little threat against their wide players. On the rare occasions we do get behind the defence a mixture of great goalkeeping and poor finishing keeps the score at 0-0.

At half-time Gaffer leaves everything the same. Well he can't make any substitutions can he?
"One goal will win this. Let's make sure we get that goal."

The boys are still looking the likelier to score and that worries us as we can both see the sucker punch being delivered. The Redbridge keeper is having a blinder and when he is finally beaten by Luke's rasping drive the ball crashes off of the crossbar and is cleared to safety

This is getting tense now and Gaffer makes a change to the formation going 3-4-3 to give us an etra body in the midfield.

Billy Stevens
Danny Hall Nick Sheppard Jimmy Smith
Ben Padgham © Adam Morley Billy Belafonte Brian Haugh,
Charlie Fisher Luke Pilbeam, Bobby Webster

Within minutes of the change Jimmy goes down with severe cramp and can't continue so he has to come off. Gaffer makes another enforced change and it's a brave change as he goes with a 3-3-3 formation in the hope that the boys can work a goal. He looks over at me and says:

"I don't want to lose Si but this is a game we need to win if we want to challenge for the title."

I just nod back without averting my gaze from the pitch as my eyes and thoughts are transfixed on the game.

Billy Stevens
Danny Hall Nick Sheppard Billy Belafonte
Ben Padgham © Adam Morley Brian Haugh,
Charlie Fisher Luke Pilbeam, Bobby Webster

It works, and Gaffer can take full credit for the goal that followed as minutes later Billy B hit the perfect diagonal ball to Charlie who took on and beat the leftback and delivered a pinpoint cross to Luke who controlled and smashed the ball home on the half volley.

Cue: wild celebrations
Cue: outpouring of emotions
Cue: Three points

Redbridge's plan was to contain us but as soon as we made the breakthrough their plan was shot to pieces and they couldn't find a way through our resolute back three. In fact the remainder of the game was played in Redbridge's half.
"Well done Gaffer, inspired change."

"You reckon? I felt we were always going to win but I needed to give the boys the belief they needed and by taking the game to them we got the breakthrough."
"That's deep thinking, nice one."

The changing room was lively afterwards but not just because we won. It was because Jimmy was back, back where he belonged amongst his team mates. It was great to see him laughing and joking with the others and back amongst his friends. I then felt a slap on my back and there was Gaffer beaming from ear to ear.

"You know what Si, we may have won today but it pales into insignificance against seeing Jimmy back in the changing room."
"Yeah I know what you mean mate."
"I gotta stop this I'm becoming an emotional wreck!"
"Shut up you tart, you'll start crying in a minute"

The minute I said it I regretted it because for the first time ever Gaffer was opening up and his face suggested I'd overstepped the mark.

"Yeah I know what you mean mate it's a really touching moment."

Gaffer smiled at me and I knew all was good again.

"Stop it otherwise I think I'll start blubbing Gaffer"

"F**k off you tart!" came the less than sympathetic retort.

And there it is. That's The Gaffer I know and we both started laughing at this point.

"I feel a session coming on Si."

"Oh great, I feel divorce proceedings coming on!"

For the record we did go out for a pint but we took our families and we ate and drank into the early evening.

Results from Sunday 18th February
Leighbridge Lions 0 – 0 Tamworth United
Redbridge Sports 0 – 1 Dalworth United
Kingsbridge 2 – 0 Oak Town Rangers

Team	P	W	D	L	F	A	GD	Pts
1 Tamworth United	12	8	2	2	37	19	18	26
2 Kingsbridge	10	7	1	2	23	10	13	22
3 Phoenix Rovers	10	7	0	3	33	16	17	21
4 Dunstable Colts	8	5	1	2	17	10	7	16
5 Dalworth United	9	5	1	3	25	20	5	16
6 Leighbridge Lions	13	5	1	7	26	31	-5	16
7 Parkfield	9	5	0	4	18	16	2	15
8 Langton Reds	10	4	0	6	31	27	4	12
9 Oak Town Rangers	14	3	1	10	16	42	-26	10
10 Redbridge Sports	13	1	1	11	13	48	-35	4

Smith Says

Sometimes you play poorly or ugly and you win and sometimes you play well and lose and sometimes you just do enough to win a game. Today we did just that and won. It wasn't pretty and we had to battle but in the end we took all three points and I'll settle for that. On Sunday morning we were down to ten players but thankfully Jimmy returned today to avert a crisis and I'm pleased to say he will returning to us for the rest of the season. Next week we should have everyone back, with the exception of Johnny, so we will have a full squad to select from. We now have ten games remaining including the cup final and we will be going all out to win as many of those games as possible and then we will see where it takes us.

The Gaffer

Redbridge Sports 0 Dalworth United 1
Squad: Billy Stevens, Danny Hall, Jimmy Smith, Nick Sheppard, Billy Belafonte, Ben Padgham © Adam Morley, Brian Haugh, Charlie Fisher, Luke Pilbeam, Bobby Webster
Scorers: Pilbeam
Man of the Match: Sheppard

Tuesday 20th February
They say lightning doesn't strike twice, well what about torrential rain because we have a case of Dalworth Déjà vu tonight as once again, exactly one week after the last downpour, our training session is called to an early halt because of the heavens opening. The only difference tonight is once rescue calls have been made to parents the boys decide to carry on in the rain. Gaffer looks at me, shrugs his shoulders and says: "What the f**k, if you can't beat em..." and we join in with the boys impromptu keep-ball session which is made all the more interesting by the addition of the condition that the player that loses the ball has to do five pressups.

Then someone decides you have to do the press-ups with someone sitting on your back. Yes, when I give the ball away Gaffer plonks himself on my back and I end up face-planting the Dalworth mud. I end up looking like an advert for the Royal Marines as my front is covered from head to toe in mud. It is fair to say that the highlight of the session is the looks on the parents' faces when they arrive at the Rec to collect their offspring, their soaked and muddy offspring.

It's a funny sight watching the parents scramble around for blankets, shopping bags, dog towels in fact any item in a desperate attempt to save their seats. I don't know why I'm laughing as Nick is covered head to toe in mud, come to think of it, so am I.

On our return to Chez Sheppard we have a welcome party as we are made to strip in the hallway and deposit all muddy items of clothing into a laundry basket. I feel like a new inmate at HMP Dalworth and I'm just waiting for the delousing powder and hose wash to complete the scene. "Sheppard 275246". On this occasion it is a warm bath that waits, well for Nick it is, I get the shower and told I should know better. Love you too darling.

Friday 24th February - Dalworth News
Redbridge Sports 0 Dalworth United **Under 15**s 1
A solitary strike from Luke Pilbeam saw Dalworth continue their resurgence and climb up the table.

Saturday 25th February

Thankfully we appear to have a clean bill of health from Tuesday, no colds, no flu and no double pneumonia.

Gaffer has an added touch of excitement in his voice today.
"Jim's available tomorrow and the twins are back too."
"Back up to a 14 man squad then Gaffer?"
"Yep, see you at 9am tomorrow at the Rec."
"See you Gaffer."

I'm really glad Jimmy's back, more for The Gaffer's sake than squad numbers.

Sunday 26th February - Oak Town Rangers vs Dalworth United

The first thing I notice walking the dog this morning is the heavy black clouds that hang ominously overhead which is a clear sign that heavy rain is to follow. I manage to get Faith around our Sunday morning 'course' without getting wet but I do fear for later.

If Dalworth Rec is anything to go by then Oak Town Rangers' ground is going to be on the soft side. Gaffer's not hanging around today which is of great disappointment to Billy B who is on his second Bacon and Egg McMuffin before Gaffer issues his call to arms and the Dalworth wagon train is rolling. Billy is the last one to alight as he stuffs the last of his McMuffin into his McMouth like a McJunkie hiding his McStash so that it doesn't get McConfiscated. In a final act of defiance to The Gaffer he lets rip a McFart before climbing aboard his McRide. Gaffer catches my attention points to the skies and shakes his head before getting in his car. It doesn't look promising.

Twenty minutes later and we've arrived at Oak Town Rangers' ground which is situated in a quaint little village. This is a proper community hub and the changing rooms are of the multipurpose variety as they double up as a nursery during the week and function rooms at the weekend as well as changing rooms on a Sunday morning. Sadly the nursery leave the toys out and Stevie Carr is planking on top of a childrens car while the others push him, much to the disgust of The Gaffer although he saves his real disdain for Billy B who is munching on a now cold Sausage and Egg McMuffin.

"Jeez Bill, do you ever stop eating?"
"Mmmmmm No Gaffer"

At least he is honest if nothing else.

Gaffer announces the starting line-up and it's a slight adjustment to our usual 4-2-3-1 formation as Gaffer adopts a more attack minded 4-1-3-2.
Billy Stevens
Danny Hall Nick Sheppard Aidan Hayes Billy Belafonte
Alex Hayes
Ben Padgham © Adam Morley Bobby Webster
Charlie Fisher Luke Pilbeam,
Subs: Stevie Carr, Brian Haugh, Jimmy Smith

The first thing I notice is Jimmy is on the bench which is unusual because Gaffer always started him before he left. In fact he never even substituted him. The second is Gaffer has put Aidan centre back which makes sense as Stevie hasn't kicked a ball in anger for a few weeks.

The pitch is sticky as we go out for the warm-up and the usual high intensity session isn't possible due to the balls sticking and boys slipping. The ref is running through his own routine and is taking interest in both sides' warm-ups as he inspects the pitch. We end our preparations with keep-ball.

Just as we go in the rain starts and then comes the expected downpour which only lasts a couple of minutes and is then replaced by a steady drizzle which lasts the entire half.

The ref decides that we are here so is prepared to start the game, whether or not we finish it is another matter. It is a half littered with errors and mistakes and has little quality whatsoever from either side. The only highlights of a half which can only be described as comical were Luke spraying the goalkeeper with a stream of mud and water when he miskicked in front of the goal, a Billy B free kick which didn't make the wall, due to an Oak Town player treading on the ball and submerging it after Billy had set the free kick. But the winner was Alex Hayes slide tackle which not only won the ball but took out two Oak Town players and his brother Aidan in the process.

Gaffer was at a loss at what to do at half time. You couldn't fault the commitment or the effort of the players but it just wasn't working.
"Right boys I'm going to make a change to formation and personnel".
Gaffer sticks the new line up on the wall.

Billy Stevens
Stevie Carr Nick Sheppard Jimmy Smith
Alex Hayes Billy Belafonte Aidan Hayes
Ben Padgham © Charlie Fisher Luke Pilbeam, Brian Haugh

It's an unfamiliar 3-3-4 with Stevie, Jimmy and Brian replacing Danny, Adam and Bobby.

"Right boys forget playing pretty football, it's route one this half, forget the possession football, get the ball forward quickly and hit the channels. Don't get caught on the ball, set it and launch it. It's ugly football for ugly conditions today."

Those instructions are totally against our footballing philosophy but if you are Barcelona and you play on carpets you don't have to change your ideals but on this occasion Gaffer is right.

The second half brings more drizzle and more mistakes from both sides, and the first error sees us grab the lead as Billy B launches the ball forward from midfield and the Oak Town 'keeper drops the ball at the feet of Luke who gratefully accepts the mistake to give us the lead. Moments later Charlie latches onto a long clearance from Billy S, breaks free from the Oak Town defence and lifts the ball over the keeper but somehow the ball sticks in the mud and is cleared.

Neither side is playing any football worthy of the tag 'the beautiful game' and both sides are reduced to launching the ball at will. The midfield is virtually rendered redundant as they simply watch the ball sailing over their heads. The next one to watch the ball sailing over his head is Billy S who at the time is lying in the mud due to him losing his feet. 1-1 and the farce continues, albeit in our favour, as two Oak Town defenders collide leaving Luke a free run on goal.

Usually you would put your house on Luke, but he just can't get himself or the ball out of the mud and just as he goes to shoot, a last ditch tackle takes the ball away from him and he ends up face down it. He drags himself up and you can't tell its Luke due to the heavy covering from head to toe. The distraction of a mud-covered Luke means we don't see the referee, who has pointed to the spot much to the disgust of Oak Town who immediately surround him, arguing that it was a good tackle.

To be fair it did look a good tackle but then the ref's decision is final, on this occasion at least. Luke usually grabs the ball when we win a penalty but instead he summons Billy B, has a quick word and much to our astonishment hands the ball to Billy B. Gaffer looks at me and I just shrug my shoulders.

In the meantime Billy B places the ball on the spot, crashes it into the top right hand corner and we have the lead again.

Luke who has joined us on the side to clear the mud off offers an explanation to Gaffer:

"I place my penalties; Billy smacks them, who would you have gone for?" Gaffer nods his approval and Luke is off to take his place for the restart.

The rain is continuing and with 15 minutes of the game left there is a serious concern that the game may be abandoned. Gaffer is getting into a nervous pattern of:
1. Examining the skies
2. Checking his watch
3. Looking at the subs
4. Looking at me, going to say something but saying nothing.

In the end I break the silence:

"Five minutes to go Gaffer, we've got three points in the bag."

At that point Nick slides into the Oak Town number nine as he goes to pull the trigger and promptly upends him and the ref awards a penalty to Oak Town. Was it a penalty? I think they ref has just evened things up.

Gaffer looks at me and says "You sure Si?"

I try to reassure Gaffer and equally dig myself out of a spot "Billy will save it."

This time, I'm relieved to say, I was right as the Oak Town captain put his foot through the ball and Billy saved the goal bound strike with... his face. Luckily Nick cleared the rebound for a corner because Billy couldn't see a thing due to the mud covering his face. There have been some nasty injuries this season but calling on the trainer to 'clean the goalkeepers face' was a new one on all of us. Still, Billy's sight restored, our lead still intact and all is well again. 2-1 was how it stayed and we've got another valuable three points on the board.

The boys trudged off tired, wet and muddy but happy. Gaffer kept the post-match debrief short and sweet:

"Nice one boys, training Tuesday. Oh and make sure the kits not inside out." Then began the arduous task of peeling off kit and trying to clean off as much mud as possible without the use of showers. Within minutes of entering the changing rooms pictures of Billy S's muddy face was circulating Facebook, Instagram, Snapchat and Twitter. If you look really closely you can see the imprint of the ball on his face. Billy S and his smiling muddy face were instant social media celebrities, well at least in Dalworth. The boys were lining up for the toilets, not the actual toilet, because they were trying to wash themselves in the sink and the once red kit was now brown and the only saving grace was that we didn't use the white kit today.

"Mrs Gaffer will love cleaning that!"

"Sod that Si, this is going in the dry cleaners unless I want divorce proceedings and my dinner in the dog!"

"Point taken."

We spent the next 20 minutes trying to get the kit as mud free as possible and by the time we were finished the changing room floor was covered in mud. I really pity the person who had to clean the changing rooms that day. I bet they were about as happy as Mrs S when she greeted me and Nick at the front door. We were made to strip inside the front door and carry our dirty clothing to the washing machine, however this time I called 'dibs' on the bath.

Results from Sunday 25th February

Oak Town Rangers 1 – 2 Dalworth United
Tamworth United 1 – 0 Phoenix Rovers
Kingsbridge 4 – 0 Parkfield

Team	P	W	D	L	F	A	GD	Pts
1 Tamworth United	13	9	2	2	38	19	19	29
2 Kingsbridge	11	8	1	2	27	10	19	25
3 Phoenix Rovers	11	7	0	4	33	17	16	21
4 Dalworth United	10	6	1	3	27	21	6	19
5 Dunstable Colts	8	5	1	2	17	10	7	16
6 Leighbridge Lions	13	5	1	7	26	31	-5	16
7 Parkfield	10	5	0	5	18	20	-2	15
8 Langton Reds	10	4	0	6	31	27	4	12
9 Oak Town Rangers	15	3	1	11	17	44	-27	10
10 Redbridge Sports	13	1	1	11	13	48	-35	4

Smith Says

Well that was the dirtiest game of the season and I'm not talking about the physical aspect. The boys were superb today as we adapted our tactics and formation to the atrocious conditions and managed to grind out another win, playing a style of football that is alien to us. It was a real war of attrition today and it took an excellent team effort to secure all three points and in doing so the winning run and climb up the table continues. I would like to thank everyone who turned up today and braved the elements because without your support and efforts we couldn't do this.

The Gaffer

Oak Town Rangers 1 Dalworth United 2
Squad: Billy Stevens, Danny Hall, Nick Sheppard, Aidan Hayes, Billy Belafonte, Alex Hayes, Ben Padgham © Adam Morley, Bobby Webster, Charlie Fisher, Luke Pilbeam, Stevie Carr, Brian Haugh, Jimmy Smith
Scorers: Pilbeam, Belafonte
Man of the Match: Billy Stevens

I get an unexpected call from The Gaffer tonight.
"You alright Si?"
"Yeah although I spent half a hour cleaning out the bath and shower after me and Nick had used it!"
"Yeah same here. I'm still drying out although I've got a bottle of Monkey Shoulder Triple Malt Scotch on the go and that's warming me up."
"Believe it or not I'm on the Brothers Toffee Apple Cider and that's just taking the edge off of everything."

We both burst out laughing which drew an odd look from my wife.

"Good win today"
"Yeah boys really pulled it out the bag."
"Sure did, see you Tuesday Si."
"See you Tuesday Gaffer."

Apparently I was sound asleep by 8:30 sitting in front of the TV and the fire having consumed six bottles of cider and on a night before school. Tut, tut!

Tuesday 27th February
No training tonight as Sunday's games have destroyed the pitches. Don't think anyone is overly disappointed. I know Nick isn't, as he says his legs are still aching from Sunday's game. Gaffer was going to get everyone together for a run but soon dropped the idea when he saw the weather forecast which I have to say is to my liking as I have a ton of marking to get through.

Damn you Shakespeare!

CHAPTER NINE

MARCH

"It's only a game after all"

Thursday 1st March
The managers' meeting is cancelled early doors, not sure why, but I could have done without it anyway so happy days.

Friday 2nd March - Dalworth News
Oak Town Rangers 1 Dalworth United **Under 15**s 2
Goals from Luke Pilbeam and Billy Belafonte were enough to take all three points after Will Woodcock had equalised for the Oak

Saturday 3rd March
Gaffer is on the phone and worried that we haven't trained before our clash with Tamworth United.

"We should have got them together on Tuesday even if it was for a chat Si."
"We'll be fine Gaffer." (I hope we will be).
"I suppose. We are on a ten-match unbeaten run."
"Yeah no one's going to beat us."
"I said that at the beginning of the season and looked what happened!"
"Yeah, sorry." (I'm not helping matters).
"No, you're right, we can do this."
"I'll see you tomorrow Gaffer."
"Yeah see you tomorrow Si."

Sunday 4th March - Tamworth United vs Dalworth United
Match day and it's an 8:45 meet at the Rec. The boys are very subdued and appear almost nervous as the importance of the game hits home and a feeling of anxiousness engulfs the whole group. Tamworth sit ten pts ahead of us in the table but we have 3 games in hand. A Tamworth win today and it could be season over as far as the league is concerned. A win for us and it's definitely game on. The boys are immaculately turned out which we later found out is down to Ben who has given strict instructions to the players to turn out in tracksuits polos and trainers and no add-ons

whatsoever. This shows that they understand the importance of the game in context to the remainder of the season and are taking this game very seriously even down to their appearance. There's no need for directions as everyone knows where they are going. At 9am Gaffer gives the order to go and off we roll to Tamworth.

Everyone is sitting in the changing room at 9:45 but no one is saying a word. They are just going about their match day routines. Adz has been given responsibility for the matchday sounds and Eminem's Lose Yourself is belting out. The lack of chat I thought indicated nervousness, but I think it shows complete concentration and focus.

Gaffer delivers his teamtalk and he hardly raises his voice because he has everyone's complete and undivided attention.

"We know how important this game is but it is just another game. It's the eleventh fixture of a ten match winning streak and we don't have to raise our game, we don't have to give an extra 10%, we don't have to do anything different to what we have done in our last ten matches. All that I ask is that you believe in the team and your teammates and yourselves. If we believe it, we can do it, so trust your teammates, work for your teammates and we will win the game. Good luck boys!"

The boys carry on getting changed and I grab The Gaffer's arm.

"Great speech Gaffer, it was a good idea to take the pressure off the boys."
"Thanks Si, they are ready for this game and as long as they believe in themselves we'll get the result."
"That was still what they needed to hear though."
"Thanks but if anyone is feeling the pressure it'll be next door."

Gaffer reads out the team while he pins up the team sheet.

Starting line-up
Billy Stevens
Danny Hall Jimmy Smith Nick Sheppard Billy Belafonte
Alex Hayes Adam Morley Aidan Hayes
Ben Padgham © Luke Pilbeam, Bobby Webster
Subs: Stevie Carr, Brian Haugh, Charlie Fisher

Gaffer has gone for a 4-3-3 formation with Ben and Bobby either side of Luke it's not a rigid 4-3-3 as Ben and Bobby have a license to roam.

It's a good warm-up and the boys aren't letting their concentration levels or focus drop. During the keep-ball the boys are all on each other's cases, not in a negative manner, but they want to get it right and all the communication is positive. The passes are finding their targets and it's fast and frantic but the quality is evident for all to see. Our opponents are loud and fired up during their warm-up but our boys are oblivious to the opposition as they are all tuned into the task at hand, winning the game.

At the end of the warm-up Ben quickly gathers everyone together. He is crouching into the circle of players and wagging his finger. The message he delivers is simple:

"Those last ten games count for nothing if we lose today. We want this, we need this, so let's do this!"

The game starts at a frantic pace with both teams looking to get their noses in front. Bobby hits the post after skinning the fullback and then Jimmy blocks a goalbound shot. The game is being played at a relentless pace and we think we have taken the lead when Billy B curls a free kick around the wall only to see the Tamworth goalkeeper tip his effort round the post. Half chances follow near misses and the ref brings a tense first half contest to an end.

Gaffer calls me to one side.
"I don't think we should change things but it's not fair on the subs."
"I agree Gaffer it's a team game."
"Right."

Second Half line-up
Billy Stevens
Danny Hall Stevie Carr Nick Sheppard Billy Belafonte
Ben Padgham © Alex Hayes Aidan Hayes Brian Haugh
Charlie Fisher Bobby Webster
Subs: Jimmy Smith, Adam Morley, Luke Pilbeam

It's a massive call from The Gaffer, especially when he sticks Bobby up top in a 4-4-2 formation and Charlie replaces Luke. I can see Gaffer's logic because Bobby is on fire but it's still a big decision to make and he pulls Luke to one side to explain his decision. Luke understands and smiles at Charlie: "Bang one in Charlie Boy!" "Sure thing Lukey!"

The first chance of the half falls to Tamworth and Billy pulls off an incredible triple stop when he first saves from close range and then somehow throws himself in front of the follow-up. Then just as the Tamworth number eleven looks certain to score, he spreads himself and blocks the third effort.

Gaffer is frantically chewing on his nails or what remains of them and spitting out loose bits before shouting instructions. I hand him a pack of chewing gum which he gratefully accepts. This is as an alternative to him a) biting his nails down to the wick, b) chain-smoking c) slugging at a bottle of Whisky. All of which are a possibility such is Gaffer's anxiety levels and the tense nature of the game. I don't even realise that I'm pacing up and down the technical area until Gaffer grabs my arm and says:

"For f**ks sake Si, stand still!"

"Sorry Gaffer"

Both sides are still probing for a winner when Bobby wins a corner after his long range shot is tipped over the bar. From the resulting cross Alex powers a goal bound header which is hacked away off the line. The game is looking increasingly like a 0-0 but both managers are desperate to win such is the importance of the result due to the tight situation at the top of the league. Gaffer and I agree that today it is better to win three points than lose one.

With both teams continuing to press, Danny makes a superb sliding tackle to blunt a Tamworth attack down the right. Ben picks up the loose ball and feeds a pass to Alex who drives into the Tamworth half before finding Bobby with a through ball. Bobby latches onto the pass and realises Charlie first time who has one thing on his mind. Charlie races past both centre backs and is one on one with the Tamworth 'keeper and just as he comes out to narrow the angle, Charlie goes wide to the his right, leaving him the tightest of angles. He keeps his composure and slots the ball into the opposite corner to give us the all important lead. Charlie races to the technical area closely followed by his teammates but Charlie isn't being caught and once he gets there, he and Luke perform the most outlandish dance celebration that involves touching their heads, shoulders, hips and knees while wiggling the rest of their bodies. They finish it off with a chest bump, by which time the rest of the team are performing their own rendition of the dance.

The overzealous dance celebrations, while not intended to mock Tamworth, serve as inspiration for our opponents and they come roaring back and hit the post. Moments later, with Billy S well beaten, Jimmy manages to clear the rebound. The Gaffer senses the tired legs and makes further changes.

Billy Stevens

Stevie Carr Jimmy Smith Nick Sheppard Billy Belafonte

Ben Padgham © Alex Hayes Aidan Hayes Brian Haugh

Luke Pilbeam, Charlie Fisher

The fresh legs give us new impetus and Tamworth are on the back foot, struggling to create any decent chances. Luke hits a volley from Brian's cross that cannons off the Tamworth bar and Aidan's follow up effort is cleared off the line. With the clock running down the boys play the game in Tamworth's half, hitting the lively Charlie and Luke at every opportunity.

The final whistle is greeted with muted celebrations from the boys. It's almost as though they just had a job to do, they did it and they were never in doubt of the outcome. Which is more than can be said for The Gaffer and I.

We notice a bit of a commotion and all the parents are crowding round someone or something. A gap clears and we notice that Mr Hayes is sitting on the ground. The twins also notice it and rush over to their Grandad who is soon upright and talking. He immediately reassures the concerned twins and tells them not to worry, telling everyone not to fuss. He tells the twins to go and get their snacks and pop and once they are happy that Grandad is OK they're off. Once again it's a short feedback from The Gaffer:
"Well done boys, big, big result today. See you all Tuesday"

Results from Sunday 4th March
Tamworth United 0 - 1 Dalworth United
Dunstable Colts 3 - 1 Redbridge Sports
Langton Reds 8 - 3 Kingsbridge

Team	P	W	D	L	F	A	GD	Pts
1 Tamworth United	14	9	2	3	38	20	18	29
2 Kingsbridge	12	8	1	3	30	18	12	25
3 Dalworth United	11	7	1	3	28	21	7	22
4 Phoenix Rovers	11	7	0	4	33	17	16	21
5 Dunstable Colts	9	6	1	2	20	11	9	19
6 Leighbridge Lions	13	5	1	7	26	31	-5	16
7 Langton Reds	11	5	0	6	39	30	9	15
8 Parkfield	10	5	0	5	18	20	-2	15
9 Oak Town Rangers	15	3	1	11	17	44	-27	10
10 Redbridge Sports	14	1	1	12	14	51	-37	4

Smith Says

We always knew this was going to be a tough game so I'm so pleased that we walked away with all three points. In important games like this you hope that 80% of the team is going to be on their game but today we had ALL 14 players on their game and everyone contributed to the win. We are now on an incredible eleven game unbeaten streak but we are still taking things a game at a time. We now sit in third place and while we are still seven points behind the leaders we have three games in hand and all to play for. As well as taking points off of the league leaders today second-place Kingsbridge suffered a heavy 8-3 defeat to Langton Reds which again opens things up with seven games to play

On a separate note it seems that the occasion got the better of Grandad Hayes at the final whistle and he passed out but thankfully he was OK and by the time we left Tamworth he was looking much better. We would however like to wish him well and everyone at the club sends their best wishes.

Tamworth United 0 Dalworth United 1
Squad: Billy Stevens, Danny Hall, Stevie Carr, Nick Sheppard, Billy Belafonte, Ben Padgham © Alex Hayes, Aidan Hayes, Brian Haugh, Charlie Fisher, Bobby Webster, Jimmy Smith, Adam Morley, Luke Pilbeam
Scorer: Fisher
Man of the Match: Fisher

Tuesday 6th March
Gaffer rings to say that he has got stuck on a job so is running about 15 minutes late. I told the boys and Ben said he'll start the warm-up as soon as everyone turns up. But with ten minutes to go half of the boys are still missing. Adz and Stevie aren't though and Adz challenges Stevie to a rap battle. The boys excitedly gather round them and any thoughts of training have disappeared from their young impressionable minds. Adz tosses a coin and Stevie calls "heads". Heads it is, so Stevie decides to go first.

"Yo stand back or you're gonna get cut, I'm spitting rhymes fresh from my nut,
 Adz thinks he's gonna steal my show, with old whack rhymes that just don't flow,
He just came here to look and learn, but Adz is gonna crash and burn,
He wants to learn from the king, and when you lose you can kiss my ring"

At this point Stevie turns round and presents his backside to Adz. The rest of the boys start hollering and whooping and even Adz has to acknowledge Stevie's efforts. Adz gets ready with his response but before he can start, Billy B decides to enter the battleand jumps in launching into his own adaption of the PJ & Duncan classic.
"Arse get ready, arse get ready, arse get ready to rumble!

Watch me wreck the mic! Watch me wreck the mic! Watch me wreck the mic! PSYCHE!" At which point Billy let's rip with a loud Billy B special.

Adz screws his face up and responds with "You're sick Bill. What the f**k was that?"
"A 'Crap battle', and I think I won!" says a beaming Billy.
The boys burst into laughter and even Adz can't help but laugh.

The other boys arrive including Alex and Aidan and after the twins have been bombarded with numerous questions about their Grandad, who thankfully is feeling a lot better, everyone wants to know what they've missed and the tale of Billy's 'Crap Battle' is the talk of training naturally with a few embellishments: "Did you really shit yourself again Bill?", "No" says an indignant Billy. "It was a controlled explosion, maybe a few skid marks. Why, do you want to check for me?"

Bill offers his bum for investigation but funnily enough noone takes up his offer. Ben sternly addresses the boys: "Any danger of doing any training tonight?" and whisks the boys off for a warm-up with all talk of Billy B's bum banned.

Gaffer turns up just as the boys are getting back from the warm-up and they are still sniggering out of Ben's earshot. Gaffer looks at me puzzled and I simply say "Don't ask!"

The training session is a good one and there's a lot of laughter mixed with hard work. It's an easy job managing when you are winning, you don't have to change too much and you just aim to keep things ticking over. Having a small squad helps, especially if you have one that are all capable of contributing. In this side there are no passengers and therefore you can give gametime to everyone, which means you also have a happy squad. We have a fantastic team spirit and camaraderie and there are no egos. The players also know that the team always comes first. All in all it's a nice place to be at the moment.

Wednesday 7th March
Gaffer is on the phone and straight away I can detect something is up.
"Mr Hayes has been rushed to hospital, suspected heart attack."
"Oh no, what's happening?"
"They are running tests and monitoring him. He is staying in at the moment."

"How are the twins?"
"Not good."
"OK Gaffer, keep me posted."
"Yeah will do."
Moments later Nick comes charging down the stairs.

"Dad, Dad you heard about Grandad Hayes?"

"Yeah I have."

"Poor Alex & Aidan."

"Yeah I know, but I'm sure he'll be OK, he's in the right place."

Why do we say things like that on these occasions? I know you want to reassure your kids but in reality you have no idea what is going to happen and what you are saying may be the complete opposite of the truth. But it is still considered better to give false hope than the reality of the situation. Weird that.

Friday 9th March - Dalworth News
Tamworth United 0 Dalworth United **Under 15**s 1
Dalworth gained revenge for their early season reversal by inflicting defeat on league leaders Tamworth. A second half strike from Charlie Fisher was enough to give Dalworth three vital points.

I ring The Gaffer to give him an update on Mr Hayes, but Gaffer has already heard; thankfully he is much better and on the road to recovery, thank God for that, especially after my conversation with Nick. We also have the small matter of a game on Sunday and Gaffer has said to Alex and Aidan it's their shout if they want to play.

Saturday 10th March
Gaffer is on the phone earlier than usual as he is out tonight.

"Alright Si, all set for tomorrow?"

"Yes Gaffer."

"We might not have Alex and Aidan tomorrow as Grandad Hayes is still in hospital. I've told them to ring me in the morning."

"OK Gaffer if you need anything let me know."

"Yeah thanks Si, see you tomorrow."

"See you tomorrow Gaffer."

Sunday 11th March - Phoenix Rovers v Dalworth United
It's a 9am meet at the Rec and everyone is punctual as usual. I'm pleased to see Alex and Aidan jump out of The Gaffer's Merc and the boys immediately crowd round them hugging and back slapping them. The twins look pleased to be with familiar faces but don't look their usual boisterous selves.

"You alright boys?"

"Yeah thanks Si." they reply in unison.

You can sense the twins feel uncomfortable but they are amongst their mates and with it comes a reassurance that they can be vulnerable in this group. I notice that they keep looking at each other almost as though they are each others safety blanket. Gaffer taps me on the shoulder.

"What do you think Si, do we play them today?"
"Give it a go Gaffer. I think it was a big step for them to be here so let's play it by ear."
"OK Si."

Gaffer barks the "time to roll" instruction and everyone is scampering for their vehicles. It's a 30 minute journey to Phoenix but fortunately the convoy stays packed together and everyone gets there at the same time.

It's funny how some managers' match day routines differ. Gaffer likes to get to the ground about a hour before kick off. Michael the previous manager aimed for 45 minutes before kick off but had a strict pre-match routine of ten minutes to get changed while he delivered his instructions. Twenty-five minute warm-up then back to the changing rooms for the last five points (it was always five key points, no more, no less).

Gaffer likes an extra 15 minutes in which he delivers his instructions before the boys get changed, but he sticks to the same format as Michael. The U16s manager likes to get to games a full 90 minutes before kick off which is OK if you are at home but away he is often sitting around waiting for the home team to open the changing rooms, sometimes to the disgust of his players and parents who feel they could have had another 30 minutes in bed. Gaffer, like me, is keeping a close eye on Alex and Aidan looking for any sign of emotion but the twins seem to be losing themselves in the hustle and the bustle of the changing room. He pins the team sheet up and the twin's emotive "Yes!" shows they are really excited to be starting. Gaffer opts for a 4-2-3-1 formation which I must say is my preferred formation as it is a flexible formation that gives the boys lots of freedom.

Starting Line-Up
Billy Stevens
Stevie Carr Nick Sheppard Jimmy Smith Billy Belafonte
Alex Hayes Aidan Hayes
Brian Haugh Ben Padgham © Bobby Webster
Luke Pilbeam,
Subs: Danny Hall, Adam Morley, Charlie Fisher

The twins are still beaming ear to ear and for the first time today they look like the twins we know and love. Gaffer notices this and looks at me and winks and I smile back. Well if they lose themselves in a game of football today and can take their minds off of everything else for 90 minutes then that's not a bad thing.

The warm-up is a very serious affair. There's no laughing or joking and no 'bants', it's just down to business. The boys as usual are focused but it would seem out of respect there is to be no laughing today. This is business.

Gaffer gives his last instructions:
1) Don't be afraid to express yourselves.
2) Work as a unit and work for each other.
3) Play the game in their half.
4) One game at a time.
He delivers the last one to everyone but is looking at Alex and Aidan when he says:
5) Go out there and have fun.

Things don't go according to plan though and from an early corner the ball hits Aidan on the shoulder and ends up nestling in the back of the net. This is the last thing we wanted to happen especially to a player who is at best fragile. The disconsolate Aidan is sitting on the ground head in hands but that doesn't last for long as his brother drags him to his feet and Ben, with his fist raised says to everyone: "Come on, heads up and we go again".

Within five minutes we are level as Alex bursts through three tackles and takes the ball wide of the goalkeeper. Just as we are expecting him to try to beat the 'keeper from a tight angle, he rolls the ball across the goalmouth to Luke who is standing alone in the area. Luke could have got on his hands and knees and headed the ball in, that's how much time he had, but instead he smashes the ball into the empty net.

The celebrations were muted from the players because, and to quote from Ben: "We haven't won anything yet". The players followed their captain's brief because they had unfinished business to take care of.

The pace of the game was hard to keep up with as the ball was pinging about from both sides and to be fair the busiest players were the goalkeepers, both of whom made several important saves. The half finished 1-1 and both teams looked in need of the break for a breather. Gaffer changes the formation slightly going 4-1-3-2 and give Aidan who had run his socks off a break.

Starting Line-Up
Billy Stevens
Danny Hall Jimmy Smith Nick Sheppard Billy Belafonte
Alex Hayes
Ben Padgham © Adam Morley Bobby Webster
Charlie Fisher Luke Pilbeam,

Within five minutes of the restart we have the lead when Charlie picks up a crossfield pass from Billy B on the touchline and with two touches outpaces the left back. He cuts inside the centreback with Luke screaming for the ball in the box, Charlie unleashes a thunderbolt which leaves the Phoenix 'keeper clutching at thin air. On this occasion it wasn't the Phoenix that rose from the ashes it was Charlie's thunderbolt. The boys work wasn't done yet and they pressed for a third. Gaffer made more changes and Aidan was re-introduced for Jimmy, who was struggling with a knock after making a block tackle, at the back. Billy S then pulled off an amazing point-bank save from a Phoenix corner spreading his immense frame to tip away a goal bound header. The ball went straight down the other end and Luke forced another fine save from the Phoenix 'keeper and the loose ball was put behind for a corner. Billy B's outswinging corner fell just over Aidan's shoulder and in the blink of an eye he quickly adjusted his position and then hit a stunning overhead kick into the top right corner. There were no muted celebrations this time and players, management and parents collectively went mental. The Phoenix players were as stunned as us and the goal broke them. That was it, game set and match Dalworth. As Phoenix kicked off I heard their manager say "There's no coming back from that."

The final whistle brought more celebrations and the Phoenix management were quick to acknowledge Aidan's moment of sublime skill.

"I hate losing but if you are going to lose why not to a worldie."
"Thanks,"
"Good luck for the rest of the season and good luck in the cup final,"
"You too,"
In another nice touch the Phoenix assistant manager puts his arm round Aidan's shoulders and says: "Great tekkers son" Aidan is beaming now.
The changing room, as is becoming the custom of late, is buzzing and everyone is in a state of disbelief after watching such an outstanding goal.
"Top drawer Aidan."
"Just like Pele in Escape to Victory."
"Goal of the season, more like goal of the century."

It was at this point that we all noticed the gentle almost silent sobbing coming from the scorer of the amazing goal. Alex immediately had his arm round his brother and we noticed he too had tears in his eyes. Aidan wasn't able to speak, He was too consumed with emotion and too choked. He sat head bowed staring at the floor. It was left to his brother to explain the source of his tears.

Alex initially struggled to get the words out but he somehow managed to explain that his brother had said the first thing he did when he scored was look to where their Grandad always stood and he was just overcome with emotion when he realised that he wasn't there to share the moment. This outburst of pure and raw emotion consumed the whole changing room and everyone was left speechless, but as usual Ben managed to find the words: "Leave it out Aidan; you'll love talking your Grandad through your goal tonight. It's Alex I feel sorry for he's going to have to listen to it a hundred times!"

Aidan began laughing and despite his tear-stained eyes, a big smile broke on his face. Ben's words worked a treat, and soon everyone was smiling and laughing.

There really wasn't anything Gaffer could say except "Well done boys, See you Tuesday." this was sufficient.

Once the boys were gone and we were packing away the dirty kit, Gaffer suddenly stopped and plonked himself on the bench.

"I'm f**king drained Si".
"Yeah it was a tense game, I know what you mean."
"No emotionally Si, it was as much as I could do to stop myself from shedding a tear when Aidan spoke about his Grandad."
"Yeah it's comforting to know that I wasn't the only one that felt that way."
"You don't know what you're taking on when you become a manager. I thought losing games was bad enough but when you share your players' pain like that losing games is nothing."

I'm not sure what to say back to The Gaffer as this outpouring of emotions has caught me off guard.

"It's because you care mate, it's because they are not just players they are more than that."
"Yeah I suppose so, I hope Grandad Hayes is going to be OK."
"So do I."

We both sit back and nod our heads to a question that hasn't been asked or answered and sit in silence for a few minutes. Gaffer makes the first move "Suppose we better get cleared up."

Results from Sunday 11th March
Redbridge Sports 1 - 3 Tamworth United
Parkfield 1 - 2 Dunstable Colts
Langton Reds 7 - 0 Oak Town Rangers
Phoenix Rovers 1 - 3 Dalworth United

Team	P	W	D	L	F	A	GD	Pts
1 Tamworth United	15	10	2	3	41	21	20	32
2 Kingsbridge	12	8	1	3	30	18	14	25
3 Dalworth United	12	8	1	3	31	22	9	25
4 Dunstable Colts	10	7	1	2	22	12	10	22
5 Phoenix Rovers	12	7	0	5	34	20	14	21
6 Langton Reds	12	6	0	6	46	30	16	18
7 Leighbridge Lions	13	5	1	7	26	31	-5	16
8 Parkfield	11	5	0	6	19	22	-3	15
9 Oak Town Rangers	16	3	1	12	17	51	-34	10
10 Redbridge Sports	15	1	1	13	15	54	-39	4

Smith Says
What a game today and what an absolutely amazing goal from the man of the match Aidan Hayes. Aidan showed great character to come back from scoring an own goal and his own contribution, an overhead kick, was nothing short of stunning. I wasn't sure if Aidan and Alex were going to play today but they both showed what big hearts and character they have. I also want to give credit to the other boys for their efforts today which prove that we win together, we lose together and whatever happens we are in this together. We have a break next week so enjoy a rare lie-in.
The Gaffer

Phoenix Rovers 1 Dalworth United 3
Squad: Billy Stevens, Stevie Carr, Jimmy Smith, Nick Sheppard, Billy Belafonte, Aidan Hayes, Alex Hayes, Brian Haugh, Ben Padgham © Bobby Webster, Luke Pilbeam, Danny Hall, Adam Morley, Charlie Fisher
Scorers: Pilbeam, Fisher, Aidan Hayes
Man of the Match: Aidan Hayes (for that wonder goal)

Monday 12th March
Yes, it's a Monday but I'm expecting a phone call from The Gaffer. Especially after Nick had came hurtling down the stairs two minutes ago with bad news. As expected, the phone rings.

"Alright Si."
"Alright Gaffer. Nick just told me."
Gaffer is struggling to get the words out so I help him.
"Can't believe it. How are the twins?"
"They are devastated."
"I can't believe it."
"I'm calling off training tomorrow."
"Yeah I agree."
"I'll give you a call tomorrow Si."
"OK Gaffer."

As I put the phone down I can hear Nick crying.
"You OK Son?"
Nick gives me the biggest hug ever and I join him in shedding a few tears.
"I can't believe it Dad. I thought he was getting better. Poor Alex and Aidan they'll be gutted."
"Yeah I know we'll give them all the support they need."
"I'm popping out to see Ben, Dad."
"OK Son."
"Love you Dad."
"Love you son."

A sudden overwhelming numbness engulfs me as the news finally sinks in and I have to sit down. Death affects us in many ways and I feel totally dumbstruck. I pour myself a very large whiskey and all these questions are flying round my head. "How will the twins cope?", "How will Mrs Hayes cope?", "How will this affect the other boys in the team?".

Before the last thought leaves my head I'm pouring a second whiskey and I feel that I should be doing something, but what is there to do? Gaffer is busy ringing round the boys and he later said that he was necking whiskeys to get through the calls.

He rings me again about 30 minutes after his last call.
"Sorry Si, that was really difficult, the boys are heartbroken. You don't realise how much Grandad Hayes meant to all the boys. All the kind words, advice, lifts and Ice Creams and Coke he bought them."
"He was such a kind man."
"Did you know he was in the RAF?"
"Really?"
"Yeah I always thought he was ex-military."

Me and Gaffer spent a full hour on the phone, chatting and reminiscing while both emptying our own bottles of whiskey. Gaffer had a bottle of Monkey Shoulder Triple Malt and I'm on the JD Honey. Both bottles take a real battering. By the end of the call we were about twenty parts to the wind. We also agree that we would attend whatever service they were planning and support the boys in whatever they wanted to do.

Tuesday 13th March

I'm pleased training is off tonight but somehow I've got to get through a full teaching day with no frees so I'm carrying this hangover with me all day. I nearly managed it without any dramas until the last lesson of the day when 11xc somehow managed to destroy the Bard's text whilst reading *A Midsummer Nights' Dream* after the class clown delivered the line "He hath betwixt my bottom". It took a full ten minutes to regain my own composure and then the attention of the class. By which time I had lost my train of thought, the lesson and the will to live. I took the easy way out and stuck on the 2012 film with Michelle Pfieffer and Kevin Kline, while watching the remaining minutes of the lesson tick away slumped in the comfort of my chair. I think I was the first member of staff out the front gates at 3pm as I sought solace at home and by solace I meant more alcohol.

Friday 17th March - Dalworth News

Phoenix Rovers 1 Dalworth United **Under 15**s 3.

Dalworth moved into third place with a win at Phoenix. They trailed through an Aidan Hayes own goal until goals from strikers Luke Pilbeam and Charlie Fisher gave Dalworth the lead. A spectacular overhead kick from Aidan Hayes secured all three points for Dalworth.

Saturday 17th March

The service will be next Friday at Dalworth Crematorium at 2pm. The entire squad and management are going as well as most of the parents. Gaffer rang to say that we will train on Tuesday as he wants all the boys together. He was thinking of asking the league to postpone the game next Sunday but decided against it after he spoke to Alex and Aidan's Mum who thought the boys would want to be involved next Sunday even if only as spectators. Our fixtures secretary rang Parkfield to ask if we could hold a minutes applause before the game, at Alex and Aidan's request. They kindly agreed but it is still going to be a tough day as is next Friday.

Sunday 18th March

The sun is shining so I rang Gaffer to see if he fancied taking the families out for Sunday lunch. Guess which pub he suggested? As our wives had kindly agreed to drive, I was really fearing the worse and absolutely dreading disgracing myself in front of the family.

"But they don't do food."

"They do now. New management. They've just started doing it and they do a fantastic Sunday carvery."

Oh shit.

"See you about 1pm then?"

"See you then Gaffer."

When we arrived Gaffer was already there, as was a pint of 'Bert's Badger Juice'. "Cheers Gaffer!"

To be fair it never turned out to be a session and it was a really pleasant afternoon. The wives spent it chatting away like long lost friends although I did notice my wife keeping a close eye on my ale consumption and she frequently threw a 'I'm keeping my eye on you' look. While we never reached the depths of our Christmas visit I'm still glad I wasn't driving. Well to be fair I would have been incapable of driving. After three pints the bladder decided it was time to stretch the old legs and The Gaffer must have also felt the need too as when I returned from the toilet there awaiting me was a pint of my nemesis: The potent Old Gits Toffee Apple Cider.

Gaffer smiled at me and winked as I picked up the glistening pint holding it away from me with some trepidation while examining it as you would an incendiary device. I took a deep breath and held it to my lips. I felt like a Bond villain. "Ah Old Gits Toffee Apple Cider I've been expecting you". I braced myself and took a long gulp and nearly emptied half of the glass in one go and then waited anticipating the contents to come bouncing back out of my stomach. I was pleasantly surprised that it remained in my system. However I was perturbed by my wife's expression which she followed up with a cautionary "Oi you alcoholic steady on!" "Sorry dear." I'm sure Gaffer was sniggering watching and waiting for some adverse effect caused by the Cider.

Gaffer was right, the food was very, good and the beef and trimmings helped soak up the alcohol in my stomach. We finally got onto the subject of Friday:

"We all set for Friday Gaffer?"

"As much as we can be."

"Is the wreath all done?"

"Yeah it's a red and white football from us and the boys."

"That's a nice touch."

"The boys have decided to wear white shirts and red ties too."

"Shall we do the same?"

"Yeah I think so."

"Alex and Aidan are doing a reading too, they've written a poem."

"That's a nice touch."

"Yeah I think Ben sat down with them and helped."

"It's going to be a really tough day and then two days later we've got a game."

"I can't see beyond Friday Si. The purpose of training on Tuesday is literally just a get together, nothing major."

"Be glad when it's all over if I'm brutally honest."

"Yeah. Fancy another pint Si?"

The minute The Gaffer says it my wife is eye-balling me and scowling at the same time. I haven't even had the chance to reply and Gaffer is gone. I try smiling at my wife to ease the tension and offer an arbitrary "Food was nice wasn't it dear?"

"Mmmmm apparently the alcohol is better".

Oh well. I tried.

Gaffer kindly picks up the bill and we are off. On our return I quickly grab Faith and we are off on a long walk. I should have gone to the loo before because 15 minutes into the walk I'm bursting for a piss. Thankfully there are a number of bushes on the route and I dive behind one to relieve myself. Unfortunately this is one of those pisses that goes on and on and on and out of nowhere I hear voices in the distance. I try shaking furiously but the stream of urine continues to the point that my trainers are getting wet. I even try talking to my member: "For f**ks sake, stop pissing!"

This is ridiculous. I had six pints but it appears that at least twice that amount has left my bladder. The voices are almost upon me and I can hear children amongst the adult one so I have no option but to duck down and hope that they don't decide to join me on my side of the bush. The stream is almost at an end so I pinch the old fella to temporarily halt it and wait for the voices to pass. Faith meanwhile is looking at me with an expression that says: "What the f**k are you doing you idiot?" I cut the intended walk short as I fear there may be more in the tank and I'm not getting caught out again.

"Good walk?" my wife greets me with.

"Interesting" I say under my breath, but follow up with "Yeah good."

"Cup of tea?"

"Yes please, just gotta pop to the loo..."

Results from Sunday 18th March
Redbridge Sports 0 - 2 Phoenix Rovers
Tamworth United 4 - 1 Parkfield
Kingsbridge 1 - 4 Leighbridge Lions
Langton Reds 4 - 0 Dunstable Colts

Team	P	W	D	L	F	A	GD	Pts
1 Tamworth United	16	11	2	3	45	22	23	35
2 Kingsbridge	13	8	1	4	31	22	9	25
3 Dalworth United	12	8	1	3	31	22	9	25
4 Phoenix Rovers	13	8	0	5	36	20	16	24
5 Dunstable Colts	11	7	1	3	22	16	6	22
6 Langton Reds	13	7	0	6	50	30	20	21
7 Leighbridge Lions	14	6	1	7	30	32	-2	19
8 Parkfield	12	5	0	7	20	26	-6	15
9 Oak Town Rangers	16	3	1	12	17	51	-34	10
10 Redbridge Sports	16	1	1	14	15	56	-41	4

Tuesday 20th March
It's a pretty sombre affair tonight. Alex and Aidan are in attendance and everyone is offering condolences and their sympathy. We are just going through the motions without saying much. The usual zeal and vigour are missing, understandably so, and you sense that while noone wants to be here, they wouldn't be anywhere else. Ben takes the warm-up and then it's keep-ball and a small-sided game and while no one is slacking, everyone just wants to do their bit and go home. Noone wants to lighten the mood or muck about. Even Billy pays his respect by not farting at any point. At the end Gaffer gets everyone together.
"Meet at the Crematorium at 1:45pm boys, then it's 9am here on Sunday, any questions?"

Noone has any questions and everyone drifts off to their modes of transport.
"See you Friday Si."
"See you Friday Gaffer."

Friday 23rd March
I'm up ridiculously early considering I'm not at work today, although not as early as The Gaffer who has already text me to say he is picking the wreath up at 11am from the florists. The school have been really good today and let me have the day off as paid leave. I suppose you could say I am still supporting our students in some capacity.

I'm the first one up in the household and I'm straight out with Faith, but not before I grab a flask of coffee to take with me. While it's lovely to be alone with Faith, my thoughts, a flask of coffee and the early morning sunshine, today is a day that I want over and done with as quickly as possible and if that seems harsh then so be it. Our walk takes us through a very large ploughed field and I sit on a tree stump with my coffee while Faith charges about chasing imaginary rabbits. Well I say imaginary because I can't see them, but that's not to say they aren't there.

I've really been dreading today because I know it's going to be very emotional. I've been to funerals and cremations before and I'm glad that this one is a cremation, more for the boys sakes than mine. They are naturally sad and sombre occasions, as you would rightly expect, but you try to make them a celebration of someone's life and therefore a time to reminisce and reflect on a loved one's/friends/relations achievements and the legacy that they leave behind. Today, however, I'm there to not only celebrate and mourn the passing of a friend (yes he was a friend and not just 'a parent') but support the boys and that's why it is going to be hard because not only am I going to have to deal with my own grief but that of the boys and I know that their emotions and their tears will be difficult to take on board. I try to stay out for as long as possible but Faith is keen to go home for her breakfast of scrambled eggs, cheese and chicken. Sorry, did you say spoilt?

When I get home everyone is up. My wife and daughter are getting ready for work and rushing around the house. Nick is also awake but is deep in conversation with Ben. This is Nick and Ben's first funeral and both are discussing how they are feeling and what to expect from today. My wife kisses me as she leaves, wishes me good luck and asks me to send her love to everyone especially Alex and Aidan. My daughter gives me a big hug and then, in the first of what is going to be many emotional and heart tugging gestures hugs her brother and gives him a big kiss on the head. I can feel the tears welling up inside already and we haven't even reached the crematorium. Deep breath Simon. The lump in my throat feels like it is bulging. I attempt to swallow and it's painful. I'm not sure if the pain is from the lump in my throat or the grief that is simmering inside.

With my wife and daughter gone, we play the waiting game and I put a film on to kill some time. I don't know what the film was called but it had the rapper Ice Cube in it and was set in what appeared to be the school from Hell. He played a teacher who was partial to administering discipline with a baseball bat. Note to self: buy a baseball bat, and then ended up fighting another teacher. I was drifting in and out of it but made a mental note to watch it another time when I would concentrate on it as it did look like a fairly good film. I was receiving and answering an endless stream of text messages from The Gaffer and the boys. I also drank an endless stream of coffee; at least four cups in a two hour spell.

I then took Faith out for another walk, which took her by surprise but she appreciated the extra exercise although I did cut the walk short when the coffee hit my bladder causing extreme discomfort. It was now time to get ready and as agreed I wore a white shirt and red tie under a black suit. A quick glance revealed it was now 12:00 and, against my better judgement, I took Nick down the pub for a quick drink. Not many words were exchanged as I could see Nick was really struggling with the uncertainty of the day so I tried to run through the anticipated order of events.

I could see, however, that my words of reassurance were falling on deaf ears and in the end we both lost ourselves in the ambience of the pub, straining to catch the odd conversation or simply people-watching. Whatever words were floating about were better than the unspoken ones and we were reduced to exchanging reassuring smiles in place of them. Nick looked like he was trying his utmost to keep his emotions in check. Not that Nick's eyes were giving anything away as they were covered by sunglasses for the whole time. We both drank up.

For the record Nick was drinking Coke and nothing stronger. We reluctantly made our way to the car for the ten-minute journey to the Crematorium. I remember thinking that I should be protecting Nick from this type of thing but that he wasn't a kid anymore, he was still my youngest, but standing beside me was a young man immaculately turned out and I was so proud of him.

When I originally asked him about attending I explained that he didn't have to and that noone would think badly of him if he didn't. He simply said to me he felt it was his duty to be present and I respected him for that. As far as I knew all the boys wanted to attend and all said they wanted to be present for Alex and Aidan.

When we get to the crematorium The Gaffer and Jimmy are already there with Luke, Adam and the Billys. Five minutes later and everyone is there. The boys wouldn't look out of place at a fashion show as they look pristine. Shirts are a spotless white and the red ties are perfectly knotted. No shirts are untucked or ties at half mast, as you would often see in school. Trousers are pressed so sharp you could use them as a ruler and shoes are shined to military precision. All the boys are wearing sunglasses and everyone speaks in a whisper. The boys shake hands and hug when they arrive and then stand back silent just observing and standing together in a close knit group. The parents that are in attendance congregate together, just like on match days.

The funeral procession slowly rolls into the crematorium grounds and the silence is broken by a collective intake of breath from the mourners. The first thing I notice is our wreath, a red and white football, which is very impressive and then notice a red *Grandad* wreath and the reality of the situation hits me. I quickly survey the boys and they stand heads bowed in respect. Mrs Hayes gets out first followed by her Mum and then Alex and Aidan. You can tell immediately that the twins have shed more than a few tears already. They both look towards their Mum and without saying a word she gives them permission to join their mates. The boys are engulfed by their mates and are hugged by every single one without a single word being uttered.

Everyone shuffles into the chapel to the sounds of Westlife's "You raise me up' and take their places. Alex and Aidan take their place at the front with their mum and gran and the boys pack tightly into the pews behind Alex and Aidan in another show of support and solidarity. The service begins and like most you only take in odd words and sentences as you try your hardest not to catch a fellow mourner's eye or succumb to the grief that is bubbling inside. I did take in the fact that Mr Hayes was a real family man and cherished his beloved Grandsons and that he loved nothing better than taking them to football on a Sunday morning. It was also mentioned that they reminded him of himself when he was younger and he too was a combative midfielder for Dalworth United and the RAF. I had never known that he had played amateur football for the local side nor that the family had always lived in Dalworth.

There were now a number of smiles randomly appearing on mourners faces but they were soon dispelled by the next song, the beautiful and touching *In the arms of an angel* by Sarah McLachlan. The feelings of grief come flooding out and I bowed my head trying to hold back the tears and can hear random sobs coming from the mourners. A quick glance up reveals bobbing heads struggling to contain their emotions. I just hope and pray that Nick is OK. Next on the order of service comes the moment for the twins to do their reading. They slowly and hesitantly edge towards the pulpit constantly checking each other's movements almost expecting the other one to break down and leave the other frightened and alone. They manage to get to the pulpit and then start their reading a poem called *We love you Grandad.* Alex starts and manages to get the first two lines out but is hesitant as he desperately tries to keep his composure then Aidan races through his two lines head down eyes fixed on the poem.

Alex chokes out his first line but then stops and you can hear the pain in his voice. He aggressively wipes the tears from his eyes and tries again but he is not alone as Aidan begins gently sobbing. It is truly heartbreaking and you just want to scoop them up and hug them. I can feel the tears welling up in my own eyes and I can't hold them back. I just can't look up because I know I will end up full-on sobbing. I'm trying desperately to regain some form of composure when I hear another voice reading the poem. I instantly recognise the voice as Ben's. I quickly glance up to see Ben standing inbetween Alex and Aidan reading the piece. He has his arms round their shoulders and they both have an arm round his back. I take a deep breath, take in the beautiful words and I feel uplifted. I notice in front of me that all the boys are standing arms round each other's shoulders in yet another show of solidarity. Alex and Aidan take over from Ben and finish off the poem.

The poem must have lasted three minutes tops but the reading felt like a lifetime and the clarity of that moment will be forever etched in my memory. The twins finish the poem and Ben hugs Alex and Aidan and the three boys shuffle back to their places. I don't know where the thought came into my head, but I hear Stevie shout out: 'That's gay!' when the three boys hugged. But he didn't, and I berate myself for having such an inappropriate thought. The rest of the service flew past and then came the cremation and *We'll meet again* by Vera Lynn ended the service. At this point there wasn't a dry eye in the crematorium and everyone trudged out heads bowed and sobbing. Nick went out before me and despite the sunglasses I could see the tears on his cheeks. This set me off again. Why is it that your own kid's crying will always set you off? Even the ever-composed Ben was openly weeping. I turned sideways and The Gaffer was wiping his eyes discreetly in a "must be something in my eye" manner but it didn't matter. This was friends and family in collective grief. Grief doesn't discriminate and amongst this group of people it *really* didn't matter.

In the Garden of Remembrance everyone respectfully surveyed the wreaths and words of comfort were exchanged. I went with The Gaffer to offer our condolences to Mrs Hayes and Grandma Hayes. Mrs Hayes hugged us and she thanked us for all our support and the help we had given her. It was only later that I learned that The Gaffer had paid for the function room and all the food at the pub where the wake was being held. The man never fails to surprise me and what made the act even kinder was he told her it was from the whole team. We stood for what seemed an eternity, sun beating down on our already red faces, exchanging glances but not words. Then came that awkward moment when everyone just waits for someone else to make a move. Eventually Mrs Hayes, her mum and the twins slowly made their way to their car and as soon as they disappeared everyone quickly followed suit and made their way to the wake.

It was a relief to get to the pub and most people have dropped their cars off at home and used taxis or public transport to get to the pub so that they can see Grandad Hayes off with a few drinks. Once inside, Mrs Hayes says a few quick words and then finishes with a toast. I notice one or two of the boys have helped themselves to the free alcohol on the table and then notice Alex and Aidan knocking back a whiskey they have poured for the toast. "f**k it" I think, "Why not?"

The conversation starts to flow in conjunction with the alcohol and although it is audible only to those indulging in the conversation it does fill a void. People begin to pick at the buffet except for Billy B who is on his third plate. I pick at a few sandwiches even though I don't feel that hungry and we adjourn to the garden to have a few pints and chasers and make the most of the March sunshine that is beating down on us. Everyone is exchanging stories of Mr Hayes and Alex and Aidan seem intent on lapping up every story to lock away with their own precious memories.

I catch Ben and tell him how well he did with the reading.
"Well done Ben that took a lot of courage."
"Nah, we already planned it that I would step up if they couldn't read it."
"It was a lovely poem, where did you get it from?"
Ben tapped his temple and said:
"All in here Si, all three of us put it together."
"That's a really nice touch Ben."
Ben smiled and scurried away to get some food before Billy B finished it all off.

The rest of the afternoon was as pleasant as it could be and I felt that we had given Mr Hayes a good send off. The Gaffer looked worried though.

"You OK Gaffer?"
"Just wondering how we are going to get this lot ready for Sunday, I'm beginning to think we should have called it off."
"Maybe it's what we need."
"We'll see."

Everyone began to depart the pub after more hugs and goodbyes and Nick and I began the fifteen minute walk home.

"That was a nice service wasn't it Nick?"
"Yeah."
"The twins were incredibly strong weren't they?"
"Yeah."
"You ok Nick?"
"Yeah."

It was at this point I decided to drop the conversation and we finished the rest of the walk home in silence. It wasn't an awkward silence, just a reflective silence and when we got home Nick rushed upstairs and got changed. Moments later he was back down changed and going out again.

"Just off out to meet the boys Dad"
"Oh OK son."

"Thanks for today Dad." He gave me a big hug and then was gone. It was another poignant moment amongst the many the day had brought. I smiled to myself and then poured myself a very large whiskey. Faith looked at me and her face suggested a walk which was just what I needed and so that's what we did after I had filled my silver hip flask and it was indeed a very long walk.

When I got back my wife and daughter were home which I was pleased about as I needed the company. My wife gave me a big hug.

"Give The Gaffer a ring and see what he is up to. See if he and his wife fancy going to that pub. I reckon you could both do with a night out after today. My treat."

I didn't need telling twice and The Gaffer didn't need asking twice. An hour later we were all sitting in the pub tucking into a hearty mixed grill and knocking back a few pints of whatever real ale was on the guest list. I left the pub feeling quite tipsy but with Gaffer's final words ringing in my ears: "We've somehow got to prepare the boys for the game Sunday." Sunday was going to be another emotional occasion and the football match was always going to be secondary to the boys' minute's applause. Faith was thankfully happy to go out in the garden when we got home and I went to bed emotionally drained and slightly tipsy. I slept like a baby and even Faith appreciated my need for a good night's sleep and let me lie in in the morning.

Saturday 24th March
Gaffer rang fairly early as he was out again in the evening although he openly admitted the last thing he wanted to attend was a surprise 50th

birthday party for his cousin. I would rather sit at home with a bottle of whiskey watching the EFL highlights and *Match of the Day* he moaned. Regarding the twins tomorrow he was going to leave it to them if they wanted to take any part. I agreed that it would be better not to put any pressure on them. Tomorrow will be another difficult day.

Sunday 25th March - Parkfield vs Dalworth United

It's a very subdued meet at the Rec with lots of polite smiles and acknowledgments but the usual hustle and bustle and wind-ups are absent today. Mrs Hayes and Grandma Hayes are here to support Alex and Aidan, both of whom have made themselves available for the game. As soon as everyone turns up Gaffer gives a nod and everyone is quickly in their cars and away. It is a strange atmosphere and it feels like a testimonial game, a game that everyone wants to play in out of respect for Grandad Hayes, but equally a game that everyone wants over and done with.

The changing room is quiet, *really quiet*, and everyone is speaking in whispered tones. The boys get changed quickly and I notice all of them have black tape wrapped round their arms to signify a black armband. Gaffer sticks the team sheet up and the boys quickly gather round.

Starting line-up

Billy Stevens
Stevie Carr Jimmy Smith Nick Sheppard Billy Belafonte
Alex Hayes Adam Morley Aidan Hayes
Ben Padgham © Luke Pilbeam, Bobby Webster
Subs: Danny Hall, Brian Haugh, Charlie Fisher

Alex and Aidan are smiling and both nod at Gaffer and in unison thank him.

"Right boys"

Gaffer gets ready to give a few instructions but then stops and says:

"Look, just give me your best shot today boys."

The boys make their way outside for the warm-up and just as I'm leaving the changing room Gaffer grabs my arm and pulls me back.

"I wish I'd cancelled this game Si. We've got it all wrong playing so soon after the funeral. The occasion is too much, the minute's silence, the black armbands, it's all wrong, it's too much for the boys."

I acknowledge his sentiments and just offer up: "We just need to get today over and done with." "He nods in agreement and we leave the changing room trudging along like criminals on their way to face an inevitable guilty verdict.

The claustrophobic confines of the changing room make way for the sunshine of a surprisingly warm late March day. The warm-up is completed quickly and in virtual silence as everyone goes through the motions. Then comes the minute's silence. It produces lumps in throats as the boys try desperately not to shed any tears, especially as there are no sunglasses to hide behind. But the occasion is too much and the tears do flow, but they are quickly caught by a swift sleeve. Our opponents respectfully adhere to the minute's silence but it also gives them hope as they sense the vulnerability of today's opposition. I casually look at our parents and see mother and daughter locked in embrace, openly sobbing and just pray that Alex and Aidan haven't caught their mum and grandma's pain.

The minute's silence ends after what seems a lifetime and Ben quickly gathers everyone in and although we cannot hear what he is saying he is very animated and furiously wagging his finger.

Any fears we might have had were soon erased as within a minute of the kick-off we hit the post. Straight from Parkfield's kick off we pressed high and won the ball in midfield. Aidan seized onto a loose pass and fed Adam who played a sublime throughball behind the Parkfield right back and Bobby was away. He picked his pass and found the onrushing Luke who hit a first time drive that hit the post with the Parkfield goalkeeper well beaten. Luke then forced a fine save when he latched onto a pass from Alex but saw his shot beaten away and then cleared.

The boys were playing some fantastic football and any thoughts of the previous day's events were lost amongst the task at hand, gaining three points. Then came a crucial incident when Luke raced away from the last defender only to be tripped in the box by the covering centreback. Now noone likes to see a player sent off at this level but to the letter of the law it was deliberate foul play. However the referee didn't issue a yellow card let alone a red. He then confounded everyone when he placed the ball on the edge of the box. While the players, technical area and parents launched into a variety of appeals/abuse (I think there was an outpouring of suppressed emotions) Luke was apoplectic and he didn't hold back as he was pointing at the marks in the box that indicated the foul took place inside it. He was then clutching his head and screaming at the ref and by screaming, swearing and accusing the ref of cheating. To be fair the ref came over to The Gaffer and indicated that unless he substituted Luke he would be sent off. Gaffer stuck Charlie on for the disconsolate Luke. Luke was fuming "F**king cheat!" Gaffer turned on Luke: "For f**ks sake Luke calm down."

If there was any justice Billy B would have stuck the free kick away to give us the lead but instead he curled the ball around the wall and found the crossbar. Nick was quickest to react and as the ball looped off of the crossbar and back into play he thundered the ball home with a delightful volley.

While we were celebrating we noticed that the ref had pointed to the area. Ben was the first to the ref and simply asked: "What was that for?" We could see the ref indicate a push and Ben held his arms up and said "Who?" The ref pointed at Nick and again indicated a push. Ben again argued the cause only to receive a yellow card. Luke, who had began to calm down, was up on his feet and gesturing at the ref but all his "What a f**king cheat" comment received was another yellow card.

Football is supposed to be a passionate game and tempers can become frayed but you always hope the impartial man in the middle will restore order. The next five free-kicks all went the way of the home side and with each decision our boys became more and more irate and all the emotions of the past two days came flooding out. First Alex and then Aidan received yellow cards for late challenges and then Billy B retaliated to a late unpunished challenge and received our fifth yellow card of the half.

What made the yellow card even more galling was that he also hurt himself in the challenge and hobbled off to be replaced by Danny. The home side then had their first clear chance of the game and when Jimmy blocked a point blank shot, rather than receive his teammates' plaudits he instead joined in the protests as the ref awarded a penalty due to Jimmy apparently blocking the shot with his arm.

When the protests died down Billy S and Jimmy picked up yellows, Billy for protesting too aggressively and Jimmy for the handball. The penalty was duly dispatched and we found ourselves 1-0 down at half time and with seven players on a yellow card.

Half-time Parkfield 1 Dalworth United 0 or if you want to put a positive spin on a negative game. Parkfield 0 Dalworth United 7 (in bookings).

The boys were absolutely fuming and if a swear box had been present it would have been full in minutes. We spent the entire half time break trying to calm the boys. We had thought about speaking to the ref but decided against it as neither of us was in the right state of mind, which was especially difficult when we were fuming ourselves and shared the boys' collective views of the ref's performance in the first half.

We tried our hardest to bring the boys back to task but in the end Gaffer summed it up perfectly when he said: "Don't get mad, get even".

The boys were fired up for the second half when we would have preferred them not to be but Ben added: "Remember why we are here, three points boys." Gaffer changed a few things and started the second half with a 3-5-2 formation.

Starting line-up

Billy Stevens
Danny Hall Nick Sheppard Jimmy Smith
Brian Haugh Alex Hayes Adam Morley Aidan Hayes Bobby Webster
Charlie Fisher Ben Padgham ©

Luke was looking despondent until Gaffer smiled at him and said: "Don't worry Luke, I'll get you back on soon." That was all Luke needed for the smile to return to his face.

The boys came out firing on all cylinders and were soon asking all the questions. Charlie saw a shot well saved and then Ben should have done better when well placed. Parkfield looked like they were content to sit back and catch us on the break. They were also employing every timewasting tactic in the book and we were struggling to play our usual free flowing football. Luke came back on for Ben who took a slight knock and he immediately rattled the crossbar with a thunderous shot. I found myself getting more and more irate with the near misses, poor decisions (their linesman appeared to have a spring loaded arm which sprung into action every time we looked like scoring) and the timewasting tactics.

The Gaffer however is a picture of serenity and cooly delivers instructions to the players in a really calming tone. Chance after chance goes begging and with minutes left a cross from Brian falls for Charlie who only has to get a touch on the ball for an equaliser. Just as he goes to make contact he is bundled over as the centerback goes straight through him. Just as we get ready to bombard the referee with vociferous appeals the ref surprisingly (to us) points at the penalty spot. Luke grabs the ball and then smashes the ball against the crossbar. At that point you can see any confidence that remains visibly drain from the players. Parkfield know that they have the three points and they comfortably see out the game. The final whistle sees our players slump to the ground and Luke is in tears after his penalty miss. Gaffer shakes hands with the opposing managers and then strides purposefully out to the referee. I quickly try to cut him off but I'm shocked that when he gets there he simply shakes the referees hand and says "Thanks."

The Gaffer then makes his way to Luke and picks him up off the ground and then goes round and picks the remaining grounded players up. He quickly summons them to the side of the pitch.

"OK we didn't win today but it wasn't from a lack of effort. You gave 200% today and got nothing in return. If there was any justice you would have won today but that's football for you, it can be a cruel bloody game and today was one of those days."

The Gaffer looks at Alex and Aidan: "Your Grandad would have been proud of you today boys." He again addresses the group:
"Heads up boys, I'll see you all Tuesday and we go again."

The Gaffer (rightly) receives a rapturous round of applause from the parents and a massive hug from a tearful Mrs Hayes.

Not for the first time this week I was struggling to hold back the tears. The Gaffer then went round and shook everyone's hand and then shook mine. My admiration for this man has gone through the roof this week. The boys beaten and down trudged off to the changing rooms.

I use this moment to collar The Gaffer
"Fancy a quick pint later Gaffer?"
I'm a state of shock when he replies:
"Not today Si."
What, Gaffer turning a drink down!
"You alright?" and that was the trigger point for The Gaffer to let rip
"No I'm f**king not. That was a bloody travesty Si, the boys didn't deserve that, what the f**k was that referee playing at? We're not a dirty side, he knew what the boys had gone through. Poor Luke is devastated missing that pen, I'm gutted for Alex & Aidan too."

He had put on a brave front for the boys and that secretly he was raging inside.

"Come on mate, we've gotta let it go."
"Yeah but it ain't f**king fair."
He looks almost tearful
"No it's not f**king fair, but that's life."

We go and collect our gear from the technical area and Gaffer is throwing the stuff into the bag then out of nowhere Gaffer blurts out:
"F**k it let's all go down the pub!"
"F**k yeah!" Is my response. That's the English teacher in me.

The Gaffer extends the invitation to the rest of the parents and two hours later the pub garden is overtaken by the management, players and families of the Dalworth Under 15s. I'm not ashamed to say that I drank too much, ate too much but had a fantastic afternoon (and early evening) with my extended family. The boys ended up having a kick about in the pub garden with a ball they grabbed from the boot of Gaffers's motor. They were keeping the ball up in a circle and showboating with little flicks and tricks. Some of the dads having partaken in a few pints thought it was a good idea to join in and one of two ended up on their arses. There then followed an impromptu game of dads v lads and the boys really turned it on with nutmegs and various other moves all resulting in the humiliation of the dads. That aside, we drank, we laughed and the pain we shared this week simply evaporated in the pub garden. Today's game was disappointing but it didn't matter because we win, lose, laugh, cry and mourn together.

Dalworth til I die (God I'm pissed and I've got work tomorrow).

Results from Sunday 25th March
Redbridge Sports 2 - 3 Leighbridge Lions
Parkfield 1 - 0 Dalworth United
Langton Reds 6 - 2 Tamworth United
Phoenix Rovers 8 - 2 Oak Town Rangers

Team	P	W	D	L	F	A	GD	Pts
1 Tamworth United	17	11	2	4	47	28	19	35
2 Phoenix Rovers	14	9	0	5	44	22	24	27
3 Kingsbridge	13	8	1	4	31	22	9	25
4 Dalworth United	13	8	1	4	31	23	8	25
5 Langton Reds	14	8	0	6	56	32	24	24
6 Dunstable Colts	11	7	1	3	22	16	6	22
7 Leighbridge Lions	15	7	1	7	33	34	-1	22
8 Parkfield	13	6	0	7	21	26	-5	18
9 Oak Town Rangers	17	3	1	13	19	59	-40	10
10 Redbridge Sports	17	1	1	15	17	59	-42	4

Monday 26th March
Today was a tough day at work, no I didn't have any difficult classes, I was just carrying the hangover from Hell and as soon as the buzzer signalled the end of the school day I was off.

Smith Says
Yesterday was our first defeat in what seems like ages and it was a game we didn't deserve to lose. The boys were superb, each and every one of them, and they can all hold their heads up high. I would like to give a

special mention to Luke who despite missing a penalty needs to remember that without his goals we wouldn't be where we are today. So no excuses and no apportioning blame, we gave it everything but just came up short and we move on. League leaders Tamworth suffered a comprehensive 6-2 defeat to a resurgent Langton Reds so it's still all to play for. Thankfully we've got a game this Sunday when we play bottom side Redbridge Sports so we've got an early opportunity to get back to business and hopefully winning ways.

Parkfield 1 Dalworth United 0
Squad: Billy Stevens, Stevie Carr, Jimmy Smith, Nick Sheppard, Billy Belafonte, Alex Hayes, Adam Morley, Aidan Hayes, Ben Padgham © Luke Pilbeam, Bobby Webster, Danny Hall, Brian Haugh, Charlie Fisher
Man of the Match: The squad.

Tuesday 27th March
Tonight was an incredible training session. I don't think I've seen the boys so 'at it'. They ran harder, trained harder and tackled harder as I was to find out when Aidan challenged me during a small-sided game at the end. The best way I can describe it with regards to the pain I felt on the impact is I know how James Caan's ankle felt when Kathy Bates hit it with the mallet in *Misery*. Aidan was mortified and must have apologised about a hundred times. He helped me up but I couldn't stand and fell back to the floor staying there for 20 minutes with my ankle throbbing. Driving home was very painful.

Wednesday 28th March
The following day my right ankle is black and blue and I struggled all day as I limped around the school to a soundtrack of sarcastic comments from pupils and colleagues alike. I spent most of the day stuck in my chair with my leg elevated giving the whiteboard a swerve in favour of handouts. Delegation was the name of the game as I had my students running about fetching and carrying books. I also managed to get my colleagues to do my break and lunch duties and I certainly owe a few favours after today.

Friday 30th March - Dalworth News
Parkfield 1 Dalworth United **Under 15**s 0 - Dalworth's title hopes took a dive when they suffered a rare defeat at the hands of Parkfield. Ben Mercer scored the only goal of the game to condemn Dalworth to a rare defeat.

Saturday 31st March
Gaffer rings to find out how my ankle is and just to check in but we end up on the phone for a hour just chatting about the events of the past

week. Neither of us know what to expect tomorrow regarding the players' mentality and we know we are going to have to be on the ball. Before the tragic events of the previous week the boys were seemingly unbeatable but last Sunday they looked so vulnerable and that is what we need to turn around. We both agreed that training was really good on Tuesday and that the boys looked back to their best but how they will react to last week's defeat is another matter. Gaffer is very reflective and I'm happy to let him bounce things off of me. I've seen a real change in The Gaffer this season he is a changed character.

"See you tomorrow Si."
"You will Gaffer."

CHAPTER TEN

APRIL

"You can achieve anything if you believe"

Sunday 1st April - Dalworth United vs Redbridge Sports

Today may be a game against the team cemented at the bottom of the table but it's a really important one in the context of the season and what we may or may not achieve. In reality the only anxious people in the camp are the management duo because the players are back to their cocky, jovial, mischievous best. Adam strolls into the changing room looking immaculate in his seemingly pressed tracksuit he also has a pair of bright purple Beats by Dr Dre headphones which he has covered with a massive beanie which sits precariously perched on his head. Adam removes his beanie hat to reveal a 'man bun' and is immediately met with a torrent of abuse

"Leave it out Adz!"
"Women's game is this afternoon Adz?"
"Adz you tart!"
"Adz you bumder!"
"Adz you look a right w**ker!"
"You're just a sh*t Andy Carroll, sh*t Andy Caaaaarroll..."

Ben grabs a pair of scissors from the first aid box and threatens to remove it for Adam. Adam shoots off to the toilet to remove the hairband before Ben can give him an impromptu haircut.

Gaffer calls for everyone's attention but notices a gap in the changing room. Ben points to the showers and everyone silently makes their way over to the small cubicle. Ben grabs the closed shower curtain to reveal Billy B munching on an Egg and Bacon McMuffin while crouched in the corner of the shower. Billy looks guiltily at his bemused teammates and offers up an insincere "Oops".

Gaffer is the first one to burst into uncontrollable laughter as any concerns we had are lost in a sea of smiles and laughter. Billy finishes his McMuffin and then stands up, wipes his mouth with a serviette, lifts his head up high, launches the McDonald's bag and its contents into the bin and walks out of the shower. Then, in his poshest voice, addresses his team mates:

"Excuse me Gentleman I have a match to prepare for".

That is it. The whole changing room is rocking with hysterical laughter and our opponents next door must wonder what kind of weird team talk is taking place. Billy B it appears has just been afforded 'Legend' status from his teammates. Poor old Gaffer is really knocked out of his train of thought and after going through the team accepts defeat to the antics of Billy B and simply says: "Have fun boys."

It's a really good warn-up full of smiles, laughter, focus and a high intensity. Gaffer looks at me while we are watching the keep-ball session and nods. "Nothing's stopping these boys today Si."

"I think you could be right Gaffer"

Gaffer is going with a very attacking 3-4-3 formation today.

Starting Line-up

Billy Stevens

Jimmy Smith Nick Sheppard Billy Belafonte

Ben Padgham © Alex Hayes Aidan Hayes Brian Haugh

Charlie Fisher Luke Pilbeam Bobby Webster

Subs: Danny Hall, Adam Morley, Stevie Carr

Gaffer's attacking formation leaves the team in no doubt that we are going for it today and within the first ten minutes we have carved out three clear cut chances and hit the post twice. Redbridge are struggling to string two passes together but they are forming a formidable defensive brick wall which the boys are struggling to break down. Billy S is virtually a spectator and in the end he decides to play as a sweeper just so that he can play some part in the game. We are creating chance after chance but just cannot convert one as Redbridge have all eleven players camped out in their penalty area. The boys are now snatching at shots and passing when a shot is on and shooting when a pass is the better option. They are also adopting a hit and hope approach as they frantically search for the lead. The woodwork, some inspired goalkeeping and dogged defending mean we somehow end the half at 0-0. The boys dejectedly troop off at half time. Even Ben who is the most optimistic of people is looking down.

Gaffer waits until everyone is back in the changing room and then claps his hands to get everyone's attention.

"Right everyone up on their feet!"

The boys look at each other curious as to what is going to happen.

"Right, close your eyes - and don't worry Billy I won't nick your Haribos."

Nervous laughs are suppressed as the boys look genuinely worried at what Gaffer has planned.

"Right, take a big deep breath and hold it."

The boys follow The Gaffer's instructions purely out of respect.

The Gaffer repeats the breathing exercises and then in a voice alien to The Gaffer (Surprisingly soft and reassuringly calm):

"Right I want you to visualise yourself scoring or making a match winning pass or game saving tackle."

The boys again follow The Gaffer's instruction and I notice smiles slowly appearing on the boys' faces as they imagine their match-winning impact on the game and you visibly see the stress disappearing.

"Right, we are going 3-5-2 second half and all I want you to do is keep calm and play the way I know you can. The goals will come."

Gaffer pulls another surprise by subbing Billy S for Danny and Stevie and Adam are on for Jimmy and Bobby.

Second half line-up
Danny Hall
Stevie Carr Nick Sheppard Billy Belafonte
Ben Padgham © Alex Hayes Adam Morley Aidan Hayes Brian Haugh
Charlie Fisher Luke Pilbeam

Gaffer pulls a disappointed Billy S to one side and after a quick chat the keeper is smiling again.

The second half sees the boys straight out of the traps and immediately on the attack. Whereas in the first half they seemed to be trying too hard now they seem really relaxed. The first goal comes five minutes into the half when Adam wins the ball in the middle and chips a lofted pass over the Redbridge defence. It is a straight race between the goalkeeper and Charlie and there is only going to be one winner. Charlie chips the stranded keeper to give us a lead. The goal has the desired effect as not only does it fill our boys with confidence but it means Redbridge have to come at us and that gives us space to exploit. Our midfield dynamos the triple AAA's (Alex, Aidan & Adam) are running riot and our opponents have no answer to them. The next attack sees us extend our lead when Aidan sprays a pass out to the right. Ben receives the ball, cuts inside the left back and drills a low cross into the box which Charlie manages to get a toe to, sliding the ball into the net. Brian then drifts inside to pick up a short pass from Alex and then goes on a mazy run beating three defenders before calmly slotting the ball past the Redbridge keeper.

This totally deflates Redbridge who concede a further three goals. The biggest surprise is Luke doesn't get on the scoresheet as Charlie completes his first ever hat-trick with a close range drive and then grabs a fourth with a header from Brian's corner.

There is just enough time for the customary Billy B free kick after Adam is clattered on the edge of the box.

The boys are all smiles at the end and Ben seeks out The Gaffer at the final whistle.

"Change of career Gaffer?"
"What?"
"I didn't have you down for a sports psychologist!"
"Did you like that then?"
"It was different, but very effective."
"You could see everyone was so tense so I just wanted to chill everyone out"
"Fair play Gaffer it worked."
"Cheers Skip!"

It was my turn next.

"You sly old dog, you kept that in the locker didn't you?"

Gaffer is absolutely beaming from ear to ear.

"Up there for thinking, down there for dancing" he says tapping his forehead.

I haven't got a reply for that and just replicate The Gaffer's beaming smile.

The smiles are back and so are the winning ways, happy days.

Results from Sunday 1st April
Parkfield 3 - 2 Langton Reds
Dalworth United 6 - 0 Redbridge Sports
Dunstable Colts 0 - 4 Kingsbridge

Team	P	W	D	L	F	A	GD	Pts
1 Tamworth United	17	11	2	4	47	28	19	35
2 Dalworth United	14	9	1	4	37	23	14	28
3 Kingsbridge	14	9	1	4	35	22	13	28
4 Phoenix Rovers	14	9	0	5	44	22	24	27
5 Langton Reds	15	8	0	7	58	35	23	24
6 Dunstable Colts	12	7	1	4	22	20	2	22
7 Leighbridge Lions	15	7	1	7	33	34	-1	22
8 Parkfield	14	7	0	7	24	28	-4	21
9 Oak Town Rangers	17	3	1	13	19	59	-40	10
10 Redbridge Sports	18	1	1	16	17	65	-48	4

Smith Says
Today we moved up to second place and put ourselves forward as genuine title contenders and while Tamworth still hold a seven point lead over us, the next three teams, us, Kingsbridge and Phoenix all have three games in hand. I was so proud of the boys today Once again they showed an incredible inner strength and played like champions. I'm not going to make any predictions but we will be giving it our all in the next five games. Next week we have the final of the David Dudley Challenge Cup versus the unbeaten Bridgeham at Petersfield Park home of Cheltenham Saracens FC. We will meet at the Rec at 10am for the 1pm kick off.
The Gaffer

Dalworth United 6 Redbridge Sports 0
Squad: Billy Stevens, Jimmy Smith, Nick Sheppard, Billy Belafonte, Ben Padgham © Alex Hayes, Aidan Hayes, Brian Haugh, Charlie Fisher, Luke Pilbeam, Bobby Webster, Danny Hall, Adam Morley, Stevie Carr
Scorers: Fisher 4, Haugh, Belafonte
Man of the Match: Fisher

Tuesday 3rd April
Training is buzzing tonight and it's all because of our cup final on Sunday. The boys are confident but under no illusion that it is going to be our toughest game of the season. I made the mistake of saying that I was really looking forward to the occasion and was immediately shot down by Ben who countered with: "We win the game Si and then we enjoy the occasion."

I sheepishly replied "Of course Ben". Gaffer jumped in and said "Go easy on him Ben, it's his first final!" "Sorry Si" came Ben's reply before ushering his teammates off for a warm-up. I felt quite relieved at my reprieve but then realised they were bloody patronising me. Gaffer collared me once the boys had gone off.

"You should know better Si, they are desperate to win the final."
"I know that now!"
"Nothing too heavy tonight Si, I don't want anyone getting injured."

He paused and then laughed "And that includes us too!"

The rest of the session seems to fly past and Gaffer gathers everyone in at the end.

"10am here Sunday morning I've got a surprise for you."

Everyone looks at Jimmy hoping to get a clue but Jimmy just screws his face up and shrugs his shoulders.

"Tracksuits boys."
"Gaffer, can we wear shirts and ties?" asks Ben.
"And then put our tracksuit tops on for the warm up?"

Gaffer looks at me for my input and I nod in agreement.

"Ok boys, it's your cup final"

Gaffer sends the boys off but not before they have put all the balls, bibs and cones in The Gaffer's car. Gaffer chucks Jimmy his car keys and tells him and Nick to wait in the car.

Gaffer looks like a kid waiting to see Santa and is bouncing about from one leg to the other. I'm intrigued but don't have long to wait because as soon as Nick and Jimmy are out of ear shot Gaffer blurts out:
"I've hired a luxury coach for Sunday for players and families. We are going to the Old Maid for breakfast and then onto the ground. I'll ring all the parents to make them aware but we'll make it a very special occasion"
I quickly interject: "Win the game first, and then we enjoy the occasion afterwards."

"Of course Si, of course."

Wednesday 4th April
Happy birthday to me, happy birthday to me, happy birthday dear Simon, happy birthday to me

Thursday 5th April

No managers' meeting for us tonight, it's my birthday meal at the Mexican restaurant Conchitas in town. The Sheppards and The Smiths are apparently taking over the restaurant, not sure how but imagine my surprise when we get there and all the boys are there. We take over the room at the back and with family and friends there are 41 of us. Let's just say it got messy but the highlights were:

1. The Gaffer vs Billy B Habanero Pepper Challenge.
2. Me downing five Mezcals in a row.
3. The Gaffer vs Billy B Ghost Chilli Challenge.
4. Adz dressed as Clint Eastwood ala The Good, the Bad and the Ugly, which was a good description for the nights events.
5. Alex and Aidan challenging me to the Tequila Suicide Challenge - snort salt, drink a shot and squeeze lime in your eye. I don't know which was worse 1) Accepting the challenge from two 15-year-olds or 2) Losing to two 15-year-olds.
6. Me vs The Gaffer Tequila Slammer Challenge - five slammers in a row.
7. The entire restaurant chanting 'lightweight, lightweight' at me.

The food was lovely, the worm in the Mezcal that I swallowed was alright, the company was delightful but the hangover the following morning was debilitating and for the first time in my teaching career, I'm ashamed to confess, I threw a sickie. Yes I am a lightweight of the lightest kind. In fact Ben had called me Sir Light of Lightweight from Lightweightenstein at the restaurant. I hope it doesn't stick.

Friday 6th April - Dalworth News

Dalworth United **Under 15**s 6 Redbridge Sports 0

Dalworth got back to winning ways after last week's defeat putting six second half goals past bottom side Redbridge Sports. Striker Charlie Fisher grabbed four goals with Brian Haugh and Billy Belafonte chipping in with one apiece. Dalworth now turn their attentions to their David Dudley Challenge Cup Final on Sunday when they face Bridgeham at Petersfield Park home of Cheltenham Saracens FC, kick off 1pm.

Saturday 7th April

Gaffer rings about 1pm and I already know what's coming.
"Fancy a pint and a quick chat about tomorrow?"
"Where?"
"The Old Maid."
"Just a pint?"
"Promise!"

Forty minutes later I'm sitting in the Old Maid with a pint of Cherry Beer, as chosen by Gaffer, sitting in front of me. Luckily I'm not driving because my wife kindly dropped me off on her way to her friend's house. I'm now on first name terms with the staff and I really feel at home here. I can see a time in the future when The Gaffer and I are propping up the bar, pints of real ale in our hands, stroking our beards and discussing the density and flavour of the latest guest ale with our fellow members of CAMRA. Gaffer brings me back to the present and reality.

"What are your thoughts on tomorrow Si?"
"With regards to what?"
"Starting line-up, formation, tactics, what would you go for?"
"How about a 4-3-3 formation, Billy S, Stevie, Jimmy, Nick, Billy B in defence. Alex, Aidan and Adam in the middle and Ben, Luke and Bobby up top?"

The Gaffer is screwing his face up so I can tell that he disagrees.

"I was thinking of going 3-5-2, they are really strong in the middle and they play the same formation. I'm thinking of matching them like for like."
"Yeah that makes sense. What about the starting line up?"
"Billy S in goal, Danny, Nick and Billy B at the back. Ben, Alex, Adam, Aidan and Bobby in the middle and Luke and Charlie up top."
"I can see the logic."
"Another pint Si?"
"One more can't hurt I suppose..."

One more didn't hurt but the three afterwards did and despite me trying Strawberry and Rhubarb beer as well as the good old Toffee Apple cider the consumption of four of my five a day was far outweighed by the effects of lunchtime drinking which I have never been good at.

I foolishly rang my wife to pick me up after turning down a lift from The Gaffer. My wife text me to say she was in the car park so I quickly ran to the loo and then said my goodbyes to who as usual had taken the five pints in his stride. Actually he was on his sixth as he waited for his lift. Just as I was leaving the pub I received another text saying: "You coming or what?" As soon as I sat down in the car I was bombarded with questions:

"How many did you have?"
"Did you mix your drinks?"
"You know you can't do lunchtime drinking!"
"You're such a lightweight!"

I replied to all my wife's questions with:

"Five darling."
"I did honey."
"Yes, I know, beautiful."
"Yes, I am, gorgeous."

Did you spot my deliberate attempt at flattery? To be fair it did work and I used my usual tried and tested diversionary tactic of grabbing Faith as soon as I got in and going on a long walk. Once again I foolishly forgot to use the loo before I left and on my return was bursting for the toilet.

To my surprise awaiting me on my return was not another interrogation, instead a sirloin steak in a mustard sauce with thick cut homemade chips and mushrooms and tomatoes. To top off this picture of perfection was a freshly uncorked Merlot waiting. My nostrils were dancing to the delightful smells and I could almost taste the food before it hit my mouth.

Life is good.

Sunday 8th April - Bridgeham vs Dalworth United

I'm awake at 6am and I've got butterflies in my stomach. I am the only one in the house awake but ten minutes later my phone flashes at me and The Gaffers name precedes a text message which simply reads "Cup Final Day" This is a new experience for me as last year I was on the peripheral so witnessed the cup final victories from the sidelines along with the other parents, but today is totally different because this year I'm in the dugout. Faith gets a shorter than usual Sunday walk due to the fact that I'm desperate to get everything sorted out for today and by 7:10am I'm back home with newspapers, much to Faith's disgust.

'Cup Final Day'. I pity the kids of today they don't experience the cup finals like we did. No FA Cup Question of Sport or It's a Knockout. No interviews with the team at their hotel in the morning or en-route to Wembley on the team bus. No interviews with the fans. Gone are the days of a 3pm kick off nowadays it's a 5:30 kick off with little or no build up. I make a note to self to take in every last second of the day and enjoy the experience, a winning experience of course, sorry Ben. I'm reading the Sunday newspapers and settling down with a pot of coffee and I can't believe Nick isn't up. I'm like an excited dad at Christmas waiting for the kids to open their presents and I want him to wake him up. I'm already clock-watching and it isn't even 7:30am. There are still over five hours to kick off. Nick finally rises at 8:15 and is as calm as they come unlike me who cannot contain his excitement and I bombard him:

"Cup final day!"
"Excited?"
"I couldn't sleep!"
"Fancy a fry up?"

Nick yawns, stretches and then casually replies:

"No that's OK Dad I'm going to have Porridge and Blueberries and a fruit smoothie."

I feel a bit let down by Nick's less than enthusiastic response.

"Don't worry Dad, I've got a lot of running around to do today."
Nick's smile puts the smile back on my face.
"Good idea Son"

Nick's phone starts ringing.

"Alright Ben" and off he goes.

It's now 8:30am and we've got four and a half hours to kick off and 90 minutes to the meet and I'm pacing up and down the kitchen wandering what to do next. In the end I sit down with another coffee and watch last night's Match of the Day but despite a pulsating Manchester derby and boring Merseyside derby I'm not taking the games in and all thoughts are of the final. My phone springs into life and it's The Gaffer again asking if I can get there a bit earlier. I'm glad to take him up on his offer. I give Nick a shout that we are leaving at 9:30 but he tells me not to worry as Ben will pick him up.

I get to the Rec at 9:40 and The Gaffer is already there alongside a luxurious 52-seater coach. It is really impressive and Jimmy has already customised it with a big homemade Dalworth United banner in the back window. Within five minutes of the first family arriving, the Stevens, all the boys and their families have arrived and as requested, are in white shirts, red ties, black trousers and black shoes. Headphones and earphones are draped around necks but the boys still look the business. Gaffer gives the signal to board the coach and the boys scramble for the back.

It's a short drive to the Old Maid (Are we playing a cup final or going on a session?) and when we get to the pub the function room is all laid out and breakfast is being served up of scrambled eggs, poached eggs or beans on toast. Gaffer seeks out Billy B to advise him it's an either or choice and not all three. Billy smiles and pats his stomach: "Not today Gaffer!" It's a very relaxed atmosphere and players and parents tuck into the buffet breakfast.

There are pots of tea and coffee available but one or two parents are already having a cheeky pint. Alex and Aidan catch The Gaffer's attention:

"Fancy a whisky to calm the nerves Gaffer?" Gaffer pre-empts where this is going and delivers a curt "No I don't - and you don't either!"

It's such a chilled atmosphere that it feels more like a social gathering than a cup final day. Gaffer brings the players together and they sit facing him while he gives a quick teamtalk at the pub. Then we are ready to board the coach for our final destination: Cheltenham Saracens FC. It's an interesting journey and we are attracting the attentions of passers-by as they try to peek through the tinted windows to see who the occupants of the coach are.

I wouldn't say the boys were nervous but they are quieter than usual but also seem extremely focused, again as usual. Before we know it the parents are going through the turnstiles. £3 adults and £1 children (0-16) and we are going through the players' entrance.

We have been allocated the away changing room but it's still bigger and better than we are used to. We aren't the only game here today as there are three finals, a 10:00am kick off (U13s) us at 1pm (**Under 15**s) and a 4:00pm kick off (U16') and on our arrival the changing rooms are just being tidied up so we take a stroll out onto the pitch and the boys take this opportunity to take a few selfies.

Playing in a stadium in a cup final to a bigger crowd than usual can have a detrimental effect on players and the nerves can really kick in. Our boys still look very calm at the moment but I'm sure the adrenaline and nerves are starting to surface.

The Gaffer is nowhere to be seen but he is in the changing room hanging out the players' kit and training gear. The shirts are on the hangers provided and the rest is neatly folded and laid out. I go looking for The Gaffer and when I find him in the changing room the first thing I notice is that there are 15 sets of kit laid out.

"Fifteen sets of kit, have we made a new signing?"
"No you div, Johnny is on the bench."
"What, but he hasn't even trained let alone played?"
"He's not going to play but I want him to be part of the day."
I nod. "That's a really nice touch Gaffer."
"Yeah he played his part getting us here so he deserves to be included in the squad."

Gaffer sends me out to get the boys in and they quickly shuffle into the changing room. The Gaffer has put the team up and the boys locate their squad number and go and sit in their allocated spot.

The team is as follows:
1 Billy Stevens
2 Danny Hall
3 Billy Belafonte
4 Alex Hayes
5 Nick Sheppard
6 Adam Morley
7 Ben Padgham (c)
8 Aidan Hayes
9 Luke Pilbeam
10 Charlie Fisher
11 Bobby Webster
Subs:
12.Stevie Carr
13 Jimmy Smith
14 Brian Haugh
15 Johnny Day

The boys spread themselves out in the changing room, appreciating the ample space and soaking up the atmosphere. Despite a few nerves they still can't resist the 'bants'.

"Here Bill look, two pegs one for your clothes and one to hang your McDonalds on!"
"P*ss off!"
"Adz do you need my hanger for all your clothes?"
"Yeah well you don't need to hang Primani gear up do ya, just toss it anywhere!"
"They've got loads of spare loo rolls in the bogs."
"They heard Bill was coming!"
"Look Johnny's got his own spot"
Stevie points at the physio's table.
"Yeah, well I saw your spot outside.......the bench!"

It's all lighthearted and noone takes offence. Gaffer is closely examining the team sheet. He half changed his mind from his original formation and is now going with a 3-4-1-2, which switches to 3-5-2 when we are defending:

Billy S
Danny Nick Billy B
Ben Alex Aidan Bobby
Adam
Luke Charlie

Gaffer leaves the boys to get changed and we go and stand outside the changing room.

"Think they are ready Si?"
"Hope so Gaffer."
"Have we done all we can in our preparations?"
"I think so Gaffer."

I can't resist it: "Fail to prepare, prepare to fail!"

Gaffer smiles and adds: "Yeah, the rest is up to them."

The boys are out and after a few waves to family and friends we are going through the warm-up with Oasis' *Don't Look Back in Anger* blaring out of the PA . The ground is starting to fill up nicely. Well the parents are coming out of the bar. The warm-up is punctuated with a few errors and you can see the boys examining the crowd and surroundings. You can tell the nerves are kicking in. This morning went so slowly and it dragged, now it feels that the seconds are whizzing by. The music comes to a halt and the announcer gives out both line ups before *London Calling* by The Clash takes over the airwaves. We make our way back to the changing rooms and I wave at my wife before we enter the tunnel. The boys looked the part in the warm-up but I remind myself that games aren't won in a warm-up.

Gaffer grabs everyone's attention and gives his final words:
"No regrets boys. Don't leave anything in the changing room. Don't be afraid to express yourself on the pitch. Work hard for each other and just give it your best shot. That's all I ask."

There's a knock on the changing room door and the ref's assistant is calling us out to do a boot check. Both teams are lined up in the tunnel and just as we are about to go out Ben turns around to his teammates:

"This is it boys, we've worked hard for this, let's go to work!"

This statement literally sends a chill down my spine and I turn to Gaffer "They are ready."

Raucous applause from the bigger-than-anticipated crowd greets both teams as they make their way onto the pitch and they line up for the handshake. We shake hands with the Bridgeham management and take our place in the away dugout. I nudge The Gaffer and point out the size difference between us and Bridgeham who look like they have had their players in growbags. Not one of them look to be under six feet and at least five of them are bigger than our tallest player Billy S.

"Not a lot we can do now Si, unless you've got some stilts!"
"True Gaffer."
"Just need to keep the ball on the deck."

Kick-off
Right from the start Bridgeham are hitting a few 'testers'. Thankfully, for our defence, they are overhitting the longball and Billy is a grateful recipient. However Danny and Billy are dropping in alongside Nick to cover loose second balls and this means Ben and Bobby are covering the ball into the fullback position and not giving us options on the wings.

The boys are trying to press high and not let their opponents have comfortable possession on the ball but the quick longball is forcing them back. We then start trying to hit Luke and Charlie quickly but they are being swamped by the three Bridgeham centrebacks and the midfield isn't getting close enough to our forwards to support them. To be fair neither side is making the ball stick in the final third and the game is becoming quite a dour spectacle and not the final we had hoped for. Gaffer learns into me.

"Both teams are cancelling each other out."
"Yeah there's no space out there."
"We need to get Ben and Bobby wide and get the ball to them."
"That might be the key."
"I'll say one thing Si, whoever scores first may go on to win this."
I look at The Gaffer and give him a "Did you really say that" look.

Brigdeham then win the first corner of the match and we are lucky to get away with it as Billy B lets his man go and the resulting header flies inches over the bar.

With half time approaching Gaffer says:
"I'm changing this at half time otherwise we will end up losing to a set piece. We've got to focus on our strengths and not concentrate on our weaknesses. If we don't change anything then nothing changes"

Half-time 0-0

Gaffer quickly gets his troops together.

"I'm going to change it up. We know they are dangerous in the air but we've got to play to our strengths. I'm going four at the back to cover the long ball and to push Ben and Brian wider and further forward. They are killing us in the air so I want low crosses from the by-line. Luke, Charlie, I still want you to press high and stop them hitting the longball. We have to play the game on the deck, that's how we win this game."

The knock on the door signals the officials are ready for the second half and Stevie, Jimmy and Brian are introduced in place of Danny, Adam and Bobby.

Second Half line Up

Billy S

Stevie Jimmy Nick Billy B

Ben Alex Aidan Brian

Luke Charlie

The change has the desired effect and Nick and Jimmy are coping with the longball with one attacking and the other dropping off for the second ball. Ben and Brian are staying out wide and seeing more of the ball, but Luke and Charlie still aren't getting any joy from the physical Bridgeham defence who are all over them. Our first real effort comes from a Billy B free kick which is tipped over the bar and then Brian hits a long range effort which goes just wide of the post. Alex is then adjudged to have fouled the Bridgeham number ten when it seemed as though he had won the ball fairly. From the free kick which is delivered to the far post the ball is headed back across the goal and the faintest of touches takes it past Billy to give our opponents the lead.

The boys don't let their heads drop and come back strongly and Luke dummies a throughball which runs through to Charlie. He plays the ball back into the path of Luke. He hits a first time shot and it beats the goalkeeper but comes crashing back off the post. Charlie then chests a cross from Ben back to Aidan who hits a low shot which is tipped round the post for a corner.

Billy swings the resulting corner over. Nick loses his marker and heads a powerful header down into the ground and past the 'keeper but just as we are about to celebrate the goal a defender heads the ball over the bar. I look at The Gaffer and he has his head in his hands in disbelief. I'm starting to believe that it's not our day and just as that thought enters my head

Bridgeham grab a second and it's a goal worthy of winning any game. A long ball from the right is headed clear by Jimmy and before it bounces Bridgeham's captain volleys an unstoppable shot past Billy. Gaffer looks at his watch and Bobby replaces Billy B with ten minutes left and he switches to a 3-4-3 formation in a last ditch attempt to salvage something.

Billy S
Stevie Jimmy Nick
Ben Alex Aidan Brian
Luke Charlie Bobby

The boys again come back strongly but when Charlie hits a volley against the crossbar it just confirms that today is not our day.

"How long lino?"
"About a minute."
"OK sub please."

I look puzzled at The Gaffer especially when he summons Johnny off of the bench.

Gaffer smiles and says "Go on Johnny, grab us a couple."

Johnny replaces Charlie and although he doesn't touch the ball he gets his minute on the pitch. I nod to The Gaffer "Nice one, you've made his day."

The final whistle brings the expected mad celebrations from the Bridgeham players, management and parents, but not before their management have shaken our hands and then they are off. A few of our boys have slumped to the ground and I spot a few tears but Ben is picking up the boys and dragging them off to where our parents are congregated. Ben and the players applaud their parents and the gesture is reciprocated. The mutual applause is genuine and heartfelt and The Gaffer and I join the boys in thanking the parents.

The presentation is the anticipated long, drawn out occasion that you expect after you have lost. The boys collect their runners up medals and then are magnanimous in defeat applauding our opponents as they collect their winners' medals and trophy. At this stage all you want to do is collect your medal and retreat to the sanctuary of the changing room where you can suffer with the rest of your team mates and where you don't have to hide your pain and emotions. We begin the slow trudge to the changing rooms while Bridgeham sing, dance and celebrate on the pitch against a backdrop of clicking cameras and phones.

We know we have at least ten minutes before we have to listen to the Bridgeham celebrations through the walls of the changing room. The Gaffer uses this time to deliver his take on things:

"I'm so proud of you today boys and while the score suggests otherwise, you're winners in my eyes. I don't think there is anything more you could have done and it really was just one of those days and today belongs to Bridgeham. I know you're hurting now but I want you to use that hurt. The cup is gone but now we begin the fight to retain our league title so get your heads up boys because tomorrow we go again."

The Gaffer's call to arms receives a round of applause from the boys and rightly so because his speech has had the desired effect and although today we are the losing changing room, the boys know that they can still finish the season as winners. We go round the room and personally thank all the boys.

"Well done Ben." Ben looks up to me from the bench.
"Cheers Si, did you enjoy the occasion?"
"No I didn't, did you?"
"No I'm proud of everyone and Gaffer was right we gave it everything, but I'm left with a runners up medal when I wanted a winners one and an experience that left me deflated."
I come back with: "We live to fight another day though Ben"
(I have no idea where that came from)
"No Si, we live to get it right next time."

We shake hands at this point because what do you say?

"Not everyone can win", or "It's not all about winning" because today was all about winning and we lost. I totally believe that you have to learn to lose before you can truly appreciate winning and we've achieved that with these boys because they don't look for excuses if they lose, it's never the ref's fault or the linesman, even though they may have influenced the outcome. No, they always look at themselves first and foremost and they learn from it and move on. They want to win every game and it hurts when they don't, especially today after losing a cup final. It hurts me and Gaffer too but it's up to us to put them back together now.

When we come out of the changing rooms the parents have formed a guard of honour and the boys are applauded onto the coach. The biggest cheer though, and rightly so, goes to The Gaffer. When we are all on board Gaffer produces a microphone and addresses the coach.

"Thank you for coming today I'm sorry we didn't bring home the trophy but the boys did all that was asked of them and it just wasn't to be and in honour of their achievements I'd like to invite everyone round to mine for a barbecue in recognition of the boys' achievements. So go home, grab some alcohol and I'll see you round mine in a hour."

I turned to my wife smiling and she gave me the dreaded look, but then smiled and said: "I'll drive, you and Nick have worked hard today, but just remember: you've got work tomorrow!"
"We could get a taxi then you can have a drink too?"
"I suppose we could."
Nick interjects: "Yeah, then we can all have a drink!"
Nick is shot down with a firm and unified response: "No".

So a hour later I'm at The Gaffer's, thankfully my daughter has offered to walk Faith, and every single player and their families are in attendance and the makeshift tables that The Gaffer had put up were soon overflowing with every form of alcohol known to man (and woman). Opposite the alcohol was another table that contained an absolute mountain of meat and all the trimmings. I'd only heard about EU food mountains, now I've seen one. I certainly didn't envy the prospect of cooking it and Gaffer's face was soon bright red from slaving over an absolute beast of a barbecue.

I did offer my services but Gaffer already had some assistance in the form of Billy B, who it would seem, can not only eat food but cook it and cook it rather well. The Billy Burgers that he was creating were in big demand and had many takers. Soon the drink is flowing and the disappointment of today is fading in a sea of food and alcohol. The boys, unlike previous get-togethers, are quite subdued and they are chatting about the game and going through the key points.
"That was a lucky deflection for the first." , "The second was a worldie and on another day would have flown over the bar.", "If one of Charlie's efforts had gone in it would have changed the game."
It was interesting to hear their views and it's reassuring that they saw the game as we did. Gaffer finally calls a halt to the cooking about 6pm and grabs a bottle of whiskey and two glasses. He hands them to me and pours two very large whiskeys.

"Cheers Si."

Gaffer then gathered everyone together and thanked them for coming and then the Hayes twins stepped forward and raised their glasses signalling a toast and said:

"We may have lost today but I know Grandad would have been proud of all of us. To Grandad"

Everyone raised their glasses and Mrs Hayes, after raising her glass then went mental when she realised that the liquid in the twins' glasses had a very whiskey look to it as she soon discovered her two offspring had both downed a glass of The Gaffer's expensive Monkey Shoulder Whiskey.

"Alex, Aidan what the f**k"
"But Mum, it ain't a toast if it ain't alcoholic!" responded Alex.

Everyone burst out laughing, even the twins' mum who couldn't help chuckling at the cheek of them. As usual the evening descended in total chaos and a game of football took centrepiece with dads v sons. The dads' sole advantage is weight and physicality but when a large frame is full of a) food and b) alcohol it is no match for a) pace and b) technical ability and it is safe to say that although noone kept score it was a resounding victory for the sons.

At 9o'clock the party is still in full swing until someone, obviously one of the few sober people amongst the guests, reminds everyone else that we all had school or work (or in my case school *and* work) in the morning. At about 9:30pm the gathering drew to an end and a convoy of taxis descended on The Gaffer's abode. Gaffer was in his element and with military efficiency he was soon directing families to the taxis.
"Billy S taxi's here."
"Charlie grab your family."

I eventually got home at 11pm after helping out with the massive tidy up operation and I let Faith out in the garden. I was emotionally drained, totally stuffed, extremely tipsy and absolutely knackered. It should be pointed out that my wife was *also* pissed due to her inauguration as the chairwoman of the Dalworth Ladies Prosecco Appreciation Society, a role she gladly accepted and then took on with great vigour and dedication. Two bottles later the new chairwomen had hit the brick wall, literally, as she totally missed the front door when we got home. It had been a long day but there were many highlights.
1 The luxury coach.
2 Johnny's substitute appearance.
3 Gaffer's speech.
4 The food and drink at Gaffer's.
5 Billy B teaching Gaffer how to make a Billy Burger.
6 Billy S catching out his intoxicated dad with his "What's the time Dad?"

THE GAFFER

routine resulting in his dad spilling his drink down him and then clumsily chasing Billy round the garden.

7 Adam's Batman, Stevie's Superman and Danny's preposterous Pokemon onesies that they wore to the barbecue.

8 Ben's dad attempting to recreate Pele's overhead kick from Escape to Victory and failing miserably.

9 Ben's dad getting told off by his wife for attempting to recreate Pele's overhead kick from Escape to Victory.

10 Billy eating three gigantic Billy Burgers in quick succession (for the record, a Billy Burger consists of two beef patties, three slices of cheese, two slices of bacon, gherkins, tomato ketchup, burger sauce and mustard) and then asking Gaffer what was for pudding. Legend.

11 The Hayes twins' toast.

12 Alex Hayes startlingly good rendition of Oasis's *Wonderwall.*

13 Adam's dance moves and Charlie and Luke's attempt to copy them.

14 The newly-formed Dalworth Ladies Prosecco Appreciation Society.

The barbecue was exactly the gathering we needed after recent events and despite the fact that it got very messy it was as good a day as expected taking into account the result. Today didn't go our way but we'll regroup and go again. No treble or double this season but we still have the league to go for and I wouldn't write us off yet.

As my head hits the pillow I think tomorrow is going to be a long long day. Why do I do it to myself?

Results from Sunday 8th April
Parkfield 3 - 4 Oak Town Rangers
Kingsbridge 5 - 2 Phoenix Rovers
Langton Reds 2 - 3 Leighbridge Lions
David Dudley Challenge Cup Final
Bridgeham 2 - 0 Dalworth United

Team	P	W	D	L	F	A	GD	Pts
1 Tamworth United	17	11	2	4	47	28	19	35
2 Kingsbridge	15	10	1	4	40	24	16	31
3 Dalworth United	14	9	1	4	37	23	14	28
4 Phoenix Rovers	15	9	0	6	46	27	19	27
5 Leighbridge Lions	16	8	1	7	36	36	0	25
6 Langton Reds	16	8	0	8	60	38	22	24
7 Dunstable Colts	12	7	1	4	22	20	2	22
8 Parkfield	15	7	0	8	27	32	-5	21
9 Oak Town Rangers	18	4	1	13	23	62	-39	13
10 Redbridge Sports	18	1	1	16	17	65	-48	4

Monday 9th April

It was a bloody tough day today. Thankfully Easter has come at the right time and I haven't got work. The day started badly though when the Queen of Prosecco awoke hangover-free and infuriatingly chirpy and the tone was set from there.

"Cup of tea darling?"
"Please."
"Bacon and Egg sandwich?"
"Mmmm no I'll have cereal."

Have I missed something here, did my wedding vows say Love, Honour and take your wives hangover?

Smith Says

Well we didn't win but we gave a fantastic account of ourselves and as a manager that's all you can ask. I strongly believe we deserved to win the game and created enough chances to warrant winning. Bridgeham were a very good side and they took their chances and that was the difference. Sometimes in football you play badly but still win and sometimes you play well but lose and on those occasions you have to accept it just wasn't your day and unfortunately yesterday wasn't our day.

So it's all down to the league and yesterday's win for Kingsbridge over Phoenix Rovers means it looks like it will be a straight battle between them, us and Tamworth United for the title. We still have it all to play for and I strongly believe we are in with a good chance. It's up to us to keep going and get as many points as possible and hope it is enough.

Once again I would like to thank the parents for their support and the players for their efforts and I hope you had a good day yesterday, despite the result

Bridgeham 2 Dalworth United 0
Squad: Billy Stevens Danny Hall Billy Belafonte Alex Hayes Nick Sheppard Adam Morley Ben Padgham (c) Aidan Hayes Luke Pilbeam Charlie Fisher Bobby Webster Stevie Carr Jimmy Smith Brian Haugh Johnny Day
Man of the Match: Fisher

Tuesday 10th April

All the talk at training was of the hangovers of the mums and dads - and apparently one or two of the players - and then it switches to the remaining games as the players try to predict the points total they may or may not need. Gaffer soon puts a stop to that and reinforces his one game at a time strategy. This Sunday we face Langton Reds and we finally have a full compliment of players because Johnny Day is back training. Gaffer makes it perfectly clear to Johnny that the onus is on him to make himself available when he is ready.

The Bridgeham game is a distant memory now and all thoughts are on the Langton match. The standards The Gaffer requested at the start of the season are firmly in place and the boys are giving 110% in everything they do. When Alex misplaces a pass his brother Aidan is on his case but not in a detrimental way. He is geeing him up and everyone is doing the same. The stand-out player tonight is Luke who is on fire and Nick is having trouble containing him in the small sided game.

"For f**ks sake Luke stop moving about!"
"Sorry Nick I'm getting ready to tear the Langton defence a new one."
Gaffer looks at me with a puzzled look on his face: "What did he just say?"
I just shrug my shoulders and nod.

At the end Gaffer calls everyone in.
"Everyone OK for Sunday?" He pauses and then seeks out Johnny and awaits a response.
Johnny doesn't disappoint.
"I'm ready for battle Gaffer."
"I'll include you then Johnny."
"Cheers Gaffer."
"See you at 9:30 Sunday boys."

Wednesday 11th April
My wife shouts at me that The Gaffer is on the phone. Gaffer on the phone on a Wednesday?
 "Alright Gaffer"
"Alright Si, Si I was wondering if you could help me with Jimmy?"
"Eh?"
"Jimmy needs your help."
"What?" My mind is swimming. What is wrong? How can I help? Why can't Gaffer deal with it.?
"Si, Jimmy's got English homework on *Of Mice and Men*"
"What's the problem?"
"He's got an essay to do, the question is: 'Choose a character who you think is a victim of loneliness because of the society in which he or she lives. Write about this character, explaining the reasons for your choice'"
"OK Gaffer give me twenty minutes and I'll email some bits over to you."

"Thanks Si."
"No problem."

Friday 13th April - Dalworth News
Bridgeham 2 Dalworth United **Under 15**s 0
Dalworth fall at final hurdle. An unbeaten Bridgeham put their name on the David Dudley Challenge Trophy with a 2-0 win over Dalworth at Cheltenham Saracens FC. In a tense encounter, second half goals from Steve Curtin and Bridgeham captain Harry Coates ensured it was Bridgeham lifting the trophy. Dalworth had their chances with Luke Pilbeam and Charlie Fisher both hit the woodwork but they couldn't find a way past a resolute Bridgeham defence.

Manager Vinny Smith said after the game: "The boys can hold their heads high as they gave it their best shot but just came up short against a very good Bridgeham side. I'm proud of each and every one of the players but on the day it just wasn't to be."

Dalworth United Squad: Billy Stevens Danny Hall Billy Belafonte Alex Hayes Nick Sheppard Adam Morley Ben Padgham (c) Aidan Hayes Luke Pilbeam Charlie Fisher Bobby Webster Stevie Carr Jimmy Smith Brian Haugh Johnny Day.

Gaffer's on the phone a day early which can only mean one thing:
"Fancy a pint Si? I'm bored."
"Fancy coming round here Gaffer? I'm knackered."
"See you in 15."

Luckily I've got some whiskey in and the reason I've got whiskey in is because of The Gaffer who has educated my taste buds into the ways of the firewater. There's soon a knock at the door and I open up to see a smiling Gaffer carrying a pack of Brothers Toffee Apple Ciders. We end up sat at the kitchen table, glasses in hand drinking whiskey chasers and swigging out of bottles of toffee apple cider. Gaffer thrusts a bit of paper in my direction:

Run-in:
Dalworth United (28 points - Maximum points 40)
Langton Reds (H)
Dunstable Colts (A)
Parkfield (H)
Kingsbridge (A)
Tamworth United (35 points - Maximum points 38)
Dunstable Colts (H)

Kingsbridge (31 points - Maximum points 40)
Phoenix Rovers (A)
Dunstable Colts (H)
Dalworth United (H)
Phoenix Rovers (27 points - Maximum points 36)
Leighbridge Lions (H)
Kingsbridge (H)
Parkfield (H)

I examine the paper and look at The Gaffer puzzled.

"What happened to the one game at a time approach?"
"Sod that. We are so close I wanted to see the bigger picture."
"You don't need to be a mathematician to work out that if we win every game we are champions."
"Yeah you are right but I reckon it could boil down to our last game."
"No good worrying about that though if we lose our next three games!"
"I reckon ten points will do it."
"Yeah but we have to aim for twelve"
"I think we are going to do it Si."
"Calm down tiger and have another whiskey."

We both start laughing and have another drink. Don't tell him, but I think he could be right.

Sunday 15th April - Dalworth United vs Langton Reds
The first game of the run-in and with neither of our title rivals playing, a chance to get closer to both of them. That is of course if we win, but defeat could leave us with an impossible task. Gaffer has all 15 players at his disposal but his starting line up is an indication of his intent and he is going for it with a 3-5-2 formation with three defenders on the bench.

Starting line up
Billy Stevens
Stevie Carr Nick Sheppard Jimmy Smith
Ben Padgham (c) Alex Hayes Adam Morley Aidan Hayes Bobby Webster
Charlie Fisher Luke Pilbeam
Subs: Danny Hall, Billy Belafonte, Johnny Day, Brian Haugh

While there may be a greater offensive intent the messages to the boys are still the same:
1. One game at a time boys.
2. Express yourselves and don't be afraid to take chances.

3. Work hard and work for each other.
4. Enjoy yourself.

He then stops and his manner changes as he raises a fist and adds: "Who would have thought four games into the league campaign that we would find ourselves challenging for the title? We've worked bloody hard to get here and I don't want you to fall at the final hurdle. I don't want us to have any regrets about those first four games. I don't want to hear any 'what ifs, or 'if onlys'. We fight through to the end."

Now cast your mind back to The Gaffer's inaugural speech which fell flatter than a pancake. Well this time the changing room is rocking and the boys are up for the challenge. The noise that emanates from the room is enough to unsettle our opponents. Fists are waved, the Hayes twins head-butt reappears, faces are screwed up and contorted and Billy B lets go one of the loudest farts in history. This is a sign for our warriors to leave the changing room, a changing room which is fast filling up with an odious gas.

"F**king hell Bill, what you been eating?"
"You nervous Bill?"
"That's jank Bill."
Bill stands up and does his best King Leonidas impression, roaring "Dalworth! Prepare for battle! For tonight, WE DINE IN HELL!"

The smiles, laughter - and disgust - are soon replaced by the stern and focused looks of a set of boys on a mission. Nerves? not these boys. Straight from the kick off they are flying. Ten passes later we are one-nil up and the first time Langton touch the ball is when their goalkeeper picks it out of the net. Our opponents are well and truly on the back foot and they don't create one chance in the first half. After Luke's opening goal he hits the post twice while his striking partner Charlie hits the bar and has one cleared off the line.

The Langton 'keeper is the busiest player on the pitch and pulls off three good saves from Ben, Bobby and Alex. How the score remains 1-0 is beyond me and The Gaffer can't help but be pessimistic: "This has got sucker punch written all over it..." But any doubts The Gaffer has are kept from the players.

Half time 1-0
"Keep doing what we are doing and we don't lose the game. They can't defend like that for another 45 minutes. Score the second goal and it's game over"

Gaffer makes four changes, surprisingly, and gives Johnny a second half start and gives Danny a half in goal.

Second half line up
Danny Hall
Johnny Day Nick Sheppard Billy Belafonte
Brian Haugh Alex Hayes Adam Morley Aidan Hayes Bobby Webster
Charlie Fisher Luke Pilbeam

The second half is a virtuoso display from Brian who scores our second within five minutes of coming on. Alex rolls a pass out to him on the wing and he goes on a mazy run beating three players before drawing the 'keeper out and sliding the ball into the far corner. The goal breaks the Langton spirits and they fail to register a single shot on goal all game. (For the record this stat is my own and not taken from any website). Brian is having his own personal duel with the Langton defence and he hits the woodwork twice, brings two good saves from the Langton keeper and has a shot cleared off the line. The only surprise for us is that our third and final goal doesn't come until ten minutes from the end when Brian runs onto a long clearance from Danny and lobs the oncoming keeper to make it 3-0 and game over. The boys comfortably see out the game and we are a step closer to our goal. The Gaffer is looking very smug at the final whistle and says: "One down, three to go, and we are on level terms with Kingsbridge." I'm not so convinced: "It's still bloody tight though."

On a positive note we've managed to get through a game injury-free which is an added bonus.

A handshake and a quick chat with the Langton management team and we're off to the changing rooms. Gaffer is full of praise for the boys' performance today and the superlatives are flowing, especially for Brian who was on fire.

"Great game Bri."
Brian is ever the perfectionist and comes back with:
"Thanks Gaffer, but I should have had three or four today."
Gaffer looks at me and laughs. "Never satisfied are they Si?"

The boys are just taking it all in their stride and Ben as usual is he voice of reason and puts things into perspective "Three games to go Gaffer, unfinished business, jobs not done until we are top of the league,"

"Fair play Ben, point taken. See you Tuesday Boys."

Results from Sunday 15th April
Dalworth United 3 - 0 Langton Reds
Dunstable Colts 0 - 0 Parkfield

Team	P	W	D	L	F	A	GD	Pts
1 Tamworth United	17	11	2	4	47	28	19	35
2 Dalworth United	15	10	1	4	40	23	17	31
3 Kingsbridge	15	10	1	4	40	24	16	31
4 Phoenix Rovers	15	9	0	6	46	27	19	27
5 Leighbridge Lions	16	8	1	7	36	36	0	25
6 Langton Reds	17	8	0	9	60	41	19	24
7 Dunstable Colts	13	7	2	4	22	20	2	23
8 Parkfield	16	7	1	8	27	32	-5	22
9 Oak Town Rangers	18	4	1	13	23	62	-39	13
10 Redbridge Sports	18	1	1	16	17	65	-48	4

Smith Says
That was a fantastic performance from the boys. From the first whistle to the last the boys were in control of the game and we could quite easily have reached double figures. But while more goals would have been better for our goal difference, the three goals we scored today were enough to put us into second place. We are now back in pole position and today's performance suggests the boys are more than capable of retaining their title. I've said all along one game at a time and now we are three games from winning a league title. What makes this feat even more incredible is that we took one point out of a possible twelve at the beginning of season and have since taken thirty points out of a possible thirty three. What is certain is that our next three games are going to be very interesting. Next up for us is Dunstable Colts, who I believe will have a say in where the title goes as they have to play all of the top three. Lets hope it is not our title hopes they destroy and that on Sunday we can take a step closer to being in the shake up.

Dalworth United 3 Langton Reds 0
Squad: Billy Stevens, Stevie Carr, Nick Sheppard, Jimmy Smith, Ben Padgham (c) Alex Hayes, Adam Morley, Aidan Hayes, Bobby Webster, Charlie Fisher, Luke Pilbeam, Danny Hall, Billy Belafonte, Johnny Day, Brian Haugh
Scorers: Haugh 2, Pilbeam
Man of the Match: Haugh

Tuesday 17th April
The boys are very excitable at training tonight and all talk is of winning the title. Gaffer is trying to put a lid on it and keeps saying one game at a

time but it's not working. The boys aren't resting on their laurels though and are working like Trojans. The tackles are missing as no one wants to be out injured for the run in, but they are working hard and the intensity is frightening.

"Save some for Sunday boys."

Gaffer's pleas are falling on deaf ears and the boys want this title almost as badly as we do. Johnny looks as though he is struggling though and sits out the last ten minutes, thankfully it's not his ankle but his left calf and he sticks an ice pack on it.

"See you here at 9am Sunday boys."

Gaffer is the excitable one now and can't resist tempting fate when he delivers his own prediction:
"Can't see anyone stopping us Si."
"Did you really have to say that Gaffer?"

Gaffer just gives me a wicked smile and carries on packing up the equipment.

Friday 20th April - Dalworth News
Dalworth United **Under 15**s 3 Langton Reds 0: Dalworth put their cup disappointment behind them by beating Langton Reds 3-0 with a brace from Brian Haugh and a solitary strike from Luke Pilbeam. The win lifts Dalworth into second place in he league.

Saturday 21st April
Gaffer is on the phone quite late, in fact Match of the Day is starting in ten minutes.

"Bad news Si, Johnny is out with his calf and Luke has food poisoning and is doubtful."
I know it's wicked and can't resist it.
"What was that you said about no one stopping us?"
"I was thinking of opponents, not f**king injuries and food poisoning!"

I realise at that point I shouldn't have said anything and quickly try to lighten Gaffer's mood.

"Don't worry Gaffer we still have enough strength in depth."
"Yeah but it creates doubt in the team."
Now it's my time to go on the offensive.

"F**king hell Gaffer we've won games with the bare eleven this season. The boys have stood up in the face of adversity every time, they'll be fine."
"Yeah I suppose you're right. See you tomorrow Si."
"See you tomorrow Gaffer."

Well the boys seem fearless but I think the nerves are showing with Gaffer.

Sunday 22nd April - Dunstable Colts vs Dalworth United
I'm having a bloody 'mare this morning and I get to the Rec late due to Faith rolling in Fox s**t. It's a very unpleasant experience cleaning her up and it leaves me gagging through the entire cleaning process. I did ask my wife if she would do the cleaning duties due to me being late but her "No way it's your dog and you let her roll in it" response left me in no doubt as to whose job it would be.

When I eventually get to the Rec I'm pleased to see that Johnny and Luke are both there. Johnny in a spectator role but Luke is desperate to play and has made himself available.

Gaffer looks at his wristwatch when I turn up.

"What time do you call this?"
"Ten past nine and don't ask!"

To be fair he doesn't and we are on our way.

The team is already up and there's no surprises. It's a 4-4-2 formation and Luke is up top with Charlie.

Starting line up:
Billy Stevens
Stevie Carr Nick Sheppard Jimmy Smith Billy Belafonte
Ben Padgham (c) Alex Hayes Aidan Hayes Brian Haugh
Charlie Fisher Luke Pilbeam
Subs: Danny Hall, Adam Morley, Bobby Webster

For the first time all season the nerves are present and it is a quieter than usual changing room.

We are out for a longer than usual warm-up because Gaffer wants to make sure that Luke is OK and he is putting him through a little fitness test, it is understandable because Luke looks really sluggish during the warm-up. Gaffer is not sure about him and gets a second opinion.

"What do you think about Luke Si?"
"He doesn't look right does he?"

"No, do you think we should start him?"
"I don't know Gaffer, he doesn't look 100%"
"If we start him and he's struggling I can stick Bobby up top."
"Yeah we've got lots of options, there's goals all over the pitch."
"OK I'll start him."

Luke does look like he is blowing out of his arse when he comes off. Ben is the last off the pitch and he confirms what we have been saying: "Keep your eye on Luke, he doesn't look right."

Kick-off
It is a tense affair and Dunstable are on top early doors. Billy S pulls off a brilliant double save to keep the score 0-0 and this is the turning point as we start to work our way back into the game. Alex and Aidan start dominating the middle and stifling any Dunstable threat. Brian and Charlie both go close forcing fine saves from the Dunstable 'keeper and then Billy B curls a free kick narrowly over.

Then out of nowhere Dunstable take the lead when a long clearance goes over the top of our defence. Jimmy reacts first and he looks clear favourite to get to the ball but then he pulls up clutching his hamstring. The Dunstable striker now has a clear run on goal with Nick in hot pursuit. Billy S tries to narrow the angle just as Nick slides in but it's all in vain as the striker slides the ball under Billy to give Dunstable the lead. Worse still Jimmy has to come off and Gaffer has to shuffle his pack. Aidan drops into Jimmy's place and Adam takes Aidan's place in midfield.

Billy Stevens
Stevie Carr Nick Sheppard Aidan Hayes Billy Belafonte
Ben Padgham (c) Alex Hayes Adam Morley Brian Haugh
Charlie Fisher Luke Pilbeam

The look on Gaffer's face is one of pure worry but then there is also the same look on my face. Thankfully the boys aren't concerned and just crack on and when Brian puts in an inviting cross into the Dunstable box the one person you want on the end of it is Luke. How he missed the chance I will never know but he somehow managed to let it go between his legs when it would have been easier to score.

Gaffer is immediately looking at the bench and wondering what his next move might be. Luke's next move is to hit a weak shot at the Dunstable goal and you can see that he is struggling. Ben is yelling at The Gaffer and gesturing that he take Luke off. Gaffer signals back that there are two minutes of the half left and signals to wait until half time.

Half Time Dunstable Colts 1 Dalworth United 0

At half time Luke staggers to the changing room and promptly throws up, loudly. When he emerges from the toilet he slumps onto the bench and apologises to everyone. Ben as always is the diplomat and just says to Luke: "Shut up you tart, the reason we are challenging for the title is because of your goals." Luke smiles and then slumps even lower.

"Right Bobby, you take Luke's place. Danny you take over from Stevie. It's only one goal, we can get it back. Don't panic just keep playing the way we know we can and we can still win this game."

Second half

Billy Stevens

Danny Hall Nick Sheppard Aidan Hayes Billy Belafonte

Ben Padgham (c) Alex Hayes Adam Morley Brian Haugh

Charlie Fisher Bobby Webster

Gaffer is worried and when we are back in the technical area he looks at the subs, well sub, at his disposal.
"Not got a lot of options have we unless we need a defender."
"Don't worry we can still do this."

What was it I said about tempting fate? Because just as the last words leave my mouth the Dunstable number eight hits a 25-yard screamer that gives Billy no chance and we are 2-0 down. For the first time our troops look uncertain.

We are more vocal than ever as we try to rally them into a response.
"Keep going boys, we can do this."
"Keep pressing, the chances will come."

Ben then shouts something out and we both cup our ears indicating we can't ear. Then there is a break in play and Ben comes sprinting over to our side.
"Swop Brian and Bobby over."
"What?"
"Stick Brian up top and get Bobby on the left wing."
"Why?"
"Trust me."
Gaffer looks at me and shrugs his shoulders and says "What do you think?"
"Give it a go, we've got nothing to lose"

Gaffer shouts out to Brian and Bobby to swop and both go scampering to their new positions looking happier.

They usually say when you're at the bottom nothing runs for you, well today the footballing gods have decided to test our mettle. When Dunstable win a corner the ball floats invitingly into Billy's hands. Billy tries to start a quick counter attack only for the referee to pull back play as he points to the penalty spot. The fact that both teams look in puzzlement at the ref speaks volumes.

Ben asks the ref "What's that for?"

The ref points at Nick and indicates pulling. Nick argues his innocence: "He was pulling me!"

"Penalty." Nick at this point looses it and Ben has to pull him away before the ref changes the yellow card he is about to issue for a red.

"For f**ks sake" says The Gaffer out of ear shot of the ref

"This could be our f**king season gone"

Once the ref restores order Dunstable's number nine places the ball and prepares himself to take the spot-kick. He takes a long run-up and blasts the ball to Billy's left. Billy throws himself to his left and blocks the shot unfortunately he knocks the ball straight into the path of an onrushing Dunstable player who stabs the ball to Billy's right. Billy sticks out one of his long legs and blocks the shot again. This time the ball falls to Nick who blasts the ball away for a corner.

Billy is engulfed by his team mates. The injustice of the situation galvanises the whole team who are pumped up now and the resulting corner is headed clear by Nick. The ball falls to Charlie on the edge of the box and he quickly sprays it out to Bobby who is charging down the wing. Bobby races the length of the pitch and with no other option available cuts inside the Dunstable rightback and sets off towards the penalty box. He has one defender and the goalkeeper to beat but then draws both out to his left, cutting his angle down. Just as it looks like the chance has gone, he rolls a diagonal ball towards the penalty spot and Brian smashes the ball past the defender on the line. Every single one of the boys, including Billy S, make their way to the touchline by our technical area where management, players and subs celebrate the goal wildly.

"Heads on, we don't f**king lose this" shouts Ben.

From the kick-off the boys are flying into tackles, Alex and Charlie both pick up yellow cards in quick succession for robust challenges and Dunstable are visibly rocking. Charlie forces a fine save from their goalkeeper and then Nick has a header cleared off the line. It's not all one way traffic and as we push forward for the equaliser there are gaps at the back and when the Dunstable 'keeper sends a long clearance, the centre forward breaks clear and rounds Billy rolling the ball towards the empty net and then breaks off to celebrate. What he doesn't see is Danny scrambling back to clear the ball and Danny bravely slides in and hooks the ball clear but in doing so collides with the goal post. This is Danny's last action and Stevie replaces him with ten minutes to go as a precautionary measure.

The boys are desperately pushing for an equaliser as Dunstable drop deeper and deeper and when Charlie hits the post I'm beginning to think its the Brigdeham game all over again. Then Brian hits a long range effort which the Dunstable goalkeeper somehow scrambles clear and a defender knocks it off for a corner. I can see Ben asking the ref "How long?" and he turns and signals "Two minutes."

Billy swings the corner over and Nick heads the ball towards the bottom corner where it is blocked on the line Charlie gets to the ball first and it again hits the defender on the line and goes for another corner.

Both The Gaffer and I are restricted to moans and groans and for "f**ks sakes", and with every second that ticks past our title dreams are evaporating. Gaffer responds to the latest chance that goes begging by looking up to the skies and screaming: "You're f**king kidding me!"

Every single Dalworth player is in the Dunstable penalty area, with the exception of Billy B of course who is taking the kick, even Billy S has taken his place in the area amongst the other expectant players. There are now 21 players jostling in the area trying to find a inch of space. Players are bumping into each other and Gaffer is now crouched trying to get the clearest view possible. The anticipation is killing me and I'm biting my fingers and spraying the area with discarded nails. Billy swings the ball over and it lands in the middle of a melee of players. The next thing I know the boys have turned away in hot pursuit of Ben who is charging towards the technical area. I look at The Gaffer and make the most stupid statement I have ever made in my life:
"Have we scored?"

Gaffer looks at me and comes back with "Der, yes you div!"

At this point Ben dives into the technical area closely followed by the rest of his teammates.

The ref has given up trying to restart the game and blows the full time whistle which is the signal for even more frantic celebrations. It may just be a point but it feels like it is a massive point, a season-saving point in fact, and it is celebrated in such a manner. The Dunstable management work their way through the carnage of the Dalworth technical area to offer their congratulations.

"Well done, you deserved that good luck for the rest of the season."
Gaffer shakes hands and smiles "Thanks and I hope you win your last games."
The Dunstable head coach laughs and says "Yeah I bet you do!"

Back in the changing room the stories of the boys' heroics are being retold. Billy S's double save from the penalty. Brian's first goal and Ben's equaliser, this is the story I'm most interested in as I still don't know what happened.

"The corner came over and their bloke headed it and it went in off my face. Next thing I know it's in the back of the net and I was off once I realised I had got the final touch."
"Have to call you the rebound kid Ben." says Nick.
"That's one off your knee and one off your face, you're bloody lethal when you don't know what you're doing Benny Boy!"

Gaffer is quick to add: "I don't give a damn what it comes off, it went in and we still have it all to play for" and then follows up with: "Two games to go"

Amid all the celebrations sit our casualties. Luke is whisked away by his parents at the final whistle, having already changed, and doesn't look good. Jimmy has an ice pack strapped to his right leg. He is in a lot of discomfort and not walking properly and Stevie's right knee has ballooned after he collided with the post.

Gaffer scratches his head. "I'll be happy if we finish the season with 11 players at this rate."
"Luke'll be OK for next game, not sure on Jimmy or Stevie though."
"I'll ring you tomorrow Si and we'll decide on training when we know the state of play."
"OK Gaffer."
"See you Tuesday boys."

Results from Sunday 22nd April
Dunstable Colts 2 - 2 Dalworth United
Phoenix Rovers 1 - 0 Leighbridge Lions

Team	P	W	D	L	F	A	GD	Pts
1 Tamworth United	17	11	2	4	47	28	19	35
2 Dalworth United	16	10	2	4	42	25	17	32
3 Kingsbridge	15	10	1	4	40	24	16	31
4 Phoenix Rovers	16	10	0	6	47	27	20	30
5 Leighbridge Lions	17	8	1	8	36	37	-1	25
6 Langton Reds	17	8	0	9	60	41	19	24
7 Dunstable Colts	14	7	3	4	24	22	2	24
8 Parkfield	16	7	1	8	27	32	-5	22
9 Oak Town Rangers	18	4	1	13	23	62	-39	13
10 Redbridge Sports	18	1	1	16	17	65	-48	4

Smith Says

I've just looked up the definition of 'a tense affair' and it says Dunstable Colts vs Dalworth United. At 0-2 down and our opponents getting ready to take a penalty for a 3-0 lead, you would have been forgiven for thinking it was game over. But Billy's double save followed by Brian's goal to make it 2-1 set up for a very tense ending and when Ben equalised with the last 'touch' of the game it really felt like a victory.

We are now no longer in control of our destiny. Kingsbridge are in the driving seat and Tamworth have the points on the board but we won't stop fighting until its mathematically impossible. I still believe we can win the league If we can win our last two games but we will still take it one game at a time.

This coming Wednesday Kingsbridge have the chance to jump above us but their opponents Phoenix Rovers are still mathematically in with a chance as long as the top three don't win another game. Kingsbridge then face another tough game when they play our opponents of today Dunstable Colts. Our opponents next Sunday are Parkfield who were the last team to beat us in the league so I expect another tough fixture, despite their league placing. It is all so tight at the top and makes for an exciting finale, one of which I'm pleased we are still involved in.

On the injury front Jimmy suffered a pulled hamstring and will sadly miss the rest of the season. Johnny's ankle was really sore so he rested as a precaution but should be back for our final two games. Stevie has a bruised knee and we will know more in a few days and Luke was suffering the after effects of an illness but again should be available for our next game.
The Gaffer

Dunstable Colts 2 Dalworth United 2
Squad: Billy Stevens, Stevie Carr, Nick Sheppard, Jimmy Smith, Billy Belafonte, Ben Padgham (c) Alex Hayes, Aidan Hayes, Brian Haugh, Charlie Fisher, Luke Pilbeam, Danny Hall, Adam Morley, Bobby Webster
Scorers: Haugh, Padgham
Man of the Match: Stevens

Gaffer is on the phone tonight just reiterating the injury issues.
"I might call training off tomorrow Si, we've got no Jimmy and I've told Johnny, Luke and Stevie to rest up so that leaves a flat eleven for training and I don't want to risk any injuries."
"It makes sense Gaffer, at this stage of the season all we need to do is keep things ticking over."
"I'll make a decision tomorrow Si."
"Yeah makes sense."
"Alright, call you tomorrow Si."
"OK Gaffer."

Monday 23rd April
Gaffer rings while I'm marking. A glass of Shiraz is helping the pain of marking year 10's *An Inspector Calls* homework and the call comes as welcome relief, giving me an excuse to down tools.
"Alright Si."
"Alright Gaffer."
"Training's on tomorrow Si, I spoke to the boys and they want to train."
"I guessed so, Nick said the boys were up for training."
"See you tomorrow Si."
"See you tomorrow Gaffer."

Funnily enough, in my head I was saying: "Actually Gaffer, fancy a pint?" but in reality it came out as: "See you tomorrow Gaffer." I missed my opportunity so it's back to year 10's interpretations of the differences between the social classes in *An Inspector Calls*. Oh wait, Everton are playing Newcastle on Sky.

Tuesday 24th April
The pressing issue for The Gaffer is the loss of two centre backs at such a crucial stage of the season. Aidan has covered admirably but putting him at centre back means we lose a bit of bite in the midfield. We are also down to 13 fit players which again is a worry with two very important games left. With all this in mind training is a very light affair as the last thing Gaffer wants is another injury. The boys of course are not happy and they can't resist a few sarcastic comments thrown The Gaffer's way:

"Gaffer shall we use a beach ball?"
"Gaffer shall we play netball? That's non-contact."
"What about that walking football they play?"
"Anyone got any cotton wool I can wrap myself in?"
Gaffer isn't biting and is his usual diplomatic self:
"F**k off you p*ss taking twats!"

Gaffer does give in at the end and we play a 6v6 game. I'm roped in to make up the numbers. Gaffer takes on the role of referee and plays it out with great gusto, penalising anything that looks like a tackle. The boys start winding The Gaffer up rolling around the pitch clutching faces and legs in an attempt to test his patience. In the end he has the last laugh and issues eleven red cards and training is over. While it may not have been the most productive of sessions, it has been good for team morale as the laughing and smiling faces that leave the Rec prove.

Gaffer catches me before I leave
"Fancy watching Phoenix vs Kingsbridge tomorrow? I'll come and pick you up Si. Call it a scouting mission."
"Yeah why not."
"Pick you up at 5:30 then. There's a pub by the ground so we can have a debrief session afterwards."
"OK, See you tomorrow Gaffer."

Wednesday 25th April
It was a very successful scouting mission but not as successful as the result as Phoenix won 2-0. While it put them a point in front of us, it was still a good result and sees us back in the driving seat. During the game I was bouncing about and didn't shut up as I virtually commentated the whole match.

"Si, for f**ks sake stand still you're doing my nut in!"
"Sorry Gaffer."

The debrief took place over two pints of Doombar, my treat, and I have to agree with The Gaffer that on paper we look good but we also both agree that football isn't played on paper and we know that could still be a few more twists and turns ahead.

Smith Says
Phoenix beat Kingsbridge 2-0 tonight throwing the title race wide open and while it puts Phoenix above us it certainly does us a favour in our pursuit of the title.
The Gaffer

THE GAFFER

Result from Wednesday 25th April
Phoenix Rovers 2 - 0 Kingsbridge

Team	P	W	D	L	F	A	GD	Pts
1 Tamworth United	17	11	2	4	47	28	19	35
2 Phoenix Rovers	17	11	0	6	49	27	22	33
3 Dalworth United	16	10	2	4	42	25	17	32
4 Kingsbridge	16	10	1	5	40	26	14	31
5 Leighbridge Lions	17	8	1	8	36	37	-1	25
6 Langton Reds	17	8	0	9	60	41	19	24
7 Dunstable Colts	14	7	3	4	24	22	2	24
8 Parkfield	16	7	1	8	27	32	-5	22
9 Oak Town Rangers	18	4	1	13	23	62	-39	13
10 Redbridge Sports	18	1	1	16	17	65	-48	4

Friday 27th April - Dalworth News
Dunstable Colts 2 Dalworth United **Under 15**s 2
Dalworth rescued what could be a vital point with a last minute equaliser against Dunstable Colts. Dunstable took a 2-0 lead through Danny Jordan and Barry Dawson but then saw Dalworth goalkeeper Billy Stevens save a penalty. Brian Haugh reduced the deficit for Dalworth before Ben Padgham claimed a last ditch equaliser.

Saturday 28th April
Gaffer is really early today in fact I'm still out on my morning walk with Faith.

"What's wrong s**t the bed?"
"No pissed it you twat, Johnny's not available tomorrow the ankle's still not right but Stevie is OK."
"That's good."
"What do you reckon tomorrow? Go with three at the back or drop Aidan in at centre back?"
"Three at the back, it's a game we need to win and I think we need to press Parkfield from the off."
"What formation then?"
"3-5-2"
"Yeah, Bobby or Brian?"
"I'd play them both Brian is on fire at the moment and Bobby's pace is dangerous. I'd play Brian behind Luke and Charlie and Ben and Bobby on the wings."
"What like a 3-4-1-2"
"Yeah we really need to get at Parkfield from the kick off. We owe them."

"Stevie or Danny at right centre back?"
"Danny was superb last game start him."
"Ok Si, thanks for that see you tomorrow."
"See you tomorrow Gaffer."

Sunday 29th April - Dalworth United vs Parkfield
For the first time this season Nick mentions the, up until now, banned 'C' word, no not that 'C' word. 'Champions' .
"Do you reckon we'll do it Dad?"
"We *can* do it Nick and that's all that matters.'
"We are going to have to win our last two games."
"Yeah I reckon you're right there Son."
"We will."

When we get to the Rec Gaffer is already there setting things up. The team is already up in the changing room and I'm surprised that the starting line up is exactly how I suggested. A 3-4-1-2 formation with Brian behind Charlie and Luke.

Starting line-up:
Billy Stevens
Danny Hall, Nick Sheppard Billy Belafonte,
Ben Padgham (c) Alex Hayes Aidan Hayes Bobby Webster
Brian Haugh
Charlie Fisher Luke Pilbeam
Subs: Stevie Carr, Adam Morley

I can't help but notice what an attacking threat this line up carries and if I was the opposition I wouldn't want to be facing them or be the opposing manager trying to stop them.

The changing room is loud but focused due to Ben who has brought a Mini CD system which is playing a mixed tape of Pop Punk classics. Blink 182's Rock Show is currently playing but it is background music to get changed to and not music to work the team up.

Gaffer goes through his instructions and he is the next one to mention the 'C' word.
"Two games, two wins and I think we could be champions, anything else and we are also-rans."

The boys sit listening intently and nodding in all the right places.
"I don't have to tell you what to do because you know what to do, now go out and do it!"

The boys file out the of changing room and go through the warm-up with consummate ease because that's what is expected of them. You can tell that they are itching to go and this is a game they want to win not only because it will put them three points closer to the title, but because they feel they owe Parkfield for the defeat a month ago.

Kick-off

We are flying again but it is too frantic and the boys are trying too hard. Whenever we play well we do it playing open and freeflowing football but today it looks like we are trying to win the game in the first half and it is degenerating into a battle. Gaffer is trying to get the boys "relax", "take an extra touch", "shorten up the passes" But we continue to seek out Luke and Charlie route one instead of working the balls through the quarters.

At the moment we are playing into our opponents' hands and mixing it up with them. The quality is missing. Danny launches another route one ball forward and it's flicked on by Charlie who finds Brian. Brian races away but is tripped just outside the area. For the first time in the match Billy B steadies himself, takes his time and curls the ball over the wall and into the top corner to give us the lead. If we had hoped this was the goal that would relax us then we were wrong because moments later a header by Nick which was intended for Billy S bounces over him but luckily rolls past the empty goal for a corner.

Nick is determined to make amends and wins the header but collides with the Parkfield number nine and worryingly both hit the deck in alarming fashion. Both sets of the management team are quickly on the pitch and there is a long delay as both players receive treatment. Nick has come off worse and is visibly groggy. It looks like he has broken his nose. Luckily for me my wife is in attendance today and rushes him off to hospital for treatment. The Parkfield number nine also has to come off and is replaced.

"Do you want to go with him Si?"
My wife cuts in: "No point in all of us going." Me and his sister will take him and I'll keep you updated."

So Nick is off and Stevie replaces him with Danny going central.

Gaffer is shaking his head "I hope he is OK."

"Yeah I'm sure he will be but I can't believe that's all three centre backs injured." I felt a bit callous when I said that as my son is on his way to hospital and I'm bemoaning our luck at losing another centre back.

We get through to half time and Gaffer brings on Adam in place of Danny and puts him in midfield with Aidan at the back. He issues a few instructions and the boys are heading out again.

"It's all going wrong again Si, like at the start of the season."

"The boys won't let you down Gaffer, You'll see."

That last comment was made in hope rather than belief but what do I know because a minute after the kick off and Luke increases our lead after Brian slots an inch perfect pass behind the centreback for him to run on to and bury. Ten minutes later and it's 3-0 with Brian adding a quite remarkable third.

I don't know if you've seen the video with Ronaldo hitting successive volleys against the bar, well Brian picks up the ball outside the box and hits a shot that hits the bar but loops back to him and without hesitation he volleys the rebound into the top bins. As the boys line up for the kick-off he yells over to The Gaffer: "I want the assist for that one as well!"

Further goals from Charlie, a near post header from a Bobby cross and following a brilliant run and finish from Ben, see us over the line before Parkfield grab a consolation which leaves Billy punching the ground in frustration as Billy B switches off and lets a Parkfield player nip in front of him to head home. The game finishes 5-1 to us and I'm quickly away as the changing room rocks with a chant of: "We are top of the league, I said we are top of the league!"

When I get to the hospital Nick has had his broken nose put back into place and I'm handed a leaflet about the signs of concussion. Before I can ask the question the Doctor pre-empts me and says: "No football for ten days." There is more to life than football and your health is certainly more important but I'm dreading telling Nick that his season is over.

On our return home I ring The Gaffer and break the bad news. He isn't as worried as I thought he would be.

"Is Nick OK though?"

"Yes he's struggling to breathe and he's a bit sore but OK"

"Good. Well we can get round it, even though we've lost all three centre backs, its the boys I feel sorry for missing out on the last game".

Gaffer tells me that the boys outpouring of emotion took him by surprise after the game especially as we have won nothing yet.

"They were singing and screaming at the top of their voices and jumping up and down on the benches. Even the usually calm and collected Ben was bouncing up and down."

"I think it shows how much it means to them."
"We've got this far it would be a shame to fall at the last hurdle."
"Agreed."
"Oh and by the way Dunstable did us a favour and drew with Kingsbridge so unless we lose heavily another one bites the dust."
"So it really is in our hands."

Nick is still a bit groggy but when I relay the Dunstable v Kingsbridge result he perks up.
"Roll on next week Dad, I'm not missing the title decider."
I glance at my wife, this is a conversation that can wait.

Results from Sunday 29th April
Dalworth United 5 - 1 Parkfield
Kingsbridge 1 - 1 Dunstable Colts

Team	P	W	D	L	F	A	GD	Pts
1 Dalworth United	17	11	2	4	47	26	21	35
2 Tamworth United	17	11	2	4	47	28	19	35
3 Phoenix Rovers	17	11	0	6	49	27	22	33
4 Kingsbridge	17	10	2	5	41	27	14	32
5 Dunstable Colts	15	7	4	4	25	23	2	25
6 Leighbridge Lions	17	8	1	8	36	37	-1	25
7 Langton Reds	17	8	0	9	60	41	19	24
8 Parkfield	17	7	1	9	28	37	-8	22
9 Oak Town Rangers	18	4	1	13	23	62	-39	13
10 Redbridge Sports	18	1	1	16	17	65	-48	4

Smith Says
The boys produced a stunning performance today to beat Parkfield 5-1 and put us in the driving seat with one game to go and it's our title to win (or lose). The destination of the title depends on three key games. Unfortunately the injury curse that has plagued us all season struck again when centre back Nick Sheppard broke his nose. Nick has been a vital part of our success and he will be sorely missed for our last game.

It all boils down to three games now:
Tuesday 1st May - Tamworth United vs Dunstable Colts
Sunday 6th May - Phoenix Rovers vs Parkfield, Kingsbridge vs Us
By the time Tamworth have played their game we will know what is required of us.

Dalworth United 5 Parkfield 1

Squad: Billy Stevens, Danny Hall, Nick Sheppard, Billy Belafonte, Ben Padgham (c) Alex Hayes, Aidan Hayes, Bobby Webster, Brian Haugh, Charlie Fisher, Luke Pilbeam, Stevie Carr, Adam Morley

Scorers: Belafonte, Pilbeam, Haugh, Fisher, Padgham

Man of the Match: Fisher

Sunday evening and it's me ringing The Gaffer.

"Alright Gaffer?" he detects the apprehension in my voice.

"Everything OK?"

"Nick saw your column and he told me to tell you that he will be available next Sunday."

Gaffer whispers down the phone to me: "Is Nick there?"

I try to throw Nick off the trail while giving Gaffer an affirmative.

"Yes, it was a very good game today."

"Gotcha, well it's your shout Si."

"Yeah thanks for that, I'll see you Tuesday Gaffer."

A beaming and bruised Nick ran upstairs and as he departed all I could think was: "How and when do I tell him?"

CHAPTER ELEVEN

MAY

"It ain't over til it's over."

Tuesday 1st May

Today is our last training session of the season and more importantly Tamworth's last game. We have agreed that we would settle for anything other than a Tamworth win but for now we are trying to engage everyone's attention, including our own, with a training session. Training is therefore a strange affair Nick and Johnny are present. Nick as a spectator and Johnny as a passenger and also present is the elephant on the training ground.

We try every trick in the book but everyone's thoughts are on events at Tamworth and Gaffer is treating tonight's training session like a certain Scottish play, talking about tactics, formations even the weather. Anything but results elsewhere. We stumble from drill to drill until Gaffer lets the boys play a 6v6 keep ball drill.

"Keep your eye on it for me Si, I've just got to make a quick phone call." and he's making his way over to the trees. I'm guessing what he is doing. Whoever he is calling isn't answering, but he is persistent and keeps dialing.

The boys have finally got their focus on training and are playing some quick one-two touch football. The game is flowing nicely when it is disturbed by a "YES!, f**king get in!" in the distance and Gaffer is sprinting towards us.

The game has ceased and the 13 of us are slowly walking towards the onrushing Gaffer who has dropped his pace considerably to a gentle jog. Once Gaffer arrives he stoops to catch his breath but with hands on his knees he still manages to push out: "2-2". "Tamworth 2-2". "That's the result we wanted!"

Surprisingly the boys don't show the level of excitement that The Gaffer is showing and appear to take it all in their stride. They seem almost disinterested and pick up their keep-ball game again. Gaffer seems disappointed at the tepid response from the boys.

"Bloody hell Si, they don't seem bothered!" Nick leans over and puts it into context: "All that's happened Gaffer is we know what we have to do. Tamworth are top now and will stay there if we lose our last game."

Gaffer considers this and shrugs his shoulders, straightens up and says "Fair point Nick." The rest of the session passes off without any more interruptions and Gaffer concludes with: "All down to Sunday now boys."

Result from Tuesday 1st May
Tamworth United 2 - 2 Dunstable Colts

Team	P	W	D	L	F	A	GD	Pts
1 Tamworth United	18	11	3	4	49	30	19	36
2 Dalworth United	17	11	2	4	47	26	21	35
3 Phoenix Rovers	17	11	0	6	49	27	22	33
4 Kingsbridge	17	10	2	5	41	27	14	32
5 Dunstable Colts	16	7	5	4	27	25	2	26
6 Leighbridge Lions	17	8	1	8	36	37	-1	25
7 Langton Reds	17	8	0	9	60	41	19	24
8 Parkfield	17	7	1	9	28	37	-9	22
9 Oak Town Rangers	18	4	1	13	23	62	-39	13
10 Redbridge Sports	18	1	1	16	17	65	-48	4

Thursday 3rd May
Gaffer's on the phone, on a Thursday.
"Johnny has said he should be OK for Sunday, what do you think?"
"If he has said he is OK then include him. We've got cover."
"OK I'll include him Si."
That's the shortest call ever.

Friday 4th May - Dalworth News
Dalworth United 5 Parkfield 1
Dalworth took one step closer to retaining their title with a convincing 5-1 win over Parkfield. Goals from Billy Belafonte, Luke Pilbeam, Brian Haugh, Charlie Fisher and Ben Padgham ensured they took all three points before Colin O'Driscoll grabbed a consolation goal.

Gaffer's back on the phone:
"Did you know Nick rang to say he is available to play?"
"Did he? He said he thought he was OK to play but left it at that."
"Do you want me to leave him out?"
I pause. "No. Include him, but only use him in an emergency and when I say emergency I mean if we have no other options. I'll let him know he is in the squad."

"OK Si, your shout though."
"Cheers Gaffer."
"Fancy a pint tomorrow Si?"
"Mmmm just a pint."
"Or two."
"What time?"
"Lunchtime."
"Yeah why not."
"We can discuss the team."
"Yeah OK."
"See you tomorrow Si."
"OK Gaffer."

My wife is out shopping tomorrow with a friend so why not. I try to kid myself The Gaffer is very persuasive but really I didn't take a lot of persuading and If I'm honest I'm looking forward to a couple of pints after the week I've had. Rumour has it that OFSTED are due so everyone is on edge and marking. Books are being frantically checked and re-checked and checked again.

Saturday 5th May
Gaffer is infuriatingly prompt and annoyingly chirpy when he turns up. When I told my wife I was going out with The Gaffer she wasn't happy.
"You said you was going to sort the garage out this weekend. You won't do it tomorrow so that leaves today."
"Don't worry I'll get it done in the morning."
"You'd better because I'm sure you'll be in no fit state to do anything in the afternoon."
I tried to plead my case.
"I've said to The Gaffer I'm only going out for a couple of pints."
"More like a couple of gallons."
I realise I'm wasting my time and also setting myself up to fail.
"OK darling."

The look that my wife gives me leaves me in no doubt of the grief I will face if I turn up steaming drunk.

So it's bang on twelve and Gaffer is ready and waiting. I on the other hand am sweating like the proverbial pig and have three more boxes that need sorting. In my infinite wisdom against my better judgement and with Gaffer's assistance, said three boxes are cunningly hidden in the eaves away from sight and more importantly my wife's eyes for when the inevitable inspection follows.

I pour The Gaffer a quick whiskey which he downs equally quickly, pour him another and then shoot upstairs to get washed and changed. Ten minutes later we are off out the front door and I've necked a quick whiskey too, Gaffer insisted saying it was rude to drink on his own. We are not going to our usual haunt The Old Maid but a pub restaurant five minutes' walk from me. The weather is surprisingly hot and the pub is packed but we manage to nab a table in the garden. My aching body is in need of some liquid refreshment which Gaffer provides in the shape of a couple of ales and two whiskey chasers.

"You trying to get me shot?"
"No, you said a couple of pints, you didn't say anything about shorts!"
He says it with a wicked grin. I like his way of thinking and the same wicked smile spreads over my face. I also notice, strategically placed under his arm, a food menu.
"I'm starving, fancy something? My treat." He then adds while laughing: "It'll help soak up the alcohol!"

Food selected, two mixed grills, and Gaffer's scampering off to the bar. When he returns he has another two pints and two more whiskeys which he places in front of me.

"Right, tomorrow's game, do we put Nick and Johnny on the bench?"
"Yeah definitely I think it's a case of 'use in emergency'. What formation you thinking of going with?"
"I was thinking of a 3-5-2. What do you think?"
"The boys know it inside out besides I don't think it's the formation that will win the game."
"Yeah you're right we are light in defence but our attack is very strong, so let's play to our strengths"
"Who would you put at the back?"
"I'm thinking Danny, Aidan and Billy."
"That does make sense, what about midfield?"
"I reckon Ben, Alex, Brian, Adz and Bobby."
"Yeah that's OK."
"Charlie and Luke up top."
"Goes without saying."
"That's a side to win a title." Gaffer is now beaming as the importance of tomorrow hits home.
"I f**king hope so!"

The food when it arrives looks delicious and fills the large plates. I use it as an excuse to go to the loo and get another two pints in, well two pints each to save going back to the bar. Gaffer is very reflective as he cuts into his steak.

"If you'd said to me we'd be in this position after four league games I would have said you was mad."
"Well we are so we better not blow it."
"I want this so badly not for the glory but we deserve it."
"The boys want it just as badly."
"You're right I hope they do it for their sakes."
"Well let's make sure we get it right our side and they can do the rest."

The rest of the afternoon is spent chatting about the Dalworth presentation night and the awards and the season in general. When we leave the pub I'm pleased to report that I am totally stuffed but compos mentis and feeling quite proud of the fact.

Sunday 6th May - Kingsbridge vs Dalworth United
So this is it and after seventeen games it all boils down to one game. If we win we will be champions but if we lose and surprise package Phoenix Rovers win, then they will take the title. If we both lose then Tamworth win it. It's that close.

The nerves I had on cup final day are surprisingly missing and I'm looking forward to today. Everyone has worked so hard for this and it's time to finish the job. I stumble downstairs to walk Faith and find her tucking into her breakfast. She looks up at me from it and gives me a 'What time do you call this?' look. Nick pokes his head round the corner.

"I've walked Faith and done her breakfast Dad."
"Eh? Oh, OK son."
"Your newspapers are on the table, do you want a pot of coffee?"
"Eh? Thanks and yes please."
"I'm OK to play Dad." I see what is happening here.
"Can't take any chances son, you know what the Doctor said."
"Last game of the season Dad, no point holding anything back."
"Erm, we'll see."

A pot of coffee and breakfast and then we are heading out the door for the meet at the Rec.

When we get there you can feel the tension building. Well Gaffer's tension is building. He is racing around the cars doing a head count and checking on everyone's well being. He then goes round again and double checks. He then targets Nick and Johnny and has a chat with them. I'm fully expecting

Gaffer to pull out a register and take names. Gaffer finally checks in with me.

"All present and correct, let's roll."

I've got Alex and Aidan with me today and they are remarkably subdued and along with Nick all seem to be in their own zone.

Gaffer's first task on arrival is to put the heavily anticipated team sheet up. It is, as expected, a very attacking line up in a 3-5-2 formation. There's a big responsibility on Aidan who is in the middle of the defensive three. The subs bench is made up of three defenders, two of which shouldn't really be playing. Gaffer is studying the teamsheet even though he picked it and you can see the cogs going round as he weighs up his options for during the game. He turns to me:

"It looks a well balanced side doesn't it Si?" he is definitely looking for a nod of approval from me and I duly oblige.

"It's a team to win a title Gaffer." He smiles and says: "Hope so Si."

So do I Gaffer, so do I.

Starting Line-Up:

Billy Stevens,
Danny Hall Aidan Hayes Billy Belafonte,
Ben Padgham (c) Alex Hayes Brian Haugh, Adam Morley Bobby
Webster,
Charlie Fisher, Luke Pilbeam,
Subs: Stevie Carr, Nick Sheppard, Johnny Day

Gaffer takes centre stage and addresses his troops:
"This is it boys. Last game of the season and you know what you have to do, nothing's different today, it's just another game and all you need to do is exactly what you've done all season, do that and the title is ours."

Gaffer then goes round the changing room and gives out individual instructions.
"Bury those chances."
"Win your tackles."
"Boss the middle."
"Keep it tight at the back."
"Good communication from the back."

The warm-up is focused and everyone is at the races and giving their all.

It finishes with keep-ball and all is going well until Stevie turns his ankle treading on the ball. Gaffer is straight on it but in vain because Stevie is limping heavily and a nasty bruise is already developing.

"F**king hell! Eleven fit players for the most important game of the season."

Stevie is helped back to the changing room and moments later the rest of the team troop in. Stevie's ankle is already engulfed in ice and Gaffer is looking increasingly worried. At this vital stage of the season is, for once, lost for words. Luckily Ben isn't and takes over with his own inspirational speech.:
"Look we've worked bloody hard to get to this stage and we've never done it the easy way. So what if we've got eleven fit players, they are the best eleven players on the pitch. Come on boys, this is what we do. It's our way, it's the Dalworth way. Let's finish off the job and then we can be crowned champions!"

The changing room at that point was rocking and it was the loudest noise I'd ever heard from us. I looked at The Gaffer. "What a speech that was." It wasn't planned but it was from the heart, and it was enough to instill confidence throughout the team.

Eleven determined players left that changing room followed by two very brave subs and a Manager and Assistant Manager determined not to f**k up.

Kick-off
For such an important game the boys were remarkably composed and are stroking the ball about nicely probing for gaps in the Kingsbridge defence, looking to expose any frailties. In games like this you need players to take control and you can see straight away that we have leaders all over the place. Aidan is controlling things at the back and pulling players into position. Brian is pulling the strings in the middle and Charlie and Luke are dragging the defence all over the place.

Brian is the first to go close when he picks the ball up outside the box and curls it inches over the bar. Charlie then beats a defender and drags the ball past the goalkeeper but agonisingly wide of the far post. Gaffer leans over to me and whispers: "It's coming." Then we get a warning shot when a hopeful shot hits Danny's foot and loops over Billy but thankfully runs wide of the goal.

After 25 minutes we do take the lead when Brian plays a defence-splitting ball through to Luke who rounds the keeper but just as it looks like he is going to try to squeeze in a shot from an acute angle he cleverly squares the ball for Charlie who smashes the ball home. The celebrations are strangely muted and Ben is already tapping his temple and yelling at the players to concentrate as they line up for the kick off.

He follows it up with a: "We've won nothing yet boys." The Gaffer on hearing this just nods his head and gives Ben a thumbs up gesture.

The boys are still pressing hard but Kingsbridge look dangerous when they counter, however Aidan is in determined mood at the back and is winning everything. Then seconds later we are in dreamland when Alex, not willing to play second fiddle to his brother, dispossess a Kingsbridge midfielder and drives into the opposing half. He plays a clever one-two with Luke and then smashes an unstoppable shot past the Kingsbridge goalkeeper. We immediately look at the boys' response but they are still somewhat subdued and just return to their positions eagerly anticipating the restart.

I turn to The Gaffer, look at my watch and say: "I'll take 2-0 at half time." As soon as I've said it I regret it and with the last kick of the half Danny heads into his own net from a corner. Danny trudges off inconsolable but Ben is straight on him and has an arm round him.

"Dan ,get your f**king head up, we've got another half to go and we need you on your game."

Gaffer is cool, calm and collected and issues his instructions with a calming tone.

"45 minutes to go boys. Forget the goal we conceded because we're still in the driving seat. All we need to do is carry on doing what we are doing and we'll get over the line."

Gaffer surveys his options and realises with Stevie out of the game and Nick and Johnny only available as back up that he has no options and sends the same eleven out for the second half.

The boys start it like the first and they are controlling the game with Luke and Charlie threatening every time they get near the Kingsbridge goal. The pressure pays off when Bobby latches onto a long ball from Billy S, beats two defenders and in the blink of an eye he is gone. He picks his moment and fizzes a low cross across the box, Luke unfortunately miscues his shot, but to our good fortune the Kingsbridge keeper totally misjudges the shot and it rolls under him and into the net.

There are still no excessive celebrations, only from me and The Gaffer. We can almost taste victory. Well, that is until Billy B gets under a long clearance and heads towards our goal. Danny anticipates the danger and rushes across to cover but gets to the ball second and flattens the Kingsbridge centre forward in the area. The resulting spot kick is slammed home and our lead is reduced again.

Danny, despite two errors isn't hiding and is throwing himself into tackles to redeem himself. His next tackle is timed to perfection but as he slides in to intercept, the Kingsbridge winger is a fraction late and leaves Danny with a nasty gash across his knee. He immediately springs up but then spots the blood flowing down his leg and goes back to ground as the sight of a flap of skin hanging off his leg leaves him then feeling quite queasy.

Nick is up and stripped-off before The Gaffer can say: "Nick you're on."
I grab Nick by the arm.
"Don't head the ball and don't tell your bloody mother."
"OK Dad" and off he sprints, desperate to get into the action. Danny's Dad bundles him into the car and he is off to A&E for treatment.

All kinds of emotions are racing through me and I know that I'm seconds away from elation or despair. Ben must be aware of this as he beats a defender, cuts inside and unleashes a thunderbolt of a shot which the goalkeeper somehow deflects wide of the post. The oohs and aahs resonate down the line of Dalworth parents but before the last has faded, Ben is swinging a corner over and Aidan is bulldozing his way past the Kingsbridge defence before powering a header into the top corner.

This was the signal for wild celebrations amongst the management and parents and even the players until Ben shouts: "Still 15 minutes left boys." That is the trigger for the levels of concentration to return.

Danny's dad told us later on that Danny was bouncing up and down on the back seat of his car and he genuinely thought that he had further damaged his knee. He shouted: "Danny, what's up? What's up?" to which Danny replied: "Aidan's just scored its 4-2!"

Apparently the source of this news was Jimmy who was on strict instructions from Danny to keep him posted with updates.

Gaffer looks at his bench more in hope than anything hoping to find a fit Jimmy, Johnny or Stevie, even a Danny to supplement his severely stretched defence.

"Do we put four at the back Si?"

"Leave it Gaffer they are playing well." again I regret saying it because three minutes later it's 4-3 and despite the enormity of the game you can't help but clap the wonder strike that the Kingsbridge number hits from a full 30 yards out.

Ben does his best Batman impression when he strikes his fist in his hand and yells: "We don't f**king concede again!" I hope he is right but they do say that attack is the best form of defence and Brian agrees with that when he hits the post with a curling drive. The tension is killing me now and out of nowhere I need the loo so I'm hopping about, half out of excitement and half because I need the toilet. I check my watch and we've still got five minutes to go. We look comfortable but it only takes one mistake, one lapse of concentration or another moment of genius to shatter our dreams.

We are moving towards injury time when Kingsbridge win a corner. The ball is floated in and after a mad scramble Aidan pokes the ball away and straight into the path of the scorer of Kingsbridge's wonder goal. Without hesitation he smacks the ball towards our goal and past the despairing dive of Billy S.

Just as our title dreams begin to evaporate, Nick appears out of nowhere and deflects the ball over the bar with his head. My first thought is: "I'm a dead man." but as Nick bounces upright I breathe a sigh of relief. The second corner is curled into our box and yes you guessed it, it is headed clear by Nick. My second breath is punctured by the shrill blast of the ref's whistle and there it is, at last! The celebrations can commence and the boys are jumping up and down.

I turn to The Gaffer: "We've only bloody gone and done it!"

He laughs and says: "Alright Michael Caine, calm down."

The Kingsbridge management offer their congratulations and handshakes. "Well done, you deserved it." Gaffer turns to me and for a moment we both freeze, unsure of our next move, he then offers his hand. Thinks twice, withdraws it and then we hug. Two grown men hugging, but it is a hug of relief, it is the hug of champions.

I feel a tap on the shoulder and turn round to see Nick standing there all awkward like a naughty child.

"You OK son?"

"OK? I'm f**king banging Dad!"

"Please, please, please don't tell your mum though."

"No need to Dad." as he points to where our parents are stood and I see the smiling face of my wife. Nick just laughs and he is off in the direction of his mum.

Gaffer points to the direction of the changing rooms, and we all bounce off to the comfort of them to continue our celebrations. Gaffer stops to address the parents and I overhear the words 'barbecue' and 'brink' it's going to get messy again tonight.

In the changing rooms we find Ben slumped on the bench head in hands. "You OK Ben?"

He looks up and simply utters: "I'm f**king drained Gaffer."

We both laugh and leave Ben to his recovery. Alex and Aidan are dancing about in the changing room and the boys break out into a chorus of "And it's hi ho super Dalworth, everywhere we go we're winning. I see our trophy shining but we won't cause a fuss cos we're marvellous" followed by "Champione, champione ole, ole, ole." Then Aidan and Alex start a "Let's go f**king mental" chant which is followed by the spraying of water or any other liquid they have and lots more jumping about.

Gaffer says he has to quickly pop out to take a call.

"Thanks, leave me here to get soaked."

Moments later he returns carrying a case of non-alcoholic champagne. He hands it out and says: "Come on outside boys."

Within minutes we are covered in the stuff as management, players and parents join in the celebrations and let's face it, without the parents, there would be no celebrations, so why not include them.

Billy then lifts a leg and says "Uncork this" before letting rip a Billy B special. Billy's Dad then clips him round the ear. "Heathen." but it's all in good spirits. Gaffer then stops and remembers our wounded colleague. "Danny! Does he know?"

Jimmy holds up his phone and says: "He knows, and when I text him he apparently shouted out: "We've f**king done it" in a packed Dalworth A&E waiting room, much to the embarrassment of his dad."

"Right then, barbecue at mine this afternoon!" yells Gaffer amid the chaos.

"Abso-f**king-lutely." say the twins in unison.

"Paaaaar-tay" screams Luke.

"Faaaaaaaar-tay"n yells Billy B before letting rip.

The boys quickly get changed and the food laid on by our hosts is devoured by our very own plague of locusts in record time as everyone's focus is on getting ready for this afternoons celebratory barbecue at The Gaffer's. We manage a quick chat with our hosts and they are very complimentary. "Best team won the league in the end." I have to agree with them.

We then wish each other a good summer and make a promise that we will attend their pre-season summer tournament and we are off. Goodbyes are quickly exchanged in the car park and within seconds everyone is gone.

I kid you not, one hour later (sorry Faith I'll give you a longer walk later) and we are sitting in The Gaffer's garden, enjoying the sunshine and supping the first drink of the day. Sky usually open the season's proceedings with a 'How the League was won' programme. Well we are conducting Dalworth's own version with every player putting their own stories in.

"Remember that goal I scored against Tamworth?"

"What about that goal line clearance against Dunstable?"

"What about my penalty save against Dunstable?"

All of a sudden a big cheer goes up and a chant of "Oh Danny, Danny, Danny Danny, Danny, Danny, Danny Hall" roars out. Danny, who has come straight from hospital, is showing everyone his freshly stitched leg and telling the tale of his hospital trip. When Danny had his knee stitched the nurse said: "That's the mark of a brave young soldier"

Danny couldn't resist correcting her: "Nah! That's the mark of a champion!"

The barbecue is soon in full swing and Billy B is putting in another guest appearance alongside The Gaffer and issuing a new challenge to everyone. The Man vs Food (which for the record is Billy's favourite TV programme) inspired 'Billy B Meat Feast challenge' which consists of the following: two Billy B burgers, four hot chicken wings, two foot long Korkers dog rolls and five spicy beef kebabs skewers.

Not many dared attempt it and only two people succeeded. That was our two chefs in residence. Billy is then issued with a similar challenge, the Stevie 'No meat, No treat' challenge which consists of eating a large bowl of mixed salad. Billy politely turns it down with a firm "F**k off! No meat, no eat!" and a positively Prehistoric sounding "Billy B only eat Meat."

The food is slowly disappearing and then all thoughts turn to the serious matter of drinking. Gaffer in his infinite wisdom puts Alex and Aidan in charge of the bar and they are working on a one for you and one for me system until they are joined by Grandma Hayes who oversees matters, ending the twins' fun. The fact that we have won the league is a great reason to celebrate but in reality the coming together of this extended family is an equally feasible reason to celebrate. I love spending time with this lot, it really warms my heart, and no that's not the drink talking. Well not yet.

Gaffer is holding court with the dads who are hanging on his every word. My wife and Gaffer's are deep in conversation with the rest of the mums about hair, the soaps, microblading and, of course, Prosecco. As for the boys, Billy B is holding court at the food table showing Billy S, Stevie, Johnny, Danny and Brian how to make a Billy B Burger. Alex and Aidan are conducting a survey as to the merits of The Gaffer's whiskeys of which there are six different types. Adam is showing Jimmy, Luke, Charlie and Bobby how to breakdance. Nick and Ben are deep in conversation about something or other. They notice I'm on my own and stroll over to me.
"You alright Si?"
"Yeah. You Ben?"
"Want a drink Dad?"
"Yeah OK Son."
Nick comes back with three Toffee Apple Ciders.
"Really Son?"
Nick screws his face up and in a pained voice says: "Yeah it helps with the crippling headache I've got."
"WHAT!"
Nick breaks into a smile "Only joking Dad!"
"You and The Gaffer did well this season Si." says Ben.
"We didn't do anything really."
"Yeah you did. Several times this season it all fell apart, but you both pulled it together and that's why we are champions."

There's nothing I can say to that and all I can manage is a "Thanks."

It makes me think that what we did achieve was special and again I get a very warm feeling. Oh s**t! I need the loo again. With heads and stomachs succumbing to the ill effects of too much alcohol, Gaffer decides to make a brief speech which is the signal for our resident connoisseurs Alex and Aidan to fill their glasses, to the top, with another one of Gaffer's whiskeys.

"Thanks for coming today. I just wanted to thank all the parents for your support all season and I'm sure you'll agree it was worth it in the end. I'd also like to thank the boys. I said a lot of harsh words at the beginning and you could have given up on me but you didn't and in the end we became a unit, an unstoppable unit at that. I'd also like to thank Simon who has kept me sane and been a tower of strength all season. It has been a very testing season and we all worked hard to meet the many challenges we faced on and off the pitch and with that I'd like you all to raise a glass to the one person who can't be here today but deserves to be part of this celebration. Ladies and Gentleman raise your glasses for Grandad Hayes."

It is a really nice gesture and one that earns The Gaffer a cuddle from Mrs Hayes and her mother. That is after Mrs Hayes realises that the twins have a glass of whiskey each and the race is on for the twins to empty their glasses before their mum catches them. The twins won. The rest of the evening descends into idle chit chat, impromptu dancing and drinking. Lots of drinking.

To be fair it is the parents doing the drinking despite the boys having one or two, even the twins. Every now and then the boys break out into a chant which our resident choir master Adam starts:
"They're here, they're there, they're every-f**king-where Alex and Aidan, Alex and Aidan..." and my personal favourite:
"He eats, he sharts, his left foots deadlier than his farts Billy B, Billy B..."

By the end of the evening every one of the players had had a personal ditty composed by Adam. About 8o'clock things come to an end and everyone stumbles off home. Gaffer has hired a twelve seater minibus to ferry families home. We are one of the last ones to leave and I don't envy the cleaning up job The Gaffer has until my wife thrusts a black bag in my hand and informs me that we are part of it. Thirty minutes later and the gardens restored to its pre-barbecue state.

"Fancy another drink Si?"
"I don't know I've got to walk the dog."

Gaffer points through to the kitchen where the two wives are working their way through a newly opened bottle of Prosecco. Gaffer looks at me, then an unopened bottle of Honey Whiskey.
"If you can't beat them join them."
"But the dog" I plead.
A shout then comes from the kitchen: "I've sorted it. Katie's walking Faith."

Gaffer smiles, pours me a very large whiskey and we both slump into two matching and extremely comfortable leather armchairs. I lift my glass and Gaffer does likewise.

"Cheers!"
"Well, we did it then Si."
"Yeah I'm not sure how though."
"With this group of players it would have been criminal if we hadn't."
"The boys were good weren't they?"
"The boys were f**king brilliant Si."

We both smile a contented smile, slump back and spend the next two hours drinking whiskey and talking about everything and nothing until I'm summonsed to go by my now equally tipsy wife. We say our goodbyes and before I know it I'm tucked up in bed and reliving the game in my head. My wife kisses me goodnight and says: "Well done you. I'm really proud of you." and with that I drift off into a sound and contented sleep.

Results from Sunday 6th May
Kingsbridge 3 - 4 Dalworth United
Dunstable Colts 2 - 1 Langton Reds
Phoenix Rovers 0 - 0 Parkfield

Team	P	W	D	L	F	A	GD	Pts
1 Dalworth United	18	12	2	4	51	29	22	38
2 Tamworth United	18	11	3	4	49	30	19	36
3 Phoenix Rovers	18	11	1	6	49	27	22	34
4 Kingsbridge	18	10	2	6	44	31	13	32
5 Dunstable Colts	17	8	5	4	29	26	3	29
6 Leighbridge Lions	17	8	1	8	36	37	-1	25
7 Langton Reds	18	8	0	10	61	43	18	24
8 Parkfield	18	7	2	9	28	37	-9	23
9 Oak Town Rangers	18	4	1	13	23	62	-39	13
10 Redbridge Sports	18	1	1	16	17	65	-48	4

Monday 7th May
Smith Says
Well we did it, we bloody did it and we did it the hard way or as its now known 'The Dalworth Way'. I cannot find the words to express my gratitude to the boys but I can say I am so bloody proud of what they have achieved. The hard work they put in warranted nothing less than first place and I'm so glad they got what they deserved. The game itself was a tense affair but typical of this season, with the exception of those early games, we battled against the odds and won in the face of adversity. If I'm honest

at no point during the game did I think the boys were going to relinquish the title. On Saturday 26th May we go to the Cheltenham Civic Centre for the league presentation, tickets are £10 for adults and £5 for siblings and the players have free entry.

Then on Saturday the 16th June we have the Dalworth Presentation at the Leisure Centre. Tickets for this event are £5 for adults and £2 for children or you can purchase a family ticket for 2 adults and 2 children for £12.

If you let me know how many tickets you require for each event I will order them. I look forward to seeing you at both events.

Kingsbridge 3 Dalworth 4
Squad: Billy Stevens, Danny Hall, Aidan Hayes, Billy Belafonte, Ben Padgham (c) Alex Hayes, Brian Haugh, Adam Morley, Bobby Webster, Charlie Fisher, Luke Pilbeam, Stevie Carr, Nick Sheppard, Johnny Day.
Scorers: Fisher, Alex Hayes, Pilbeam, Aidan Hayes
Man of the Match: Aidan Hayes

Friday 11th May – Dalworth News
Dalworth clinch the title against all odds by Roger Wilkinson
Kingsbridge 3 Dalworth United **Under 15**s 4
Dalworth retained their title on Sunday with a 4-3 win at Kingsbridge. It was an amazing achievement considering they had made such a disastrous start taking only one point from their first four games. They were languishing in ninth place when they went on an incredible run which saw them win twelve of their next 14 league games drawing one and losing one and take 37 points out of a possible 42.

In a tense encounter on Sunday goals from Charlie Fisher and Alex Hayes gave Dalworth a 2-0 lead before a Danny Hall own-goal reduced arrears on the stroke of half-time. Luke Pilbeam restored the two goal advantage before a Billy Achong penalty put Kingsbridge back into the game. Aidan Hayes again increased Dalworth's advantage before an Eddie Godden goal for Kingsbridge set up a tense finish but Dalworth held to their 4-3 lead and in doing so retained their league title.

Manager Vinny Smith was ecstatic at the end and was full of praise for his team:
"While the table will show that we were the best side in the league it doesn't show the battle they fought and the adversity they overcame to retain the title. The boys literally gave their all and the spirit they displayed and the efforts they gave through the season won them the title. They simply never gave up and I'm so pleased they got the reward they deserved.

Manager Vinny Smith's predictions at the start of the season may not have been fulfilled but he can certainly be proud of what his team have achieved this season.

Result from Sunday 13th May
Dunstable Colts 2 – 0 Leighbridge Lions

Team	P	W	D	L	F	A	GD	Pts
1 Dalworth United	18	12	2	4	51	29	22	38
2 Tamworth United	18	11	3	4	49	30	19	36
3 Phoenix Rovers	18	11	1	6	49	27	22	34
4 Kingsbridge	18	10	2	6	44	31	13	32
5 Dunstable Colts	18	9	5	4	31	26	5	32
6 Leighbridge Lions	18	8	1	9	36	39	-3	25
7 Langton Reds	18	8	0	10	61	43	18	24
8 Parkfield	18	7	2	9	28	37	-9	23
9 Oak Town Rangers	18	4	1	13	23	62	-39	13
10 Redbridge Sports	18	1	1	16	17	65	-48	4

CHAPTER TWELVE

THE LEAGUE PRESENTATION

"It's all about next season now."

Sunday 20th May
Guess where I am and guess who I'm with?

Gaffer was on the phone Sunday morning moaning about the lack of football. Unless you are involved with a club you don't realise how much time it can take up. I know because I was involved this year and I know because Gaffer has just gone into great detail what his week entailed. Match days, training days, managers' meetings, phone calls, the Smith Says column for the website.

I'm just beginning to wonder what the purpose of this call is when Gaffer says: "Fancy a pint later?"
I have a list of jobs as long as my arm:
1. Wash cars.
2. Mow the lawn.
3. Bath Faith.
4. Marking homework.
5. Paint the spare room.
"Yeah I'd love one."
"What about your jobs?"
"They can wait."
"Old Maid at Twelve."
"Sounds good."

I know what The Gaffer means though, as there is also a gaping hole in my week without football. The euphoria of winning the league and the highs it brought have been replaced with the lows of a footballlless existence. So we replace football with a session at the Old Maid and use the time to discuss the League Presentation next week and sample the guest ales 'Summer Lightening', a couple of Belgian 'Rhubarb' and 'Cherry' flavoured beers.

"Should we get the boys suited and booted next week?"
"Yeah they look good and they love dressing up."

"OK, I've got a coach to take us."
"Good idea, means we can all go together."
"That's the League Presentation sorted. Fancy another pint?"
"Yeah why not."

We spent three hours in the pub garden talking about anything and nothing and I realised that we were both missing the football like crazy. Our season ultimately brought us success but I take my hat off to all those managers and coaches who don't win a thing and sometimes suffer relegation. Their's is a true labour of love and I have great admiration for someone who gives up their own valuable time without the return that we were fortunate to receive.

Saturday 26th May - League Presentation Evening
Gaffer has again laid on a luxury coach for this event and the parents in turn have had a whip round and made a decent contribution to the cost. The Gaffer promptly uses the whip round to create a float for the evening. Alex & Aidan are quick to thank The Gaffer.

"That's a lovely gesture Gaffer, well appreciated." Gaffer is having none of it though and responds with: "Yeah help yourself to as many cokes as you want."

The meeting point as usual is the Rec and as the players and families arrive everyone is greeting each other like long lost relations (it has been three weeks after all). As soon as we are ready the boys make a dash for the coach and once on board race to the back seats and once everyone is settled we are off for the long journey to the Cheltenham Civic Centre.

It is a pretty uneventful journey with lots of small talk amongst the parents and wind ups amongst the boys.
"No seriously Ben the Captain has to do a speech this season."
Ben isn't biting and replies with:
"Yeah and Michael Owen is presenting the trophies, f**k off!".

We finally reach our destination after two holdups on the way, clamber off and stretch our legs before making our way into the very impressive venue. It isn't my first visit to the civic centre as I saw Lee Nelson here a few months ago and I've been to various pantos and shows here.

The setup of the room is equally impressive and the stage is lit up with various spot lights which serve to bounce off the trophies and provide a kaleidoscope of colours. There is also a smoke machine and bubble machine?

I nudge Gaffer.
"Bit OTT ain't it?"

We have been allocated five extremely large round tables which amply accommodate our contingent.

The venue is served by a variety of bars including a Prosecco and Champagne bar which is both extremely impressive and incredibly expensive at the same time. The order of the day is ordering multiple drinks to avoid the queues and little groups are quickly formed to attack the bar. Gaffer skilfully navigates an enormous round of drinks back to the table ably assisted by Jimmy with a tray of shots and whiskeys. Gaffer has at least ten pints on a tray and once he has safely secured them he leans over to me, winks and says: "That's my drinks sorted!"

Within thirty minutes of arriving, the five Dalworth tables are full of bottles of Prosecco and wine, pints of lager, bitter and cider, shots and measures of whiskey, vodka and gin and then there must be about fifty cans of coke spread around the table. All this is without the inclusion of plates of food which are soon to be introduced.

The league presentation isn't the type of event for mingling and everyone keeps themselves to their own teams. Apart from a few 'Hellos' and 'How are yous' with our Under 16s (runners up in their division) and the Tamworth **Under 15**s contingent, it is very much a keep yourselves to yourselves event.

That is unless you are Adz, who is looking immaculate as usual. Adz in his own opinion, feels he is qualified to pass judgement as a fashion critic and he delivers his scathing verdict on the other teams present. 'Chavs United','Primani City', 'Wannabees Wanderers' are born. His acerbic wit and cutting comments induce suppressed laughter from the rest of the boys and Adz 'clothes show' kills some time.

The announcement of the buffet signals a mad dash and due to our placement at the event the queue is already horrendous before we take our place. It is also my misfortune to be queuing with Billy B, who spends the full 15 minutes we are queuing moaning at 1) The length of the queue 2) The ever diminishing food 3) The size of the plates.

Billy's moans didn't prevent him from piling as much food as humanly possible on his paper plates. Yes he managed to fill *two* plates. Billy continued moaning while eating his food because, and I quote: "Pointless getting bloody seconds, it'll all be gone."

All of a sudden the lights go down and the PA omits a thundering roar. A slideshow begins with photos and clips from our league. It's a very impressive presentation until it throws up a quite unflattering picture of me and The Gaffer looking like a pair of drowned rats. The boys find it quite amusing though. More photos follow including one of the team collecting their runners up medals for the challenge cup.

Then comes another slide show:
"Tonights Special Guest...
163 league goals in 362 games,
40 England goals in 89 games,
Ex- Liverpool, Real Madrid, Newcastle, Manchester United, Stoke City..."
At this point Ben Padgham is salivating and is almost out of his chair.
"Premier League Player of the Season 1997-98,
PFA Young Player of the Year 1997-98..."
Ben is upright now and is standing open mouthed.
"Premier League Golden Boot 1997-98, 1998-99,
BBC Sports Personality of the Year 1998,
Ballon d'Or 2001,
Ladies and Gentleman - Michael Owen..."

Thankfully the "F**king hell" that leaves Ben's mouth is drowned out by the noise booming from the PA (As if you haven't already guessed Michael Owen is Ben's footballing hero.)

The smoke and bubble machines are spewing out their wares as the footballing legend that is Michael Owen walks out on stage.

Billy B leans forward and shouts into Ben's ear:
"You knew about Michael Owen, so how come you didn't know about the speech?"

None of the words register with Ben though as he breaks out into a panic "I'm getting the trophy off of Michael Owen!"

This isn't directed at anyone in particular but then he stares directly at his dad and says: "Whatever you do don't f**k up the photo Dad."

Apparently when Ben was younger he had his photo taken with Roberto Firmino when Liverpool played Swindon in a pre-season friendly but Dad had messed up the photo, much to young Ben's disgust. Mr Padgham has just leapt above Ben in the nervous stakes but he is edging his bets and all the parents at the table are instructed to take a photo of Ben collecting the trophy from Michael Owen.

Unlike the Dalworth presentation, where you have a genuine interest in all the other teams, tonight you are only interested in 1) Our team and 2) The under 16s. So begins an eternity of polite handclaps and drinking until we are up.

Before you know it, it's our age group and Tamworth United are up first as runners up. Then it's us and it's a very nervous Ben that leads the boys up to collect their winners' medals. The cameras and phones are flashing away as Ben collects the trophy from Michael Owen and then it's a few team photos with the main main before the boys are whisked off stage for the next team. I feel a bit let down by the whole conveyor belt process but the boys take it in their stride and seem happy enough, especially Ben when his Dad shows him a perfect picture of his son collecting the trophy from Owen. The presentation concludes with a speech from the League Chairman and then a disco which falls flat as most people prefer to just stand around talking and drinking.

Before you know it Gaffer rounds everyone up and we are off for the journey home. The lights on the coach are dimmed and the coach goes quiet with the exception of the unmissable hissing sound made by ring pulls being pulled from cans of beer. I'm assuming one or two of the dads have brought emergency supplies for the journey home, however the hissing sound is followed by giggling and it doesn't sound like the giggling sounds made by middle aged men. My curiosity has got the better of me and a quick trip to the back of the coach reveals the boys chugging from cans of Fosters which have somehow been smuggled out of the Civic Centre and onto the coach.

"Don't grass us up Si, it's only one." Alex and Aidan are smiling at me like a pair of cherubs and I reluctantly give in and wander back to my seat. Well let's face it no one likes a snake (so I'm told). The conversation around the coach is all in whispered tones. Twenty minutes into the journey we notice the boys nudging each other and pointing at a spot on the coach. They start to gather around one of the seats. I nudge Gaffer and we both wander down the coach. The cause of the commotion is none other than Ben who is sound asleep and cuddling the trophy we won with a massive smile on his face and while his dad got the perfect picture of Ben and his hero Michael Owen, the pictures the boys are taking on their phones will be hitting social media way before the Michael Owen pics.

Everyone seems to have had a good night but while we might not have a special guest at our presentation night ours will be so much better.

CHAPTER THIRTEEN

DALWORTH PRESENTATION NIGHT

"I wouldn't say we were the best team in the league, but I would definitely say that we were in the top one."

So we've come full circle and on a very mild summer night in June we are on our way to another presentation night but for me this one is different as this year I'm a part of the proceedings and I feel that I've earned the right to be part of the celebrations. My wife also acknowledges this and says: "Feel free to have a few drinks tonight, you've earned it."
"You too hun."
"I might partake in a few Proseccos!" She gives me a wink and cheeky grin and I smile back.

Nick then bounces down and he is fully suited and booted with waistcoat too. He holds his arms out offering himself up for inspection and all of a sudden I feel inferiorly attired.

"You look stunning love." Nick does a little twirl for his mother.
"You going out on a date?" I interject.

Nick replies in a very serious tone: "We've got standards on and off the pitch Dad." At which point he looks me up and down and shakes his head "Standards Dad, Standards." I feel well and truly put in my place but before I can reply he is off.

I do notice that as he disappears he leaves behind the distinct smell of Paco Rabanne One Million. My Paco Rabanne One Million, which he has pinched. Nick shames me into rushing upstairs to have a shave and stick a tie on, I also select an alternative aftershave and grab a waistcoat in keeping with 'standards'.

The Dalworth Leisure Centre is as usual a kaleidoscope of glittering colours. Who needs excess lighting when you've got a hundred trophies and strategically placed spotlights? The light reflects off the trophies, climbing the walls and illuminating the hall. The kids are already knocking back pints of Coke as quick as Dads are trying to discreetly neck pints under the watchful eyes of wives and girlfriends. These are the same wives and girlfriends who are demolishing glasses of Prosecco at a steady rate. I'm already a bit giddy as I smile inanely and take in the smells, sounds and sights. A hand slaps me on the back and Gaffer is standing there in a snug fit grey two tone suit with skinny black tie, white shirt and ridiculously shiny black shoes. Once again I feel underdressed.

"Fancy a pint Simon?"

"Of course, my treat."

"Chocks away old boy."

Our contingent is secreted in a corner of the Leisure Centre and the boys are immaculately dressed in a variety of different coloured suits adorned with waistcoats and ties. Adam Morley steals the show with a blue checked suit and waistcoat, blue shirt with a skinny black tie and black pocket handkerchief. He also has a haircut so sharp that you could cut yourself on it. It is reminiscent of a Peaky Blinders haircut. All grease and slicked back and he has a flat cap tilted on his head to top off his ensemble.

The boys are a picture of cool as they strike their poses sipping on Coke, although I do have my suspicions as to what they are actually drinking. Alex and Aidan have taken it one step further in the fashion stakes by wearing Raybans although it isn't a bad idea bearing in mind the glare from the trophies. The boys stand around posing and exchanging the odd word and glance to their clubmates while occasionally slipping a scornful look to their younger peers who are charging about like a pack of escaped Tasmanian Devils.

The disapproving looks are all in a futile attempt to keep their younger clubmates in check and to ensure they do not encroach into their 'zone'. The boys chat is quiet and meaningful and they use lots of body language and hand gestures to communicate. Any form of verbal communication is difficult due to the noise levels.

The buffet is looking amazing this year and there is not an egg sandwich in sight. There is a smorgasboard of cheese, cold meats, boiled eggs, crackers, fresh bread and savouries such as sausage rolls, scotch eggs and mini pork pies. Billy B is positively dribbling as he is at the front of the queue. He returns to the table with a tower of food and devours the lot. As the last crumb enters his mouth he is already eyeing up the dessert table and he is first in piling Bannofee Pie, strawberry cheesecake and five profiteroles into the same bowl before drowning them in a river of fresh cream.

The food must be good as there is hardly any left after the first round and it is only those quick enough in scoffing their firsts that have any shot at seconds. Step forward Billy B who, after polishing his selection of desserts, goes back to the main buffet. Billy is resigned to picking off lone bits of cheese and savouries that are scattered across the table. The same cannot be said of the desserts and any dawdlers are left clutching empty dessert bowls as the table is emptied seemingly by a plague of piranhas who leave nothing. Even the jugs of cream are empty.

Food finished, next up is the raffle and there is a collective sigh until the prizes are revealed. The raffle this year has been deliberately shortened and instead of a mountain of unwanted prizes sit's a sparse total of just ten which are as follows an in no particular order:

1. A Spa day plus lunch for two at Dalworth Country Manor.

2. A day for two at Cheltenham Races.

3. Four tickets for a VIP day out at Cheltenham FC including a signed football.

4. Two tickets for any Swindon Town FC game.

5. A family ticket for four for a day out at Longleat.

6. A month's free membership for two for Dalworth Leisure Centre.

7. A meal for two at the Taj Mahal in Dalworth.

8. A helicopter ride for two at Tamworth Aerodrome.

9. A hot air balloon ride with Champagne for two at Tamworth Aerodrome

10. A night's stay for two at The Three Lodges Lodge including a three course meal.

What? No wine, no gift sets, no unwanted and unopened Christmas presents? The raffle announcer runs through the prizes and the hall goes quiet as everyone is listening intently to the fantastic bounty on offer. He then cleverly reveals to his captive audience that they are still selling tickets and with that an army of sellers hit the floor and the scramble is on.

Ten minutes later ALL the tickets have been sold and folded for the draw. In fact this year's raffle raised almost twice the amount as any other year and not one penny was spent on prizes. I'm also pleased to announce that I won a prize, the tickets to Cheltenham races and no, I didn't put them back.

The evening is going along quickly and smoothly.
Buffet – check. Raffle – check. Presentation...

Gaffer hands me a pint or, on this occasion Dutch courage, and the presentation starts. For once it goes quite quickly due to the military-style organisation and before you know it Gaffer is getting up and he is dragging me alongside him much to my surprise.

Gaffer takes the stage.
"Well what a season that was, it's fair to say that after six games, in which we managed a solitary point from a possible twelve, and took an early exit in the league cup, I was the bookies' favourite to be the first manager to be sacked. In fact I managed more red and yellow cards than points. Then came a remarkable transformation and we went on an incredible run. A run that led us to a cup final and the top of the league. We may have only finished runners-up in the cup but we somehow managed to retain our league title against almost impossible odds."

"But this season hasn't just been about the football. I made new friends and I sadly lost one too. As a group we laughed together, cried together, lost together and won together. But at the end of the season we were very much together and for that I would like to thank the boys for giving me the opportunity to be part of such an amazing season."

"I would also like to thank the man standing next to me, who without his assistance, this wouldn't have all been possible and I would especially like to thank our parents who stood by me throughout the difficult times and who I now count as close friends. Thank you."

Gaffer shook my hand and then we both took the applause that was forthcoming. In the glare of the light I could see a shadow approaching, on closer inspection I could see it was Ben. Ben then took the microphone and addressed the crowd.

"This season hasn't all been plain sailing and it has been a bit of a rollercoaster ride but I happen to like rollercoasters (cue laughs). Anyone can be a football manager but it takes a great football manager to turn things around when things are going wrong. We are very fortunate that, in Gaffer and Simon, we have two great managers and as a token of our appreciation we would like you to accept these."

Alex and Aidan step forward and hand us both a package. Each contains an engraved tankard. On each is our name and: "We did it and we did it together - The Boys."

It is a very touching moment. For once we are both speechless and can only offer our thanks. Before we can finish our bit there's the small matter of the presentation and The Gaffer handed out the following trophies as follows:

Player of the Year: Ben Padgham
"Whenever we faced adversity this player stood strong and never folded and proved to be an outstanding leader on the pitch"

Players Player of the Year: Billy Belafonte
"Mr Dependable and owner of a deadly and lethal left foot"

Parents Player of the Year: Nick Sheppard
"The teams Rock, never missed a game and scored some very important goals"

Clubman of the Year: Brian Haugh
"Spent most of the season on the bench but didn't miss a game and at the end of the season his performances dragged us over the line"

Goal of the season: Shared by Alex & Aidan Hayes
"We couldn't separate these two goals so decided to award both outstanding goals the trophies they warranted. Alex Hayes outstanding volley vs Langton Reds and Aidan Hayes overhead kick vs Phoenix Rovers"

Man of the Match Trophy: Charlie Fisher
"One of our unsung heroes who never stopped running and created as many chances as he scored"

Golden Boot: Luke Pilbeam
"This player really stepped up this year after being a bit part player last year and proved to be a lethal finisher"

Seven trophies and eight different winners. Well, eight trophies because Gaffer paid for an extra goal of the season one so that Alex and Aidan could receive one each.

With our speeches finished we rushed to the bar to grab a quick pint or four and sat back and watched the older age groups' speeches. As usual numbers dwindled with the older age groups and the speeches got shorter and shorter. The Under 18s finished and the Chairman got up and said a few words then presented the last two trophies for the Manager of the Year and Team of the Year. Michael Harris won the trophy again after his Under 18s had achieved a league and cup double and then the Chairman began his speech for team of the year.

"The team of the year goes to a team that showed you can achieve anything if you set your mind to it, a team that never ever gave up, a team that never stopped believing in their own abilities, a team that came from nowhere to eventually win the league, a team that Dalworth Football Club are proud to call their own. Ladies and Gentleman the team of the year goes to the Under 15s."

It was at this precise moment the boys lost all their cool and the noise that came from our little corner of the leisure centre hall was absolutely deafening. Gaffer pushed Ben forward and Ben accepted the trophy as captain. It was a half decent trophy and after a quick photoshoot with the rest of the boys Ben placed it on the table in front of Gaffer where it stood proud as another reminder of our achievements this season.

Before Ben could sit down, Gaffer grabbed his arm and with the other hand gave him a photo frame. Ben's face lit up as he examined the frame. I gave Gaffer a inquisitive look. "What is it?"

But before Gaffer could answer Ben was proudly showing me his gift. It was a photo from the league presentation night and showed Ben receiving the trophy from Michael Owen. But what made this picture so special was the personal handwritten message on the photo:

'To Ben, all the best from Michael Owen'

Ben was speechless and all he could do was give Gaffer a big hug. Gaffer was beaming from ear to ear as Ben showed the rest of his teammates.

"You never fail to amaze me mate."
"Yeah it was worth it just to see the look on Ben's face, that was priceless."
"Pint Gaffer? My treat."

When the presentations had finished it was time to really enjoy the rest of the evening and once a few more drinks had been dispatched, everyone took to the dancefloor. Surprisingly our little cool cats were first up on the floor when the first 'tune' hit the speakers. 'Sexyback' by Justin Timberlake. Adam was soon doing his own Neil from *The Inbetweeners* moves and he was very, very good too.

Billy B's attempts at copying Adam were less successful but nevertheless ten out of ten for trying. Even more unsuccessful was Gaffer's attempt and as Johnny pointed out to The Gaffer: 'Sexyback had just been Returned to Sender'.

Then came the boys doing a very strange dance that involved standing on the spot and dropping their arms down and moving their arms and legs up and down while crouched over. A very strange routine. Adam took over on the next one and again showed his moves with a dance that looked like a soul shimmy as he touched his head, shoulders, stomach and knees in-between a soft shoe shuffle. The boy certainly knows his moves. What came next was pure carnage as *Night Boat to Cairo* by Madness came on and everyone was skanking including The Gaffer who finally found his tune and his feet.

Come on Eileen by Dexy's became 'Come on Dalworth' and was belted out with great gusto by all. The end of the song signalled for me and The Gaffer to beat a hasty retreat for (and in order) 1) oxygen 2) toilet 3) another pint. The boys were on the floor all night while me and The Gaffer followed a dance, pee, drink, repeat routine. Much drink flowed, new dance moves were learned and we laughed and danced the night away.

The night as always ended with the club anthem: *Hi-Ho-Silver Lining*. There must have been about 200 people on the dance floor and amongst the revellers the Under 15s were represented by the players, the mangement and a fair few parents. All forming a massive sweat-drenched circle and everyone was in fine voice for the chorus:

"And it's Hi-Ho-Super Dalworth, everywhere we go we're magic...
We are forever winning, but we don't cause a fuss, because it's obvious."

As the last notes faded into the distance I slumped into my chair, very drunk and extremely knackered. Gaffer returned from the bar with two pints and handed me one.

"Cheers Gaffer."
"We did alright in the end didn't we Si?"
"You're really asking that Gaffer?"
"Yeah. At the start of season all I wanted to do was win football matches, lots of them - and trophies. We did alright in that we won more than we lost and we did win one trophy."
"Yes we did but we achieved more than that."
"I know and the main thing is I've really enjoyed it, it's been fun."
"The boys think the world of you now."
"That in itself was a major achievement especially considering how it all started."

We both started laughing at that point.
"So we doing this all again next year?"
"Too f**king right!"
"Si, for a teacher, you don't half f**king swear a lot."

That was it and we both burst out laughing again.

The night came to an end as the army of volunteers entered the dance floor with their black bin bags and that was the signal to leave. All that was left was to say our goodbyes and the boys started filtering out with their families with Alex & Aidan's Mum dragging them out after she caught them emptying discarded drinks on the tables.

"See you Gaffer.", "See you Si." giggled the seemingly tipsy twins.

Billy B was the next to go and he departed with an "Anyone know any kebab shops that are open?"

Ben was the next to leave and said his goodbyes while clutching his Michael Owen picture tightly to his chest. His dad thanked Gaffer again and said: "I think he'll be sleeping with that tonight!"

The last of the boys left. I gathered my clan together and walked to the car park with Gaffer where our taxis were waiting.

"See you next season Gaffer."
Gaffer seemed indignant.
"Sod that. Fancy going down the Old Maid next Sunday?"
I didn't need asking twice.
"See you Sunday Gaffer."

As I climbed into the taxi I took one last look at the Leisure Centre and I felt quite sad. My wife sensed my sadness and put her hand on my shoulder. She lightened my mood when she said: "You start pre-season next month."

And that was it. The official end of the 2017/18 season. A season that although we finished champions, gave us so much more and although it was my first, it was a season that I doubt I will ever see the like of again. Well maybe not until the next one.

*"And it's Hi-Ho-Super Dalworth, everywhere we go we're magic.
We are forever winning, but we don't cause a fuss, because it's obvious"*

CHAPTER FOURTEEN

THE STATISTICS

"Possession isn't everything"

Dalworth U15s Season 2017/18

Date	Comp	H/A	Opponents	Result	Scorers
10/09/17	League	H	Tamworth United	L 3-5	Pilbeam, Alex Hayes, Padgham
24/09/17	League	H	Kingsbridge	D 1-1	Pilbeam
01/10/17	League	H	Leighbridge Lions	L 1-4	Padgham
08/10/17	League	H	Phoenix Rovers	L 2-4	Pilbeam, Day
15/10/17	DD Cup	H	Diddlecott Ravens	W 16-0	Pilbeam 3 Webster 2 Padgham 2 Haugh 2 Alex Hayes, Morley, Aidan Hayes, Belafonte, Stevens, Sheppard, Day
22/10/17	L Cup	H	Dunstable Colts	L 2-3	Fisher, Sheppard
29/10/17	League	H	Oak Town Rangers	W 4-0	Fisher, Pilbeam, Padgham, Belafonte
05/11/17	League	A	Leighbridge Lions	W 6-2	Pilbeam 4 Padgham, Belafonte
19/11/17	DD Cup	A	Global Sports	W 4–3 (pens)	
				1-1 FT	Belafonte Pens: Pilbeam, Belafonte, Padgham, Hall
03/12/17	League	A	Langton Reds	W 5-3	Belafonte, Stevens, Alex Hayes, Hall, Aidan Hayes
14/01/18	DD Cup	H	Phoenix Rovers	W 4-2	Webster 2 Alex Hayes, Belafonte
21/01/18	League	H	Dunstable Colts	W 2-1	Morley, Padgham
04/02/18	DD Cup	A	Amley	W 1-0	Pilbeam
18/02/18	League	A	Redbridge Sports	W 1-0	Pilbeam
25/02/18	League	A	Oak Town Rangers	W 2-1	Pilbeam, Belafonte
04/03/18	League	A	Tamworth United	W 1-0	Fisher
11/03/18	League	A	Phoenix Rovers	W 3-1	Pilbeam, Fisher, Aidan Hayes
25/03/18	League	A	Parkfield	L 0-1	
01/04/18	League	H	Redbridge Sports	W 6-0	Fisher 4, Haugh, Belafonte
08/04/18	DD Cup	N	Bridgeham	L 0-2	
15/04/18	League	H	Langton Reds	W 3-0	Haugh 2 Pilbeam
22/04/18	League	A	Dunstable Colts	D 2-2	Haugh, Padgham
29/04/18	League	H	Parkfield	W 5-1	Belafonte, Pilbeam, Haugh, Fisher, Padgham
06/05/18	League	A	Kingsbridge	W 4-3	Fisher, Alex Hayes, Pilbeam, Aidan Hayes

Dalworth U15s League and Cup appearances - Season 2017/18

Player	Lge Apps	Cup Apps	Total Apps	Lge Goals	Cup Goals	Total Goals	MOTM Awards
Stevens	16	7	23	1	1	2	3
Carr	17	7	24	-	-	-	1
Day	9	5	14	1	1	2	-
Smith	12	1	13	-	-	-	1
Hall	18	6	24	1	-	1	2
Sheppard	18	7	25	-	3	3	3
Belafonte	18	7	25	6	3	9	1
Alex Hayes	15	6	21	3	2	5	3
Aidan Hayes	15	6	21	3	1	4	4
Morley	17	7	24	1	1	2	1
Padgham	18	6	24	7	2	9	4
Haugh	17	7	24	5	2	7	2
Webster	18	7	25	-	4	4	4
Pilbeam	17	7	24	14	4	18	2
Fisher	17	6	23	9	1	10	6

CHAPTER FIFTEEN

Prologue

"You're only as good as your last result."

It ain't over until the fat lady sings

Wow! What a season that was. It was an emotional roller coaster from start to finish and I have to say while I felt physically and emotionally drained at the end and in need of a break to recharge my batteries, I was genuinely gutted that it was over because it had been such an enjoyable experience.

I remember starting the season full of hope and confidence but also with a large dose of trepidation, not due to the boys, but due to a sense of pressure with the task at hand. How do you follow a near perfect season? With a perfect season, of course. It wasn't the perfect season we originally hoped for but by the finish it had brought a league title and the feeling that I had been part of something really special. I have to say that apart from the birth of my kids it ranks very highly amongst my list of achievements.

Like I said at the beginning, I started this journal/diary to keep a record of events so that I could look back and see and learn from the mistakes that I felt I would inevitably make during the season. I thought that it would be a suitable reference guide but then the English teacher in me got carried away and turned it from a journal/diary into a story. I'm glad that I did get carried away with my musings, because it turned into a story of a group of individuals overcoming the odds.

I apologise for adding the personal bits, but I felt it was required to complete the full story. In my humble opinion it captured more than just a junior football team's season. It captured a far bigger picture and as I re-read it I realise that the story captured an in-depth insight into a very special group of people.

The story also showed the transformation and depth of a role that I thought would consist of just laying a few cones, picking up dirty kit and being a sounding block for The Gaffer into a far more complex position. The role of a junior football team manager, in fact any football managerial position at any level, is a far more important position than just putting on training sessions and picking a team. When you unpick and unravel the story set before you, you can see just what a fantastic job The Gaffer did especially as his first major task was to take a huge slice of humble pie and accept his own failings.

From a footballing perspective, although The Gaffer felt inferior to his predecessor, in the end he did an amazing job and made a massive impact on the team and its players. He totally changed his way of thinking and his goals during the course of the season and that is what ultimately turned the season and our fortunes. On a non-footballing level he was at times the kind and compassionate person the boys needed in their hours of need.

The Gaffer went into the season with brash statements and a win-at-all-costs attitude but, by the end of the season, he had created a fantastic ethos and nurtured a spirit that led to us finishing the season as deserved champions.

During the season I gained a very close friend and I would like to think that the friendship led to the foundations for creating an effective managerial partnership. We started off as a Mike Bassett and Dave 'Doddsy' Dodds style partnership and finished as, well a half decent managerial pairing. The Gaffer has always been a brash character for as long as I have known him. I would say he was almost flash at times but while he dug deep into his own pocket on a number of occasions and went above and beyond for the cause, he never flaunted it and he certainly never craved any attention. Well maybe at the beginning when he just wanted to be seen as an effective replacement to Michael, which as we know nearly proved the undoing of him.

It was the boys that convinced him that he just had to be the best he could be and that they would do the rest. I don't think he ever lost sight of the fact that he wanted the best for the boys, but the way he went about it was too ego-driven and it came across as being all about him and not the players and the team. The Gaffer is a very successful local businessman and the football is his downtime but, like in business, he wants to be the best at everything and he demanded immediate success. From day one the pressure was there and that created a wedge between him and the boys.

He was a strict disciplinarian at the beginning of the season but soon mellowed and he created an atmosphere that was fun but focused and driven. The early season setbacks we suffered he took personally but in reality we suffered so much bad luck early doors that even Michael Harris would have struggled. With regards to Michael, he couldn't shake off the legacy that Michael left and he felt inferior. He tried so hard to be Michael that he forgot who he was and he forgot that he was already part of the legacy from the beginning. The boys were right behind him from the start but the relationship turned sour as things went from bad to worse and at this time I was more of a peacemaker than an assistant manager.

It was almost with relief when we hit what felt like rock bottom and Gaffer opened up. From that moment the team never looked back and like I have said on many occasions, it was a real pleasure to be part of the Under 15s set up.

We started the season as colleagues but we ended it as firm friends and that included our families too. My respect for the man grew and grew and I'm really looking forward to seeing what we can achieve next season.

Alcohol
One thing I did do was record our drinking exploits, well what I remember. The Gaffer certainly liked his drink and he definitely changed my drinking habits. We had a fair few 'sessions' during the season, most of which were under the context of planning meetings. Although you could say it was all part of the bonding process, in reality we were just drinking partners, and boy did we drink! I've never been a big drinker and the occasional red wine, 'teacher's medicine' was about the limit of my tipples. Now it's real ales, ciders and whiskeys and I've given my liver a proper kicking on a regular basis this year. In fact I've just bought shares in Resolve due to my regular use of it.

Food
I've put on half a stone during the course of the season largely due to the alcohol and the banquets that I always had when I went out with The Gaffer. The barbecues were bad enough but with that meal at Christmas and the alcohol I'm sure I put on five pounds just looking at the spread we had in the Indian. I can only assume that the reason The Gaffer isn't as portly as he should be is due to his job, whereas my job is not the most energetic. I wonder if The Gaffer would consider not a dry month but a dry season and a switch to vegetarianism.

The Boys
While we eventually played our part in the team's success we couldn't have done it without the boys. Resilience is a buzzword in teaching and I'm sure if you look it up in the dictionary the definition will say Dalworth United Under 15s. The boys were bombproof all season and despite suffering bad management, defeats, injuries and personal and tragic loss they overcame extreme adversity to win the league and they did so in their

own inimitable style and with smiles on their faces. The way the boys came together when Grandad Hayes sadly passed away was a testament to the team spirit and when Ben stood in between Alex and Aidan, arms linked and read that poem it produced a memory that will stay with me forever.

It was that same camaraderie and spirit that was taken into every game, even when they were at loggerheads with The Gaffer they were always on task, with maybe the exception of the Phoenix game, and I have nothing but admiration for the boys. The number of times they came back from a near impossible situation and somehow turned it round astounded me.

The time I realised that this team was special was when we were down to nine men against Leighbridge Lions and despite the fact that we had had two men sent off and Gaffer was arguing with all and sundry, Ben and the remaining players were desperately trying to save a lost cause. The fact that they didn't was irrelevant, they never stopped trying.

Off the pitch they gave me so many laughs and at times the management-players barrier was breached by the boy's antics and, instead of being angry, you couldn't help but laugh at them. Billy B should carry a health warning as should Alex and Aidan but for different reasons and while you were often in danger of physical damage in their presence, you were equally at risk of splitting your sides. But as soon as the boys crossed that line they were deadly serious and in Ben, one of the most thoughtful and considerate people you could meet, they had a leader whose drive and focus was at times frightening.

The Parents

There is no greater love than that of football parents.

Who else would drag themselves up on a Sunday morning and drive all over the county in all types of weather to watch their offspring play a game/half a game/no game at all and pay for the privilege? Football parents, that's who. The same parents who after a hard week's work can be found standing in an open area, frozen and getting absolutely soaked, while cheering on their offspring.

But they do it, not because their offspring will make the grade and repay the kindness with a mansion when they sign Premiership terms. No, they do it because their offspring want to play football. If they are lucky they may be offered the opportunity to combat the cold by running up and down a muddy touchline waving a flag and getting dog's abuse.

If they aren't they may elect to wear umpteen layers and drink coffee or tea from a flask. Whatever the option they are always there and while the coaches also give up their spare time, they may experience glory or success, the parents are most likely to experience frost bite and hypothermia.

The relationship with your parents can make or break a manager/coach. Things will run smoothly if they are on board, but if not mutiny ensues and 'parent power' results in the old 'tin tack'. I'm pleased to say that our parents were on board and above this season and the relationship was superb. We would like to think we had some influence on our title, the boys certainly did and the parents definitely did and for that we were very grateful.

Si The Coach
I'm an English teacher and I would like to think a good one. During the course of this season as you know I added 'heavy drinker' to my CV and I also increased my vocabulary. A 'Good idea' is now a "Great shout." A "Good Decision" is a "Good call", 'Conversation' is "Bants." In fact if you spend some time in my classroom you are likely to hear my students get told to "Cease the bants". Or when Year Ten come up with an insightful view on the political influences of *An Inspector Calls,* get told "Great shout."

In fact there are numerous occasions when I have to stop myself from addressing students as 'Tarts', 'Numb nuts', 'Melts', "Lemons', 'Numpties' and a plethora of other Dalworth-inspired insults. I have to admit my popularity has risen amongst my students and I am now seen as 'safe'. That is until a student gets a question wrong and I inadvertently flick their ear as a consequence.

The comparisons between a teacher and a football coach are very similar in that the qualities you need are:
Leader,
Facilitator,
Motivator,
Communicator,
Instructor,
Assessor,
Friend,
Mentor,
Adviser,
Organizer,
Planner,
A Fountain of all Knowledge.

This season I can add Mediator to the list as on a number of occasions, namely the earlier part of the season, I stepped in between The Gaffer and players/referees/dog walkers/opposing managers. I would like to think I have displayed all these qualities and proved a degree of efficiency along the way.

I believe my teaching has improved too and I realise it's not just about grades at school or results at football. It's about teaching right from wrong. It's about teaching people how to not only succeed but how to cope with failure. It's teaching people how to be respectful in victory and gracious in defeat. It's about teaching people how to be better people. I would say my biggest success has been The Gaffer but he might disagree with that.

To those about to coach I salute you
There are thousands of brave souls like me who give up their time to provide coaching, good and bad, and then instead of opting to play Championship Manager or Fantasy Football they take to the sidelines to try to mould a bunch of keen-as-mustard players into something resembling a half decent football team. Some of those brave souls know their limitations and just try to do their best; others really think they are the next Sir Alex, Jurgen Klopp or even John Sitton in the worst cases. Living out their dreams of winning the title or cup and then moving onto bigger or better things and giving the old hair dryer treatment to anyone who gets in the way. They are the ones who share their thoughts and opinions with anyone who cares to listen and boy do they have opinions but they still give up their time and for that I have the greatest admiration even if I may not agree with everything they do.

The full-time whistle
I am looking forward to an alternative Sunday routine of long morning walks with Faith in the sunshine, massive fry-ups, numerous pots of coffee and the odd impromptu visit to the pub with The Gaffer. I'm also looking forward to next season. This time we will be better prepared and I'm sure we will hit the ground running. Our goals are already in place. What are they? Well it's to go through the season unbeaten and attempt a clean sweep of trophies. Yes, you've heard that before, but let's face it you can only achieve perfection if you set perfection as your goal and although it's a big ask, that will be our initial goal.

Fail to prepare, prepare to fail.

What happens if we don't, well it's not the end of the world we'll just give it our all and we'll work as hard as possible while having a laugh. We have to it's the only way we know it's the Dalworth way.

Got a book in you?

PUBLISHING
victorpublishing.co.uk

This book is published by Victor Publishing.

Victor Publishing specialises in getting new and independent writers' work published worldwide in both paperback and Kindle format.

We also look to re-publish titles that were previously published but have now gone out of circulation or off-sale.

If you have a manuscript for a book (or have previously published a now off-sale title) of any genre (fiction, non-fiction, autobiographical, biographical or even reference or photographic/illustrative) and would like more information on how you can get your work published and on sale in print and digitally, please visit us at: www.victorpublishing.co.uk or get in touch at: enquiries@victorpublishing.co.uk

.

Printed in Great Britain
by Amazon